THOR
CORPS

THOR CORPS. Contains material originally published in magazine form as THOR CORPS #1-4; and THOR #337, #384, #433 and #438-441. First printing 2016. ISBN# 978-0-7851-9558-0. Published by MARVEL WORLDWIDE, INC., a subsid of MARVEL ENTERTAINMENT, LLC. OFFICE OF PUBLICATION: 135 West 50th Street, New York, NY 10020. Printed in the U.S.A. ALAN FINE, President, Marvel Entertainment; DAN BUCKLEY, President, TV, Publishing and Br Management; JOE QUESADA, Chief Creative Officer; TOM BREVOORT, SVP of Publishing; DAVID BOGART, SVP of Operations & Procurement, Publishing; C.B. CEBULSKI, VP of International Development & Brand Management; DAVID GABR SVP Print, Sales & Marketing; JIM O'KEEFE, VP of Operations & Logistics; DAN CARR, Executive Director of Publishing Technology; SUSAN CRESPI, Editorial Operations Manager; ALEX MORALES, Publishing Operations Manager; STAN Chairman Emeritus. For information regarding advertising in Marvel Comics or on Marvel.com, please contact Jonathan Rheingold, VP of Custom Solutions & Ad Sales, at jrheingold@marvel.com. For Marvel subscription inquiries, please 800-217-9158. Manufactured between 1/15/2016 and 2/22/2016 by R.R. DONNELLEY, INC., SALEM, VA, USA.

10 9 8 7 6 5 4 3 2 1

writers TOM DEFALCO, RON FRENZ & WALTER SIMONSON

pencilers RON FRENZ, PATRICK OLLIFFE & WALTER SIMONSON

inkers AL MILGROM, PATRICK OLLIFFE, ROMEO TANGHAL, WALTER SIMONSON & BRETT BREEDING

colorists MIKE ROCKWITZ, GEORGE ROUSSOS, STEVE OLIFF & CHRISTIE SCHEELE

letterers BRAD K. JOYCE, STEVE DUTRO, MICHAEL HEISLER, JOHN WORKMAN JR., DIANA ALBERS & CHRIS ELIOPOULOS

assistant editors LEN KAMINSKI, JOE ANDREANI, MICHAEL LARLIN, MARC SIRY & MICHAEL HEISLER

editors RALPH MACCHIO, MIKE ROCKWITZ & MARK GRUENWALD

front cover artists PATRICK OLLIFFE & VERONICA GANDINI

back cover artist LOU HARRISON

---

collection editor MARK D. BEAZLEY
associate editor SARAH BRUNSTAD
associate manager, digital assets JOE HOCHSTEIN
associate managing editor ALEX STARBUCK
editor, special projects JENNIFER GRÜNWALD
vp, production and special projects JEFF YOUNGQUIST
research & layout JEPH YORK
production COLORTEK & ROMIE JEFFERS
book designer ADAM DEL RE
svp print, sales & marketing DAVID GABRIEL

editor in chief AXEL ALONSO
chief creative officer JOE QUESADA
publisher DAN BUCKLEY
executive producer ALAN FINE

Special Thanks to MIKE HANSEN

THOR created by STAN LEE, LARRY LIEBER & JACK KIRBY

"WHOSOEVER HOLDS THIS HAMMER, IF HE BE WORTHY, SHALL POSSESS THE POWER OF THOR..."

Months ago, a mortal architect named Eric Masterson came to Thor's defense during a brutal battle. Miraculously, Eric was able to lift Thor's enchanted hammer Mjolnir, but he was fatally injured in the fight. Thor beseeched Odin to save Eric's life, and Odin did so by combining the life forces of the two men. Thor and Eric became one being with two souls and two distinct personalities — and when Eric stamped his cane on the ground, he transformed fully into Thor.

Thor, who had once previously had a mortal alter ego in "Dr. Donald Blake," took the situation in stride. Unfortunately, pulling double duty as the God of Thunder — and the sudden disappearances that it required — began to affect Eric's personal life. His architect business suffered, he lost custody of his son Kevin to his ex-wife Marcy and his relationship with personal assistant Susan Austin became strained.

Loki, seeking to attack Thor through Eric, kidnapped Kevin. Thor battled Loki and rescued Kevin, but Loki fired a mystic blast at Eric's family that hit Susan, grievously wounding her. Enraged, Thor decided that Loki could never again be allowed to harm an innocent, and used Mjolnir to draw out the villain's life force, killing him.

In Asgard, a shocked Odin sensed Loki's death and ordered Thor banished for this murderous act. In a sudden flash of lightning, Eric Masterson stood alone, unable to feel Thor's presence within him any longer. But when he stamped his cane on the ground, Eric found himself once again imbued with Thor's power — though still retaining his own mind! Eric now serves as the replacement Thor, while vainly trying to learn where the original has been banished to.

But through all of time and space, Eric Masterson is not the only mortal to have wielded the hammer of Thor. Years ago a noble alien named Beta Ray Bill was able to lift Mjolnir, and after battling valiantly in Asgard he was given his own hammer, the enchanted Storm Breaker. And six centuries in the future, a young man named Dargo Ktor was shown Thor's long-abandoned hammer, and found himself transformed into a futuristic version of Thor when he lifted it to battle agents of the mega-corporations that ruled his time.

Now, a time-traveling villain named Zarrko the Tomorrow Man is about to bring all three replacement Thors together...

MARVEL COMICS
THE THOR WAR! PART 1 OF 4
THE MIGHTY THOR
© 1991 MARVEL ENT. GROUP, INC.
$1.00 US
$1.25 CAN/UK 65p
438
EARLY NOV
02450
APPROVED BY THE COMICS CODE AUTHORITY
THE THOR OF THE FUTURE
WALKS THE STREETS OF TODAY!
ALSO: THOR
(OUR GUY!)
VS.
STELLARIS,
THE CELESTIAL SLAYER!
SIF AND BALDER
BATTLE THE UNSTOPPABLE
DESTROYER!
PLUS: THE RETURN OF
ZARRKO,
THE TOMMORROW
MAN!
'NUFF SAID!

WHEN ARCHITECT **ERIC MASTERSON** STAMPS HIS WOODEN WALKING-STICK UPON THE GROUND, HE IS TRANSFORMED INTO THE NORSE GOD OF THUNDER. ARMED WITH HIS ENCHANTED HAMMER, HE IS AT ONCE MASTER OF THE STORM, LORD OF THE LIVING LIGHTNING, AND ONE OF THE STRONGEST WARRIORS WHO EVER WALKED THE EARTH! STAN LEE PRESENTS . . .

THE MIGHTY THOR!

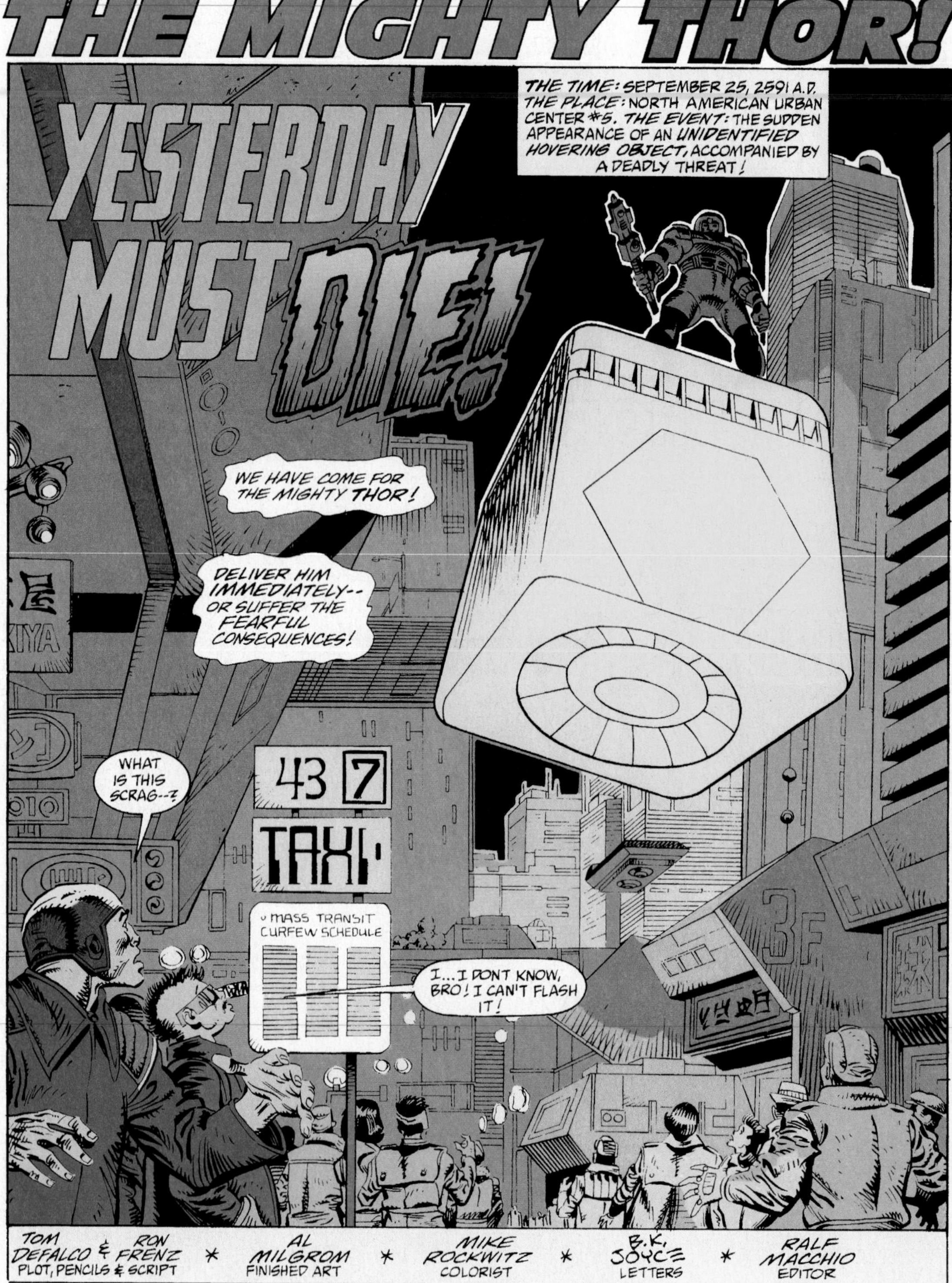

YESTERDAY MUST DIE!
THE TIME: SEPTEMBER 25, 2591 A.D. THE PLACE: NORTH AMERICAN URBAN CENTER #5. THE EVENT: THE SUDDEN APPEARANCE OF AN UNIDENTIFIED HOVERING OBJECT, ACCOMPANIED BY A DEADLY THREAT!
WE HAVE COME FOR THE MIGHTY THOR!
DELIVER HIM IMMEDIATELY-- OR SUFFER THE FEARFUL CONSEQUENCES!
WHAT IS THIS SCRAG--?
43 7
TAXI
MASS TRANSIT CURFEW SCHEDULE
I...I DON'T KNOW, BRO! I CAN'T FLASH IT!
TOM DEFALCO & RON FRENZ PLOT, PENCILS & SCRIPT * AL MILGROM FINISHED ART * MIKE ROCKWITZ COLORIST * B.K. JOYCE LETTERS * RALF MACCHIO EDITOR

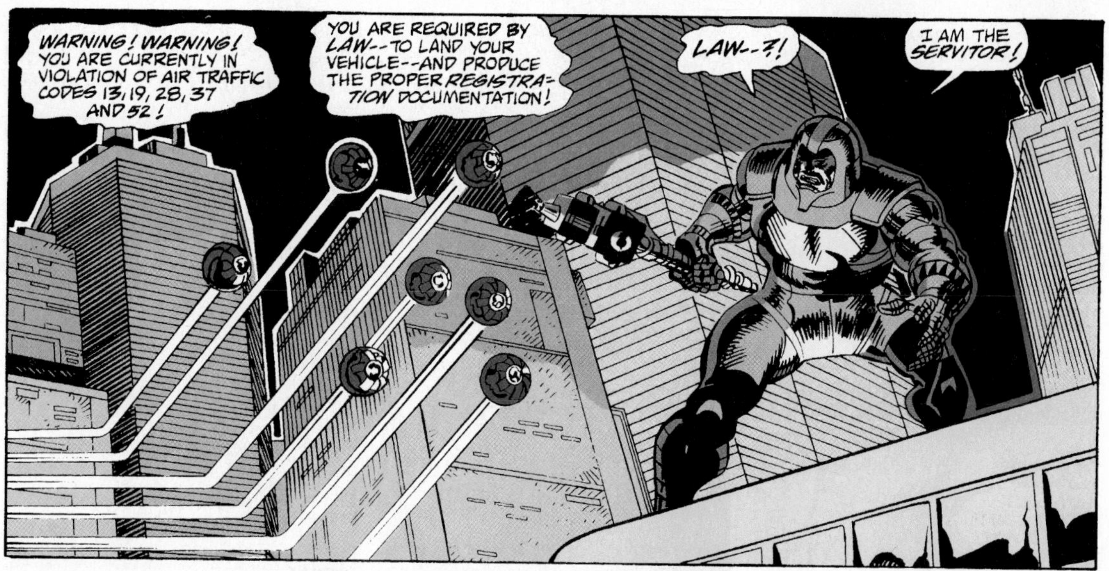
WARNING! WARNING! YOU ARE CURRENTLY IN VIOLATION OF AIR TRAFFIC CODES 13, 19, 28, 37 AND 52!
YOU ARE REQUIRED BY LAW--TO LAND YOUR VEHICLE--AND PRODUCE THE PROPER REGISTRATION DOCUMENTATION!
LAW--?!
I AM THE SERVITOR!

I RECOGNIZE NO LAW SAVE THAT WHICH RULES TIME ITSELF!

THE LAW OF HE WHOM I AM PRIVILEGED TO SERVE!

DID YOU SCAN THAT--?
H-HE SLAGGED THOSE TRAFFIC DRONES LIKE THEY WERE NOTHING!
YOU HAVE NOW WITNESSED THE UNSTOPPABLE POWER OF MY FAITHFUL SERVITOR!

PRODUCE THE THUNDER GOD BEFORE I UNLEASH HIM AGAINST THE ORGANIC POPULACE!
WHERE IS THOR? WHY DOESN'T THAT SLACKER SHOW?!

SOUNDS LIKE SOMEONE'S BUZZING MY TUNE, SALLA!
YOU...YOU MUSTN'T GO, DARGO! THAT CREATURE--! SOMETHING ABOUT HIM TERRIFIES ME!
I...I SUDDENLY FEEL LIKE I'M ABOUT TO LOSE YOU! THAT WE'LL BE SEPARATED FOR THE REST OF MY LIFE!
NO NEED TO WEIRD OUT, SALLA! YOU KNOW BETTER!

THE SCRAGGERS CAN THROW WHATEVER THEY WANT AT ME... I'LL ALWAYS FIND MY WAY HOME!
ALWAYS!
I HAVE FAITH YOU'LL TRY!
BUT I...I WON'T STAND IN YOUR WAY!

SALLA, I...
NO MORE WORDS!
DO YOUR DUTY--

--AND MAKE ME PROUD!
WHAT'S THE BUZZ, SLACKER? DID I MISS ANYTHING?
WHAT A CITY--!

STREETS SO CROWDED THAT YOU'RE ALWAYS BREATHING SOMEONE ELSE'S BREATH--
--AND VIOLENCE SO COMMON THAT IT'S ACCEPTED AS ENTERTAINMENT!
I WISH THIS TURBO-LIFT WOULD HURRY! THAT ACTION IS RAPIDLY APPROACHING CRITICAL MASS!

AT LAST! I FINALLY REACHED THE APARTMENT!
THERE'S THE CANE--! THE MOST POWERFUL WEAPON IN THE UNIVERSE... AND I STORE IT IN A JUNK ROOM!

NEVER BOTHERED TO FIND A PROPER PLACE FOR IT... BECAUSE I KNOW THAT IT'S ONLY MINE TEMPORARILY!
ITS REAL OWNER IS BOUND TO RECLAIM IT SOMEDAY!
BUT, UNTIL THEN--

--I GET TO WIELD THE POWER OF THOR!

WE'RE WARNING YOU, SLAGGART! WE HAVE YOU SURROUNDED AND--AAYIII!
MY SENSORS INDICATE THAT LIVING REINFORCEMENTS HAVE JOINED THE AUTODRONES!
A PITY THEY AREN'T AS DURABLE--OR AS EFFICIENT--AS THEIR MECHANICAL COUNTERPARTS!

I...I WAS A FOOL TO STAND SO CLOSE TO THE EDGE! I SHOULD HAVE SEEN THAT HE WAS ABOUT TO ATTACK!
AT LEAST THE OTHERS MADE IT TO SAFETY!
AT LEAST THEY'LL LIVE!!

Y-YOU SAVED ME FROM CERTAIN DEATH! HOW CAN I EVER THANK YOU?
DON'T GIVE IT A FLASH! ANYONE CAN PLAY MEGA-STAR WITH A MAGIC HAMMER... BUT IT'S AVERAGE TROOPERS LIKE YOU WHO ARE THE REAL HEROES!
I'VE GOT A FLASH FOR YOU, TROOPER... SO WILL YOU!

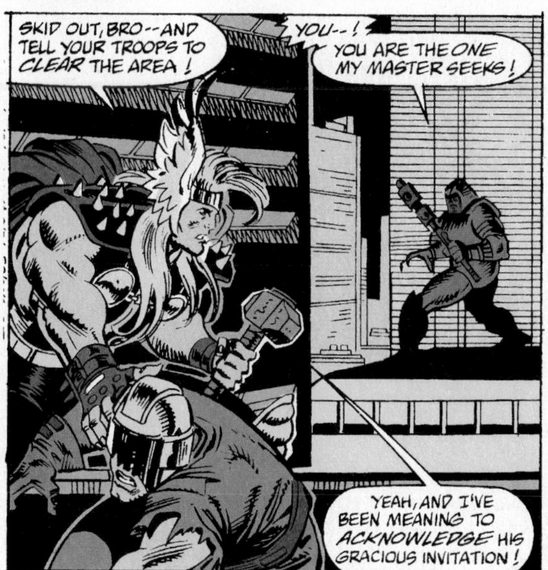
SKID OUT, BRO--AND TELL YOUR TROOPS TO CLEAR THE AREA!
YOU--! YOU ARE THE ONE MY MASTER SEEKS!
YEAH, AND I'VE BEEN MEANING TO ACKNOWLEDGE HIS GRACIOUS INVITATION!

I HOPE HE'LL ACCEPT A HAMMER IN LIEU OF A RESPONSE CARD!

SCRAGGING DRONES IS ONE BIG, SLUGGO--FLESH'N BLOOD'S ANOTHER!
STOP! THERE IS NO NEED TO CONTINUE THIS BATTLE!
A SINGLE HEAD-SLAM...AND YOU'RE READY TO SURRENDER?!

HARDLY! I POSSESS MORE THAN SUFFICIENT POWER TO DEVASTATE THIS ENTIRE POPULATION CENTER!
HOWEVER, I HAVE NO WISH TO INJURE YOU! MY INSTRUCTIONS ARE TO BRING YOU TO MY MASTER!
HATE TO DEPRIVE THE LOCALS OF THEIR EVENING JOLLIES, BUT YOU'VE GOT MY PROBES UP! LEAD ON--!

WOW! WE'RE BEING LOWERED INTO YOUR SHIP!
B-BUT...THIS STRUCTURE IS IMMENSE! IT SEEMS TO STRETCH FOR MILES!
IT...IT CAN'T BE THE SAME CRAFT!

MANY ARE THE WONDERS OF MY MASTER! HIS TIME CUBE OCCUPIES TRANS-TEMPORAL SPACE!
WHILE THE OUTER SHELL APPEARS IN YOUR ERA... THE INTERIOR EXISTS ON A SEPARATE CHRONOLOGICAL PLANE!
YEAH, BUT I'LL BET IT'S A REAL FRAZZLE TO FIND A CONVENIENT DOCKING SPACE!
YOUR MASTER SOUNDS MEGA-SLICK!

SLICK ENOUGH TO BE AWARE OF YOUR FUTILE EFFORTS TO LOCATE THE ORIGINAL OWNER OF YOUR ENCHANTED HAMMER!

GREETINGS, MY YOUNG FRIEND--!
I AM ZARRKO... THOUGH MANY, WHO LACK ANY INSIGHT INTO THE TRUE NATURE OF TIME, OFTEN REFER TO ME AS THE TOMORROW MAN!
I AM HERE TO HELP YOU!

MEANWHILE, IN THE PRESENT...
SO THIS CRAZY KINDERGARTEN KID GETS INTO HER MOM'S WALLET...AND STARTS PASSING DOLLAR BILLS AROUND THE SCHOOLYARD!
MAN, SUSAN...I WISH YOU COULD'A SEEN THE TEACHER FREAK!
I...I DON'T KNOW WHICH PAINS ME MORE! SEEING SUSAN IN THAT COMA...OR WATCHING AS KEVIN STRUGGLES TO GET A REACTION FROM HER!
THE NEWS ISN'T VERY ENCOURAGING, MR. MASTERSON...

I'VE BEEN UNABLE TO LOCATE DR. BLAKE...THE SURGEON I DISCUSSED WITH YOU!
I'M CERTAIN HE COULD HELP MISS AUSTIN!
UNFORTUNATELY, HE'S DROPPED OUT OF SIGHT! NONE OF HIS FORMER COLLEAGUES SEEM TO HAVE A CURRENT ADDRESS!
OF COURSE NOT! THE MAN NO LONGER EXISTS!

DON BLAKE WAS ONLY AN ARTIFICIAL IDENTITY WHICH WAS ONCE USED BY THE ORIGINAL THOR!
ANY OF HOPE OF RESURRECTING HIM VANISHED WHEN THE THUNDER GOD WAS RECENTLY BANISHED FROM THIS PLANE OF REALITY!
TIME TO GO, KID!
I...I'LL BE BACK REAL SOON, SUSAN!
Y-YOU TAKE CARE!

I-IS SHE EVER GONNA GET BETTER, DAD?
I WISH I KNEW, SON...
COME ALONG, KEVIN! WE'RE RUNNING LATE!

THANKS FOR BRINGING HIM, MARCY! I KNOW THIS CAN'T BE ANY PICNIC FOR YOU, EITHER!
DON'T GIVE IT A THOUGHT, ERIC!
YOU OKAY, LADY?
EVERYTHING'S FINE!
I...I'LL BE SEEING YOU!

WHEW! WHAT'S WITH THE EX-WIFE? SHE HASN'T BEEN THAT COLD SINCE WE WERE IN COURT!
SAY... I JUST HAD A WILD IDEA! I WAS ONCE MERGED WITH THE ORIGINAL THOR... WHO USED TO BE BLAKE!
NO PARK ING

MAYBE A GUY LIKE DR. STRANGE COULD DO HIS MAGIC THING AND--
NAHH! THAT PLOT IS EVEN TOO RIDICULOUS FOR A BAD COMIC BOOK!
THERE'S MASTERSON--! MY PATIENCE HAS PAID OFF!

AT LAST! AFTER STALKING HIM THE PAST FEW WEEKS, I'VE FINALLY GOT HIM CORNERED!
HE CAN'T ESCAPE ME NOW!
I COULD TRY CALLING DR. KEITH KINCAID!
HE DOESN'T REALIZE IT, BUT THOR'S FATHER USED HIM AS A TEMPLATE FOR BLAKE!

I ASSUME HIS SURGICAL SKILLS ARE COMPARABLE, AND--
HEY, MASTERSON--! WE HAVE TO TALK!
WHO--?!

I'M SURPRISED YOU DON'T RECOGNIZE ME!
I'M BOBBY STEELE!
THE MAN WHO MARRIED YOUR EX-WIFE!

JUST THEN, AN UNCONSCIONABLE DISTANCE AWAY--
--AN ARMORED ALIEN FORM SLASHES ACROSS THE ETERNAL CHILL OF DEEP SPACE!

WITH THE CASUAL PRECISION OF AN EXPERIENCED SURGEON, IT PIERCES THE MEMBRANE OF HYPER-SPACE!

COUNTLESS MINUTE, ALMOST UNDETECTABLE MODIFICATIONS ARE MADE TO ITS OUTER SHELL, AS IT IS BUFFETED BY MUTANT, EVER-EVOLVING COSMIC ENERGIES!

BILLIONS OF DREARY LIGHT YEARS ARE BYPASSED IN A MATTER OF INSTANTS, AND THEN...
FULLY RECOVERED, ME!
FIND MY PRECIOUS, BLOND BEAUTY BOY ON MUDBALL EARTH!
KILL HIM FILTHY!

SORRY FOR THE MOMENTARY HESITATION, STEELE!
I'D KNOW YOU EVEN WITHOUT YOUR CONNECTION TO MARCY!
EVERYONE IN THIS CITY KNOWS THE STARTING QUARTERBACK FOR THE NEW YORK SMASHERS!
CARE FOR A DRINK?
A LOW SODIUM VEGETABLE JUICE WOULD HIT THE SPOT!
HOW ABOUT A COLD GRAPE SODA? I ALWAYS HAVE A SUPPLY FOR KEVIN!
ONLY IF IT'S DIET! I LIMIT MY SUGAR INTAKE DURING THE REGULAR SEASON!
ERIC- CALL JERRY
Thor
TO DAD- KEV
DIET
Grape
mr.caffein

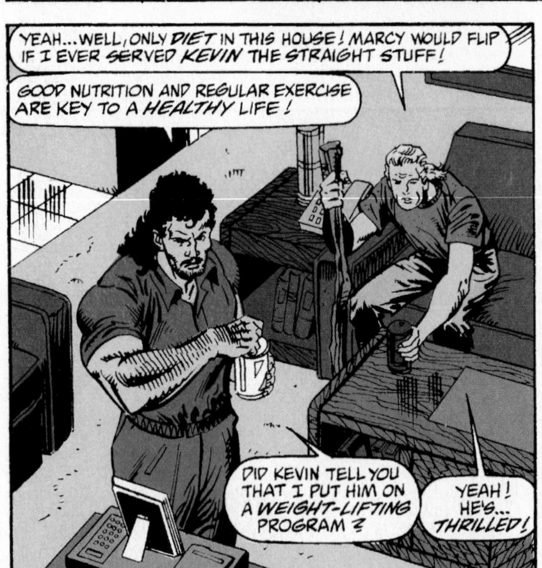
YEAH...WELL, ONLY DIET IN THIS HOUSE! MARCY WOULD FLIP IF I EVER SERVED KEVIN THE STRAIGHT STUFF!
GOOD NUTRITION AND REGULAR EXERCISE ARE KEY TO A HEALTHY LIFE!
DID KEVIN TELL YOU THAT I PUT HIM ON A WEIGHT-LIFTING PROGRAM?
YEAH! HE'S... THRILLED!

HE'S A LITTLE SLIGHT FOR HIS AGE, BUT HE'LL BULK UP!
WE ALSO DO DAILY CALISTHENICS!
SOUNDS LIKE LOTS OF FUN!
WOULD IT BE TOO MUCH TO EXPECT THAT THERE'S A POINT TO ALL THIS?

I JUST WANTED YOU TO KNOW HOW CLOSE WE HAD BECOME!
YOU SEE, MARCY AND I HAVE COME TO A DECISION...

...I WANT TO ADOPT THE KID!

AFTER ALL, THE BOY NEEDS A FATHER!
HE ALREADY HAS ONE!
I MEAN SOMEONE HE SEES EVERY DAY! NOT JUST ON WEEK-ENDS...OR WHEN IT'S CONVENIENT!

HE NEEDS A POSITIVE ROLE MODEL! SOMEONE STABLE! A MAN WHO IS A SUCCESS IN HIS CHOSEN FIELD!
I UNDERSTAND THAT YOU KEEP DISAPPEARING ON THE KID, AND THAT YOUR ARCHITECH BUSINESS HAS BEEN GOING DOWN THE TUBES...
ENOUGH, STEELE! SHUT YOUR STUPID MOUTH--

--BEFORE I SHUT IT FOR YOU!
KWAK!

M-MY HAND--!
THINK ABOUT WHAT'S BEST FOR THE BOY, MASTERSON...
AND... THANKS FOR THE SODA!

THAT STUPID, NARCISSISTIC JOCK--! HE...HE THINKS I'M JUST GONNA LET HIM STEAL MY SON!
HE DOESN'T REALIZE WHO HE'S MESSING WITH!
I'LL JUST GO SHOW HIM!

MEANWHILE...
PRETTY MUDBALL, THIS!
PITY TO MELT AND FRY!

MUST ACTIVATE TRANSFORMATION MODE--AND RETRACT ARMOR!
A WASTED TRIP IF MY BLONDE BEAUTY DOESN'T SEE MY FACE, AND REALIZE THAT--

--STELLARIS HAS RETURNED!

SENSORS ARE ALREADY TRACKING HIS POSITION!
LOCKING ON TARGET--!

ABANDONED IN SPACE, ME! LEFT TO DIE!
I FIND YOU, BLONDIE BOY!
ROT YOU! ROT YOU VERY SLOWLY!!

BOBBY STEELE MAY BE A REAL HOTSHOT ON THE FOOTBALL FIELD!

BUT THAT SMUG CREEP IS WIMP CITY WHEN COMPARED TO A MAN WHO--

--POSSESSES THE POWER OF THOR!

I'D LIKE TO SEE THAT MISERABLE JOCK GIVE ME ATTITUDE NOW!
A FLICK OF MY FINGER...AND IT'S TRACTION CITY!
I'D SNAP HIS SPINE, PULVERIZE HIS JAW BONE AND... AND...

WHO'M I KIDDING?!
IF BEING A JERK RATED THE DEATH PENALTY, WE'D HAVE A POPULATION OF ABSOLUTE ZERO!
MUCH AS I WANT TO PUNISH THAT CREEP, I...I CAN'T USE THOR'S POWER LIKE THAT!
BUT, THAT DOESN'T MEAN HE GETS OFF COMPLETELY FREE...

WHAT THE--?! WHERE'D THIS SUDDEN THUNDER-STORM COME FROM?
OH, NO! MY BABY--!

SHE'S RUINED--!
I-IT'S ALMOST LIKE THE STORM DELIBERATELY TOOK AIM ON HER!

THAT COULD RANK AS THE PETTIEST THING I'VE EVER DONE IN MY LIFE!
ALSO... THE MOST SATISFYING!

THE THERAPEUTIC EFFECTS OF REVENGE ARE VASTLY UNDERRATED!
I SHOULD LEARN TO CUT LOOSE MORE OFTEN!

THE NEXT FOOL WHO HASSLES ME, I'M JUST GOING TO HAUL OFF, AND--

KAR-BLOOOM!
SURPRISED TO SEE ME, YOU?!
PREFERRED YOUR OLD COSTUME, BLONDIE...
BUT BEARD IS NICE!
STELLARIS--?!

YOU'RE ALIVE! THOR WAS RIGHT!
HE ALWAYS KNEW THAT YOU HAD SURVIVED THAT TROUBLE IN THE BLACK GALAXY!*
THAT WHY DESERTED, YOU?
LEFT TO ROT, ME--?!
NO! IT WASN'T LIKE THAT AT ALL--!
*IT HAPPENED IN THOR #424.

A DEBT IS OWED, BLONDIE BOY!
PAYMENT IS SIMPLE, YES?

SHKA-KOW!!
REVENGE IS ALL!!

ELSEWHERE...
TIME IS LIKE A FLOWER IN FULL BLOOM TO ME, DARGO...
I CAN TEAR AWAY THE SECRETS OF ANY ERA AS EASILY AS OTHER MEN PLUCK PETALS FROM A ROSE!

THERE ARE MANY WHO WOULD AGREE WITH YOU...
BEHOLD AN IMAGE OF THE TRUE THUNDER GOD--!
HE...HE LOOKS JUST AS I'VE ALWAYS IMAGINED!
THE PERSONIFICATION OF COURAGE

"IN YOUR PARTICULAR TIME STREAM, YOU BECOME ASSOCIATED WITH A CULT WHICH HAS DISCOVERED AN ANCIENT ARTIFACT... THOR'S ENCHANTED HAMMER!"

"NO ONE IN YOUR ERA KNOWS WHY OR HOW MJOLNIR CAME TO BE EMBEDDED IN THAT STONE!"

"THE ANSWER LIES IN THE TIME PERIOD WHICH IS OUR DESTINATION... WHERE ERIC MASTERSON, A CUNNING CRIMINAL, HAS MANAGED TO STEAL THE HAMMER!"
"ACCORDING TO HISTORY, HE DIES BEFORE THE THUNDER GOD CAN RECLAIM IT...
"...WHICH IS WHY IT EVENTUALLY COMES INTO YOUR POSSESSION!"

HOWEVER, I HAVE DISCOVERED THE PRESENCE OF A VERY DISRUPTIVE ANOMALY!
A TIME VIRUS WHICH COULD ALLOW MASTERSON TO FORM A RELATIONSHIP WITH AN ALIEN...AND DRASTICALLY ALTER HIS FUTURE!
IF THIS VARIANT IS PERMITTED TO OCCUR, YOUR PARTICULAR TIME-STREAM WILL IMMEDIATELY CEASE TO EXIST!
SALLA--?!
IF MASTERSON LIVES... SHE WILL DIE!

MEANWHILE...
ROT YOU SLOW AND DIRTY, BLONDIE BOY!
YOU'RE NOT FOOLING ANYONE WITH THAT GUTTER SLANG, STELLARIS!
I ALREADY KNOW THAT YOU'RE AS INTELLIGENT AS YOU ARE DEADLY!

QUANGG
NOW BACK OFF--!

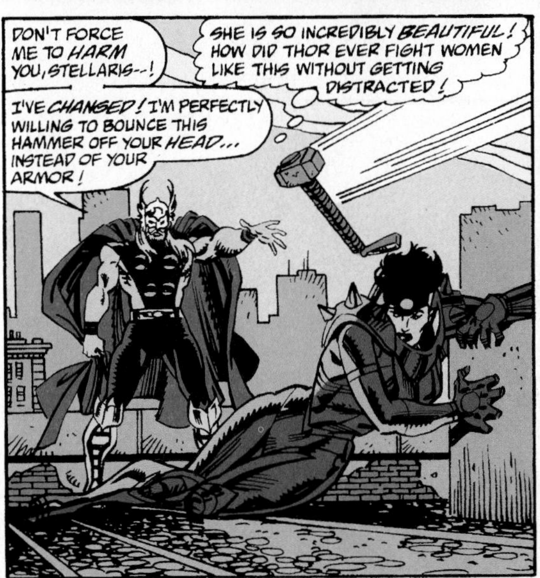
DON'T FORCE ME TO HARM YOU, STELLARIS--!
SHE IS SO INCREDIBLY BEAUTIFUL! HOW DID THOR EVER FIGHT WOMEN LIKE THIS WITHOUT GETTING DISTRACTED?
I'VE CHANGED! I'M PERFECTLY WILLING TO BOUNCE THIS HAMMER OFF YOUR HEAD... INSTEAD OF YOUR ARMOR!

I AM ACTUALLY PLEASED THAT YOU HAVE DISCARDED THAT CHIVALRY NOISE!
IT PUTS US ON AN EQUAL FOOTING!

WE CAN BOTH FIGHT FULL BLAST!
KA-WHOOOM!

CLEAR THE STREETS!
MOVE BACK!
W-WE WOULD HAVE BEEN *CRUSHED* IF YOU HADN'T PUSHED US--!
JUST DOING MY JOB, SON!

I CAN'T HOLD BACK ANY LONGER!
THIS IS NO GAME--!
INNOCENT PEOPLE COULD BE *KILLED* IF STELLARIS CONTINUES HER RAMPAGE!

BUT THEN, EVEN AS ERIC LASHES OUT WITH THE RIGHTEOUS FURY OF A THUNDER GOD--
UGNN
--HE IS UNEXPECTEDLY ATTACKED FROM ABOVE!

T-THAT WAS A *LIGHTNING BOLT!* WHO COULD HAVE--
NO! NO! THIS IS IMPOSSIBLE--!

FOR THE SAKE OF ALL I LOVE... THE *FALSE THOR* MUST *DIE!*
IT'S *RUMBLE TIME*, BLONDIE BOY!

NEXT ISSUE: THE *THOR WAR* CONTINUES AS ERIC IS FORCED TO BATTLE HIS FUTURISTIC COUNTERPART IN A TALE WE COULD ONLY CALL...

"WHEN HAMMERS CLASH!"

PLUS! AT LONG LAST! THE DYNAMIC, MUCH-REQUESTED RETURN OF **BETA RAY BILL!**

MARVEL COMICS

THE THOR WAR! PART 2 OF 4

THE MIGHTY THOR

$1.00 US
$1.25 CAN/UK 65p
439
LATE NOV
02450

APPROVED BY THE COMICS CODE AUTHORITY

The MASTER PLAN OF THE TOMORROW MAN: REVEALED!

WHEN HAMMERS CLASH!

PLUS: TALES OF ASGARD

FRENZ & MILGROM

WHEN ARCHITECT **ERIC MASTERSON** STAMPS HIS WOODEN WALKING-STICK UPON THE GROUND, HE IS TRANSFORMED INTO THE NORSE GOD OF THUNDER. ARMED WITH HIS ENCHANTED HAMMER, HE IS AT ONCE MASTER OF THE STORM, LORD OF THE LIVING LIGHTNING, AND ONE OF THE STRONGEST WARRIORS WHO EVER WALKED THE EARTH! STAN LEE PRESENTS . . .

THE MIGHTY THOR!
WHEN HAMMERS CLASH!
DUPED BY ZARRKO THE TOMORROW MAN, DARGO KTOR, THE THOR OF 2591, HAS JOURNEYED TO OUR PRESENT WITH ONE BLAZING THOUGHT--
THE FALSE THOR MUST DIE!
UNFORTUNATELY, OUR HERO ALREADY HAS HIS HANDS FULL WITH STELLARIS, THE CELESTIAL SLAYER!
JUICE UP, BEARDIE BOY! REVENGE IS ALL!
NEEDLESS TO SAY, ERIC MASTERSON IS NOT HAVING A GOOD DAY, AND IT'S ABOUT TO GET SIGNIFICANTLY WORSE--!

RON FRENZ & TOM DEFALCO — PLOT, PENCILS & SCRIPT . AL MILGROM — FINISHED ART . MIKE ROCKWITZ — COLORIST . STEVE DUTRO — LETTERS . RALPH MACCHIO — EDITOR

BACK OFF, METAL HEAD!
THE IMPOSTER BELONGS TO ME!
IF HE LIVES, MY WIFE-- MY FRIENDS-- THE EXISTENCE OF MY ENTIRE TIME-STREAM IS IN JEOPARDY!
BEARDIE BOY, MINE!
LEFT TO ROT IN SPACE, ME!
MUST PAY, HIM!
WRR
KLIK
Y-YOUR ARMOR SEEMS TO BE MUTATING--!

I AM!

SHEESH! I WISH THAT WOMAN WOULD MAKE UP HER MIND!
IF THIS KEEPS UP, I'M GONNA NEED A SCORECARD TO KEEP TRACK OF EVERYONE TRYING TO CLOBBER ME!

WHEW! AT LEAST THIS CLOWN IS CONSISTENT!
WHO ARE YOU, MAN?
DON'T TELL ME THAT SOMEONE LICENSED A THOR MOVIE WHILE MY BACK WAS TURNED... AND YOU'RE WEARING THE NEW COSTUME!
IT ISN'T AS BAD AS THE TELEVISION VERSION, BUT IT LACKS A CERTAIN FINESSE!
I'LL GIVE YOU FINESSE... RIGHT IN THE HEAD!

MY! MY! AREN'T YOU THE ANGRY YOUNG MAN! I OUGHTA-- HEY! LOOK OUT
KZAK
A BLAST FROM ABOVE--!

I HATE TO INTRUDE UPON YOUR PRIVATE PARTY, PRETTY BOY--
--BUT I HATE BEING IGNORED EVEN MORE!

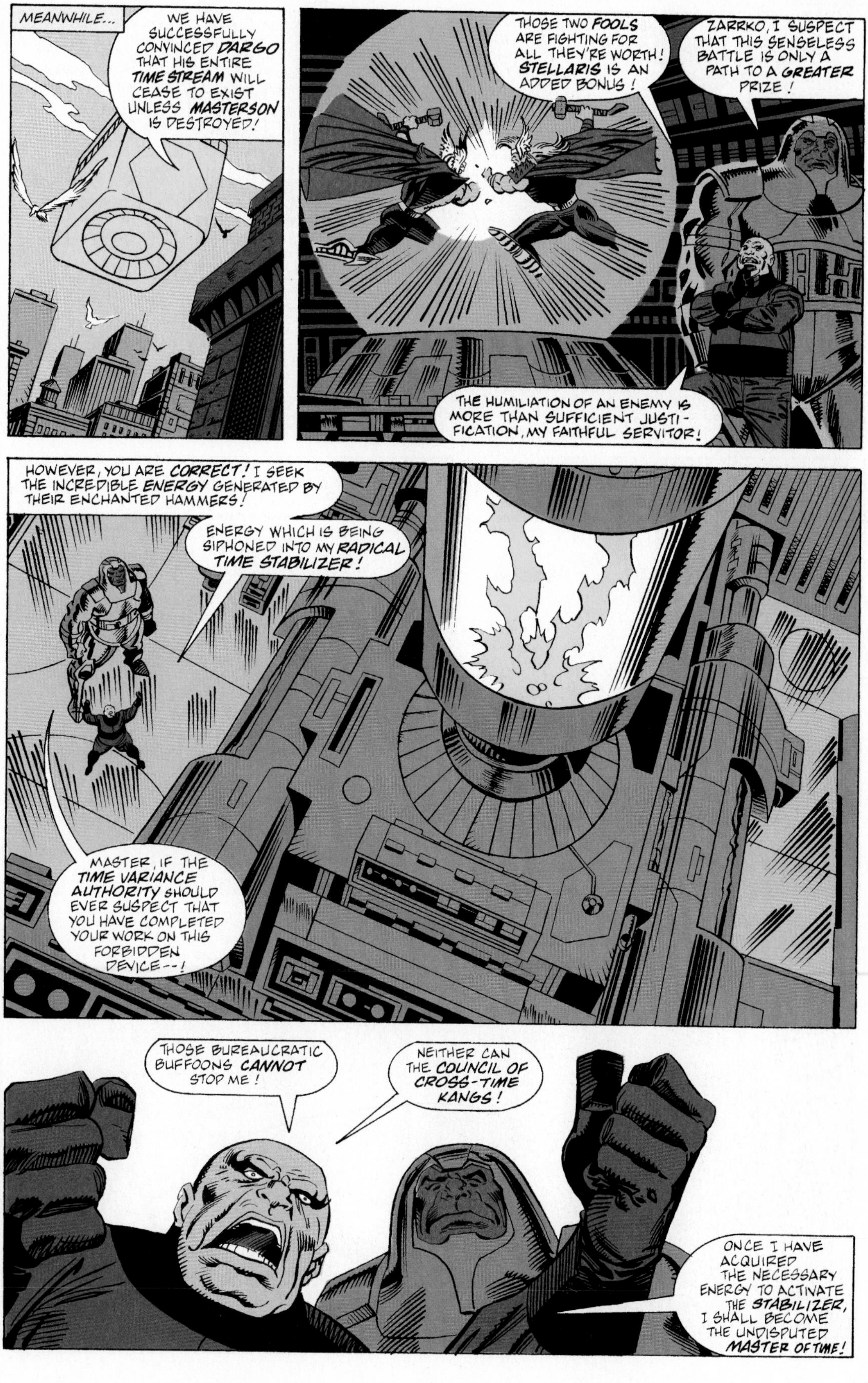

HOWEVER, YOU ARE CORRECT! I SEEK THE INCREDIBLE ENERGY GENERATED BY THEIR ENCHANTED HAMMERS!

ENERGY WHICH IS BEING SIPHONED INTO MY RADICAL TIME STABILIZER!

MASTER, IF THE TIME VARIANCE AUTHORITY SHOULD EVER SUSPECT THAT YOU HAVE COMPLETED YOUR WORK ON THIS FORBIDDEN DEVICE--!

AND, AT THAT MOMENT...
MEN! I JOURNEY COUNTLESS LIGHT YEARS TO VENT A LITTLE RIGHTEOUS INDIGNATION, BUT THOSE TWO ARE MORE INTERESTED IN ACTING OUT THE ANCIENT TRIBAL RITUAL OF MALE BONDING!
MAY AS WELL DISCARD MY BATTLE HELMET, AND ENJOY THE SHOW!
YOUR HAMMER--! CLOSE UP IT LOOKS EXACTLY LIKE MINE! BUT THAT'S IMPOSSIBLE--!

ANYTHING IS POSSIBLE TO ONE WHO WIELDS THE POWER OF A THUNDER GOD!
I AM THE THOR OF YOUR FUTURE!
IS THAT ANY RELATION TO THE CHEF OF THE FUTURE?

WISE UP, SONNY BOY! I ALREADY SAT THROUGH TERMINATOR II ... AND I'M NOT FALLING FOR ANY TIME PARADOX JAZZ!
LET'S JUST SEE HOW YOUR CHEAP IMITATION STANDS UP TO THE REAL THING--!

QUITE WELL BY ANY STANDARD!

GET THAT CAMERA INTO POSITION! IT'S PURE LUCK THAT WE HAPPENED TO BE IN THIS NEIGHBORHOOD TO GET THIS EXCLUSIVE FOOTAGE! WE'RE PRACTICALLY GUARANTEED AN EMMY, AND-- YEOW!
KAR-PWOOM

EEYIIIII

WHAT HAVE I DONE--?!
NICE SHOT, SONNY BOY! WHAT ARE YOU GOING TO DO NEXT--TRASH A KINDERGARTEN?!
DON'T BE SO FAST TO CAST BLAME, OLD MAN! IT WAS YOUR BEAM THAT I DEFLECTED!
NEVER MIND THAT NOW! GET OUT OF MY WAY!
IT'S TIME FOR ME TO DO MY HERO THING!

I'M GOING WITH YOU! IT'S MY RESPONSIBILITY TO SAVE THOSE PEOPLE!
HAMMERS HIGH!
SHEESH! YOU CALL THAT A BATTLE-CRY?!
YOU GOT A BETTER ONE?
NO, BUT THAT'S NOT THE POINT.

A TRUCE IN MID-BATTLE--?!
HAVE THESE FOOLS NO DESIRE FOR A CRUSHING VICTORY? NO PRIDE IN THEIR WARRIOR'S CRAFT?!
A FEW INNOCENT DEATHS ARE A SMALL PRICE TO PAY FOR THE GLORIOUS THRILL OF BATTLE!

BAH! THOSE TWO LACK THE STOMACH TO PROVIDE ME WITH ADEQUATE SPORT!
PERHAPS, I AM ALREADY SUFFICIENTLY RESTED TO RENEW MY WAR ON THE MURDEROUS CELESTIALS, AND-- WAIT! MY INTERNAL SCANNERS JUST DETECTED SOMETHING INTERESTING!

WHAT MANNER OF VEHICLES ARE THESE?
THOUGH THEY ROAR WITH PASSION AND FURY... THEY CLING TO THE GROUND WITH A CERTAIN HAUGHTY NOBILITY WHICH APPEALS TO ME!

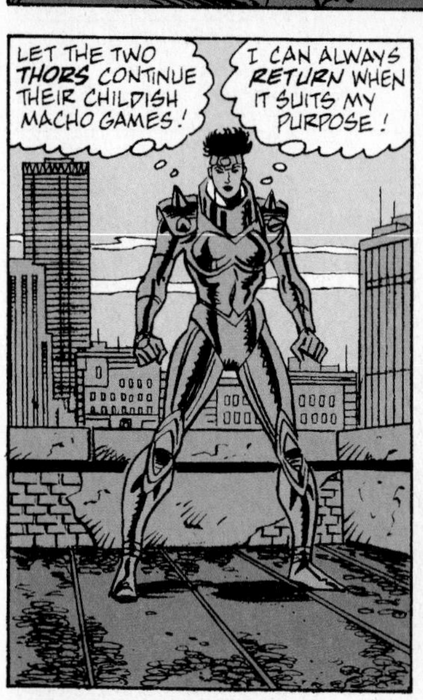
LET THE TWO THORS CONTINUE THEIR CHILDISH MACHO GAMES!
I CAN ALWAYS RETURN WHEN IT SUITS MY PURPOSE!

AS FOR NOW, I SHALL COMMAND MY LIVING ARMOR TO REFORM--

--AND RETOOL ITSELF AROUND ME!
I RARELY TAKE TIME OUT TO RELAX...

BUT WHEN I DO... YAHOO!
YOU RESCUED ME... SO THAT MEANS YOU OWE ME AN INTERVIEW!
I HAVE NO TIME FOR SUCH FOOLISHNESS, WOMAN!

THE LIVES OF ALL I CHERISH ARE LOST... UNLESS THAT MAN DIES!
DON'T GET MELODRAMATIC ON ME, PAL!
I'M SURE WE CAN SOLVE YOUR PROB-LEM... WHATEVER IT IS!
NO! I CAN'T TAKE THAT RISK!
DEFEND YOURSELF!

ELSEWHERE, AT THAT VERY INSTANT...
BY THE WAY, MARCY... I FINALLY GOT HOLD OF MASTERSON, TODAY!
DID YOU TALK TO HIM ABOUT KEVIN?

YEAH, YEAH, I TOLD HIM ALL ABOUT OUR PLAN TO HAVE ME ADOPT THE KID!
HOW... DID HE REACT?

ACTUALLY, HE WAS PRETTY COOL! HE TOOK IT A LOT BETTER'N I WOULD HAVE!

CONSIDERING THE WAY HE'S BEEN MESSING UP LATELY, I GUESS MASTERSON REALIZES THAT THIS IS WHAT'S BEST FOR THE KID!

I CAN'T BELIEVE IT WENT SO EASILY! NOT AFTER THE BITTER WAY ERIC FOUGHT TO KEEP CUSTODY OF KEVIN!
WELL... THE GUY DID BELT ME ONE!
BOBBIE STEELE! YOU CAN BE SUCH A BONE-HEADED, MACHO GOON AT TIMES!

WHAT'S THE PROBLEM, MARCY? THAT PUNCH WAS STRICTLY BETWEEN MASTERSON 'N ME!
WHAT DIFFERENCE COULD IT POSSIBLY MAKE?

STAY BACK! I'M WARNING YOU!
NOBODY USES ME FOR A PUNCHING BAG!
IF YOU WON'T LISTEN TO REASON, YOU'LL SUFFER THE BRUTAL CONSEQUENCES!
CLEAR THE STREETS, PEOPLE! YOU MUST EVACUATE THE AREA FOR YOUR OWN SAFETY! THOSE TWO WILL KEEP POUNDING AT EACH OTHER UNTIL SOMEBODY ENDS UP DEAD!
SCAN STRAIGHT, OLD MAN! YOU'RE FIGHTING SOMEONE WHO CAN EASILY MATCH YOU POWER FOR POWER!
BUT, EVEN IF OUR STRENGTH IS EXACTLY EQUAL ... I'M STILL YOUNGER!
FASTER!
AND, BASED ON THE WAY YOU HANDLE YOURSELF... A WHOLE LOT MORE EXPERIENCED!
HE'S PLAYING ME FOR A FIRST CLASS CHUMP!
BUT, IT'S MY OWN FAULT! I SHOULDN'T HAVE HELD BACK--!

I'VE HAD ENOUGH!
UNLIKE YOU, I NEVER BOTHERED TO PRACTICE ANY FANCY MOVES WITH MY HAMMER!
I PREFER THE DIRECT APPROACH!

THIS SHOCKWAVE WILL BOUNCE YOU RIGHT INTO RANGE--
THOOM

--FOR ONE OF MY GENUINE, HIGHLY PRIZED MALLET MIGRAINES!
QWOMP

KEE-RASH
THE AREA IS COMLETELY SECURE! THE BUILDINGS HAVE ALL BEEN EMPTIED!

HE-HE'S GIVING ME TIME TO RECOVER BEFORE HE PRESSES HIS ATTACK!
I ALMOST CAN'T BELIEVE THAT A MAN LIKE THIS WILL BE RESPONSIBLE FOR THE DESTRUCTION OF ALL THAT I LOVE!
ALL RIGHT, FUZZ-FACE! LET'S FINISH IT! NOW!

YOU GOT IT, PAL!
MY HAMMER AGAINST YOURS--!
WINNER TAKE ALL!

QUA-PWOOM

EVEN AS ENCHANTED HAMMER COLLIDES WITH ENCHANTED HAMMER, A WAVE OF UNCONTROL-LABLE MYSTICAL ENERGY ERUPTS SIMULTANEOUSLY ACROSS ALL PLANES OF REALITY!

NOT SINCE THE LEGENDARY BIG BANG HAS SUCH AN IRRESISTIBLE FORCE BEEN LOOSED IN THIS UNIVERSE!

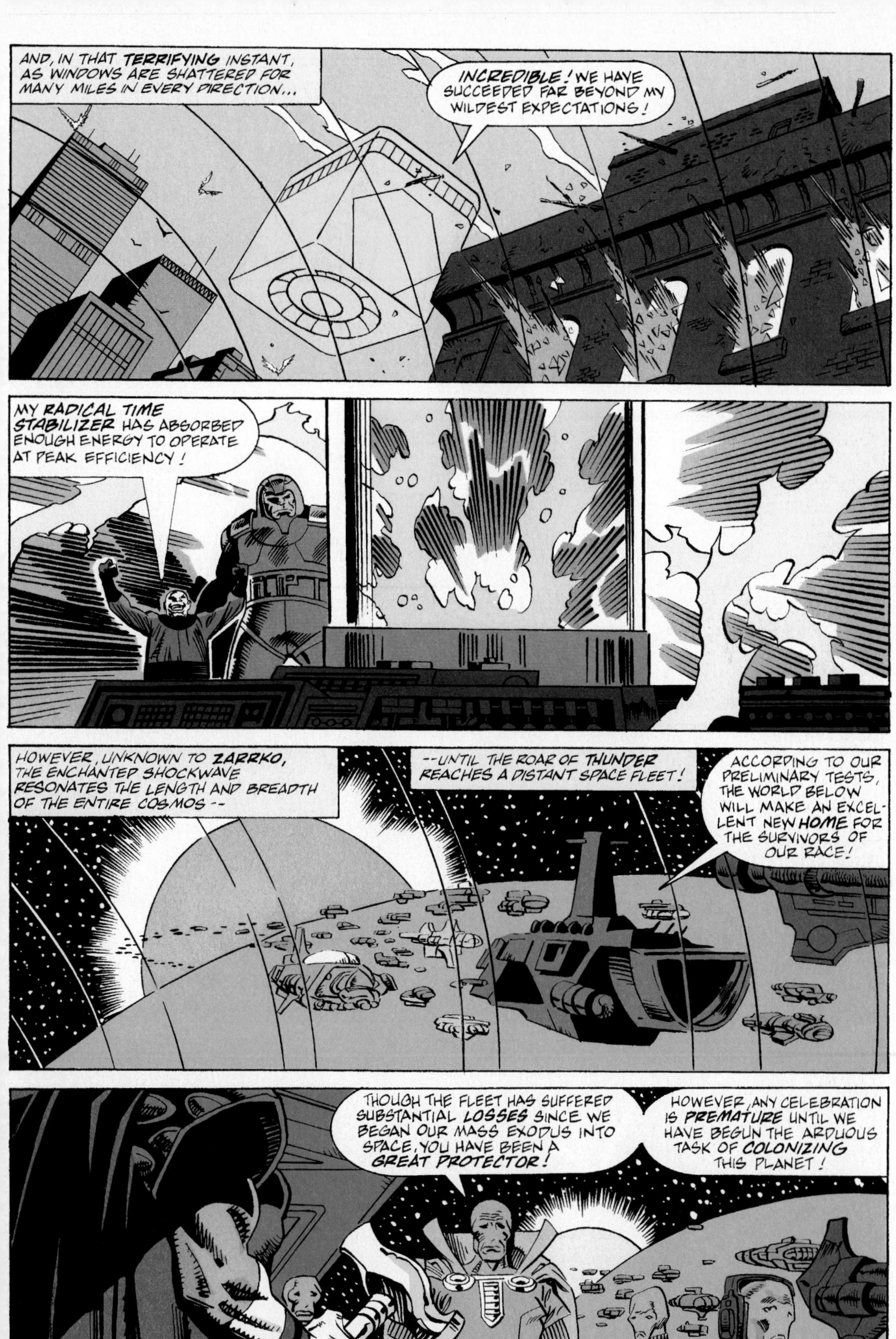
AND, IN THAT TERRIFYING INSTANT, AS WINDOWS ARE SHATTERED FOR MANY MILES IN EVERY DIRECTION...
INCREDIBLE! WE HAVE SUCCEEDED FAR BEYOND MY WILDEST EXPECTATIONS!
MY RADICAL TIME STABILIZER HAS ABSORBED ENOUGH ENERGY TO OPERATE AT PEAK EFFICIENCY!
HOWEVER, UNKNOWN TO ZARRKO, THE ENCHANTED SHOCKWAVE RESONATES THE LENGTH AND BREADTH OF THE ENTIRE COSMOS--
--UNTIL THE ROAR OF THUNDER REACHES A DISTANT SPACE FLEET!
ACCORDING TO OUR PRELIMINARY TESTS, THE WORLD BELOW WILL MAKE AN EXCEL-LENT NEW HOME FOR THE SURVIVORS OF OUR RACE!
THOUGH THE FLEET HAS SUFFERED SUBSTANTIAL LOSSES SINCE WE BEGAN OUR MASS EXODUS INTO SPACE, YOU HAVE BEEN A GREAT PROTECTOR!
HOWEVER, ANY CELEBRATION IS PREMATURE UNTIL WE HAVE BEGUN THE ARDUOUS TASK OF COLONIZING THIS PLANET!
I UNDERSTAND, IMPERIAL LEADER, AND I--

WHY DO YOU HESITATE, PROTECTOR?
DO YOU DETECT SOME HIDDEN MENACE?
MY MAGIC HAMMER-- STORM BREAKER-- IS REVERBERATING TO AN UNKNOWN CATALYST!
I SENSE THAT I AM NEEDED ON THE PLANET CALLED EARTH!

YOUR ONLY RESPONSIBILITY IS TO YOUR PEOPLE!
YOU CANNOT DESERT US!

BUT, LEADER--! THERE IS A SACRED BOND WHICH UNITES ALL WHO HAVE EVER BEEN PRIVILEGED TO HANDLE SACRED MJOLNIR!
A BOND WHICH CANNOT BE IGNORED!
IGNORE IT, YOU MUST!
YOUR DUTY IS HERE!

MEANWHILE...
WHEW!
LET'S NEVER DO THAT AGAIN!
YOU FINALLY CONVINCED ME, PAL!
ONLY MJOLNIR COULD HAVE STOOD UP TO MJOLNIR LIKE THAT!
BUT...HOW CAN ONE OBJECT EXIST IN TWO DIFFERENT PLACES AT THE SAME TIME?!

TIME IS A GREAT MYSTERY, OLD MAN! NO ONE UNDERSTANDS ITS TRUE NATURE!
MAYBE THE HAMMER BONDS SO COMPLETELY WITH ITS WIELDER THAT IT REALLY ISN'T THE SAME!
OR, MAYBE ITS ENCHANTED POWERS SIMPLY TRANSCEND THE NATURAL LAWS OF SCIENCE!
WHATEVER THE EXPLANATION, IT WON'T MATTER MUCH LONGER TO YOU!
SO! YOU'RE STILL DETERMINED TO CONTINUE THIS NEEDLESS BATTLE!

BUT THEN, EVEN BEFORE ANOTHER WORD CAN BE SPOKEN, A DAZZLING COSMIC BOLT SEPARATES THE TWO WARRIORS, AND A RESOUNDING VOICE RINGS OUT--
STOP! CEASE THIS SENSELESS STRIFE!

LOOK--!
IT CAN'T BE!
WHAT IS THIS--SOME KIND OF CRAZY CONVENTION?!

YOU MUST RESOLVE YOUR DIFFERENCES WITHOUT VIOLENCE!
YOU ARE BOTH BROTHERS OF THE SACRED HAMMER!
PRIVILEGED WARRIORS WHO HAVE BEEN DEEMED WORTHY ENOUGH TO POSSESS THE POWER OF A THUNDER GOD!
IT'S BETA RAY BILL!!
I REMEMBER HEARING THE LEGEND OF THIS GREAT WARRIOR FROM THE STARS-- BUT I NEVER BELIEVED THAT HE REALLY EXISTED!
HE'S SO ALIEN--! AND YET, NOBILITY CLINGS TO HIM LIKE A SECOND SKIN!
HE REMINDS ME SO MUCH OF THE ORIGINAL THOR!

HOW DID THE TWO OF YOU COME TO BE?!
AND, WHERE IS THE TRUE THUNDER GOD?!
I'M AFRAID THAT'S A LONG STORY!
BUT, ONE WHICH MUST BE TOLD--!

AND SO, SOMETIME LATER...
MASTER! A THIRD THOR HAS JOINED THE OTHERS!
THEY HAVE BANDED TOGETHER!
THAT IS OF NO CONCERN TO US!

WE HAVE ALREADY ACHIEVED OUR PURPOSE!
THERE IS NO LONGER ANY REASON TO REMAIN IN THIS TIME PERIOD!

WE ARE TOO LATE!
THE TIME CUBE IS VANISHING!

WHAT AM I SUPPOSED TO DO NOW ?!
EVEN IF ZARRKO WAS LYING--AND SALLA IS SAFE--I CAN NEVER RETURN TO HER! I'M TRAPPED IN THIS TIME!
DO NOT DESPAIR, DARGO! ZARRKO HAS APPARENTLY ABSORBED A VAST QUANTITY OF ENCHANTED ENERGY --AND WE CAN USE OUR HAMMERS TO FOLLOW HIM!
ARE YOU SUGGESTING THAT WE TRACK HIM THROUGH TIME--?!

FORGET IT, HANDSOME! LEAVE ME OUT OF IT!
I HAVE ENOUGH TROUBLE DEALING WITH THE HERE AND NOW!
ASIDE FROM BOBBIE STEELE TRYING TO ADOPT MY SON... I'VE GOT TO FIND OUT WHAT'S LEFT OF MY APARTMENT AFTER THE WAY STELLARIS RECENTLY TRASHED IT!
WHICH REMINDS ME ...WHERE IS STELLARIS?!

YOU COWARD! I KNEW I COULDN'T TRUST YOU!
LOOK INTO YOUR HEART, ERIC!
HONOR DEMANDS THAT YOU AID YOUR BROTHER!

YOU HAVE A RESPONSIBILITY TO THE MEMORY OF THE ORIGINAL THUNDER GOD!

TOGETHER, WE SHALL FIND AND DEFEAT THIS TOMORROW MAN!

I'M WITH YOU, BILL! IT'S MY ONLY HOPE OF RETURNING HOME!

ERIC--?

YOU GUYS ARE CRAZY BUT, OKAY--
HAMMERS HIGH!
SO BE IT! UNTIL NEXT MONTH...

$1.00 US
$1.25 CAN/UK 65p
440
EARLY DEC
CC 02450
APPROVED BY THE COMICS CODE AUTHORITY

THE THOR WAR! PART 3 OF 4

THE MIGHTY THOR®

AND NOW...

the THOR CORPS

FRENZ & MILGROM

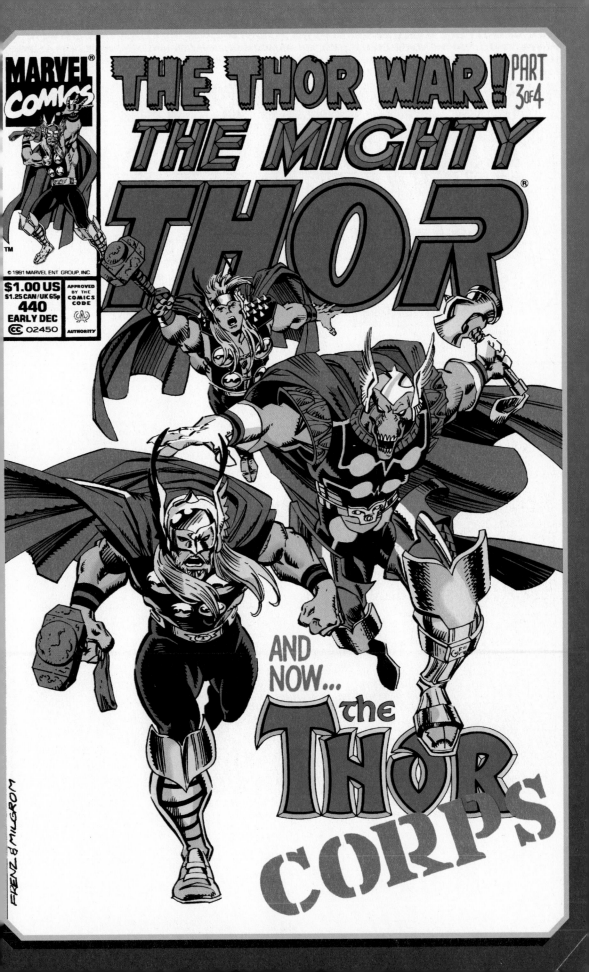

WHEN ARCHITECT **ERIC MASTERSON** STAMPS HIS WOODEN WALKING-STICK UPON THE GROUND, HE IS TRANSFORMED INTO THE NORSE GOD OF THUNDER. ARMED WITH HIS ENCHANTED HAMMER, HE IS AT ONCE MASTER OF THE STORM, LORD OF THE LIVING LIGHTNING, AND ONE OF THE STRONGEST WARRIORS WHO EVER WALKED THE EARTH! STAN LEE PRESENTS . . .

THE MIGHTY THOR!

ALL THE RIVERS RUN!
IS THIS A GREAT PLANE OF REALITY, OR WHAT?!
WHERE ELSE COULD A SIMPLE CHILD FROM AN OVERCROWDED URBAN CENTER GROW UP TO BECOME THE MASTER OF TIME?!
ALL IT TOOK WAS A DREAM... AND THE ENCHANTED ENERGY STOLEN FROM THOSE SURROGATE THORS FOR MY RADICAL TIME STABILIZER!
I WISH MY POOR MOTHER COULD SEE ME NOW!
SINCE TIME ITSELF IS SUBJECT TO YOUR WHIM, ZARRKO... YOU COULD EASILY VISIT HER AT ANY POINT OF HER EXISTENCE!

TOM DEFALCO & RON FRENZ — PLOT, PENCILS & SCRIPT
AL MILGROM — FINISHED ART
MICHAEL HEISLER — LETTERER
MIKE ROCKWITZ — COLORIST
RALPH MACCHIO — EDITOR

THAT IS TRUE, MY FAITHFUL SERVITOR...
HOWEVER, I DID NOT DESIGN MY TIME CUBE WITH INNOCENT SOCIAL CALLS IN MIND!

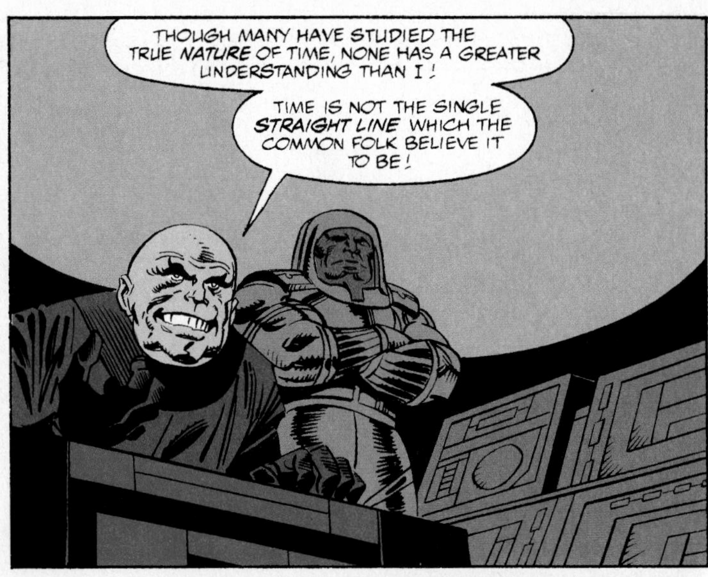
THOUGH MANY HAVE STUDIED THE TRUE NATURE OF TIME, NONE HAS A GREATER UNDERSTANDING THAN I!
TIME IS NOT THE SINGLE STRAIGHT LINE WHICH THE COMMON FOLK BELIEVE IT TO BE!

INSTEAD, IT IS A LINE WITH A MULTITUDE OF BRANCHES WHICH EXTEND FROM THE CENTRAL TRUNK AT CERTAIN CRITICAL JUNCTURES!
AND EACH BRANCH GIVES BIRTH TO AN ENDLESS GROWTH OF NEW BRANCHES!

BECAUSE THERE ARE AN INFINITE NUMBER OF VARIATIONS, ANYTHING IS POSSIBLE IN THE TIME STREAMS -- INCLUDING ALTERNATE WORLDS IN WHICH OTHER FORMS OF LIFE ASSUMED DOMINANT ROLES ON EARTH!

MY RADICAL TIME STABILIZER WILL BRING ORDER TO THIS CHAOS!
IT WILL COLLAPSE ALL OF THE TIME LINES INTO A SINGLE ENTITY!
ONE IN WHICH I SHALL BE PROCLAIMED AS THE SOLE LORD OF TIME!

MEANWHILE, BACK ON PRESENT-DAY PLANET EARTH...
TAKE HEED, FELLOW THUNDERERS--! STORM BREAKER HAS FINALLY LOCATED THE ENERGY TRAIL LEFT BEHIND BY THE ONE CALLED ZARRKO, THE TOMORROW MAN!
WHOOP-DE-DOO! I CAN'T WAIT TO GO TRAIPSING THROUGH THE TIME BARRIER AFTER THAT CLOWN!
SCRAG THE ATTITUDE, OLD MAN!

MY WIFE... AND MY ENTIRE TIMELINE... COULD DIE IF WE DON'T SLAG THAT SLUG!
LOOK WHO'S TALKING ATTITUDE!
KEEP IT UP... AND YOU'LL FIND A MALLET WHERE YOUR MOUTH SHOULD BE!

DARGO! ERIC! BE SILENT!
YOUR CONTINUOUS BICKERING ILL SERVES THE MEMORY OF THE TRUE THUNDER GOD!
WE ARE ALL BROTHERS OF THE SACRED HAMMER WHO HAVE BEEN GIFTED WITH THE POWER OF THOR!
WE ARE BOUND BY HONOR TO AID ONE ANOTHER!
WE ALREADY HEARD THAT RAP, BILL!

LET'S JUST GET THE SHOW ON THE ROAD!
VERY WELL! TAKE YOUR POSITIONS--!

IF WE ARE TO PIERCE THE VEIL OF TIME, IT WILL SURELY REQUIRE THE COMBINED ENCHANTMENT OF ALL OF OUR HAMMERS!
YOU MUST DO EXACTLY AS I DO--!

ONCE OUR HAMMERS ARE IN PERFECT TUNE, WE SHALL--

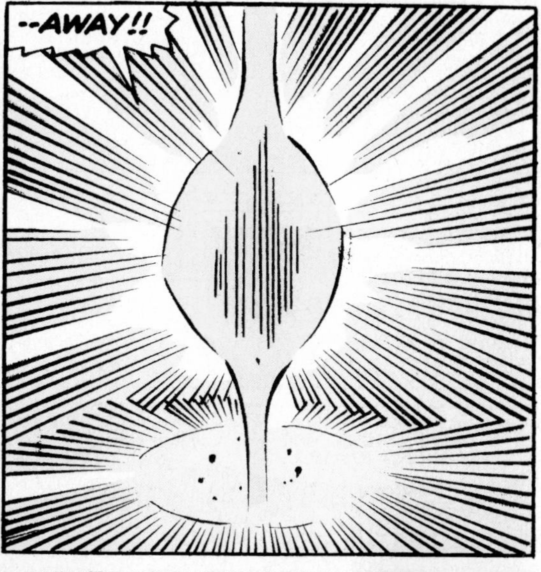
--AWAY!!

JUST THEN, AT CITY HOSPITAL...
THE LONGER MISS AUSTIN REMAINS IN THIS COMA, THE DIMMER HER CHANCES FOR RECOVERY!
I... I'M GOING TO LOSE HER UNLESS I CAN LOCATE DR. DON BLAKE, AND CONVINCE HIM TO OPERATE ON HER!
DOCTOR PARETSKY--? I HATE TO DISTURB YOU WHEN YOU'RE WITH A PATIENT...

THIS MESSAGE JUST ARRIVED! IT'S MARKED URGENT!
I... I HOPE IT'S GOOD NEWS!

YES!!

MEANTIME...
MASTER! THE THOR SURROGATES HAVE BANDED TOGETHER EXACTLY AS YOU PREDICTED!

THEY HAVE SOMEHOW ENTERED THIS MISTY LIMBO, AND ARE STREAKING TOWARD US!
AN APPROPRIATE RECEPTION HAS ALREADY BEEN PREPARED FOR THEM, FAITHFUL ONE!

I'VE GOT TO HAND IT TO YOU, BILL! I NEVER THOUGHT WE'D GET THIS FAR--!
THIS CEILING LOWERS INTO THE SHIP'S INTERIOR!
THERE MUST BE A TRIGGERING MECHANISM SOMEWHERE--!

FORGET IT, BILL! WE DON'T HAVE TIME TO SEARCH FOR IT!
I'LL JUST USE MY HANDY-DANDY URU OPENER!

CRUDE... BUT EFFECTIVE!
BE CAUTIOUS, ERIC! OVERCONFIDENCE IS A SURE PATH TO DEFEAT!
YOU MAY HAVE UNINTENTIONALLY ACTIVATED A TRAP!

STAY TOGETHER! WE DARE NOT BE SEPARATED NOW--!
LIGHTEN UP, HANDSOME! YOU'RE NOT THE ONLY ONE WHO TAKES HERO PILLS!

THE PATHETIC FOOLS! THEY SHALL FIND ONLY DEATH IN THESE CORRIDORS!
I CAN SIMPLY OPEN THE CORRIDORS OF TIME--

"--AND SUMMON SUITABLE PAWNS TO DISPOSE OF THEM!"
BROTHERS, BEWARE--!
THE SHADOWS TEEM WITH MENACE!

BILL, LOOK OUT--! I RECOGNIZE THAT GUY!
THE GREY GARGOYLE!!
WHO ARE YOU? WHY DID YOU BRING ME HERE? Y-YOU'RE SOME KIND OF GROSS PARODY OF THOR!
I ONLY KNOW THAT I MUST DESTROY YOU!

BACK, DEMON! THOUGH YOU SMITE WITH A FIST OF STONE, IT WILL AVAIL YOU NAUGHT!
SHAKK!
GREATER STILL IS THE POWER OF BETA RAY BILL!

THE PURPOSE OF THIS BATTLE ELUDES ME--
--BUT MERCURIO THE 4-D MAN MUST STRIKE WITH HIS FIRE AND ICE!
ZARRKO IS USING THE REAL THOR'S OLD SPARRING PARTNERS AGAINST US!

HE PROBABLY FIGURES THAT WE DON'T HAVE THE NECESSARY EXPERIENCE TO BEAT THEM ALL!
BUT THESE GUYS ARE DAZED... SLUGGISH... AFTER THEIR TRIP THROUGH TIME!
DARGO, BEHIND YOU--!

TOO LATE!
YOUR FRIEND HAS ALREADY FALLEN VICTIM TO THE COBRA!

HOWEVER, THIS WHELP IS A LITTLE TOO YOUNG FOR ME--

-- SO I'M GOING TO TOSS HIM BACK!
PWAK!
AYE! RIGHT INTO THE HUNGRY FISTS OF TYRUS THE TERRIBLE-- THE RIGHTFUL RULER OF ALL ROCK TROLLS!
UGNN

AT LAST! AT LONG LAST! TYRUS SHALL WREAK HIS UNHOLY VENGEANCE UPON THEE, LITTLE MAN!
THOU SHALT PAY FOR ALL OF MY PAST DEFEATS... AND HUMILIATIONS!

IT IS FAR MORE ENTERTAINING TO WATCH A BATTLE THAN TO PARTICIPATE IN IT!
SAFER, TOO!
AW! THE YOUNG FOOL DROPPED HIS HAMMER--!

WHAT A PITY!

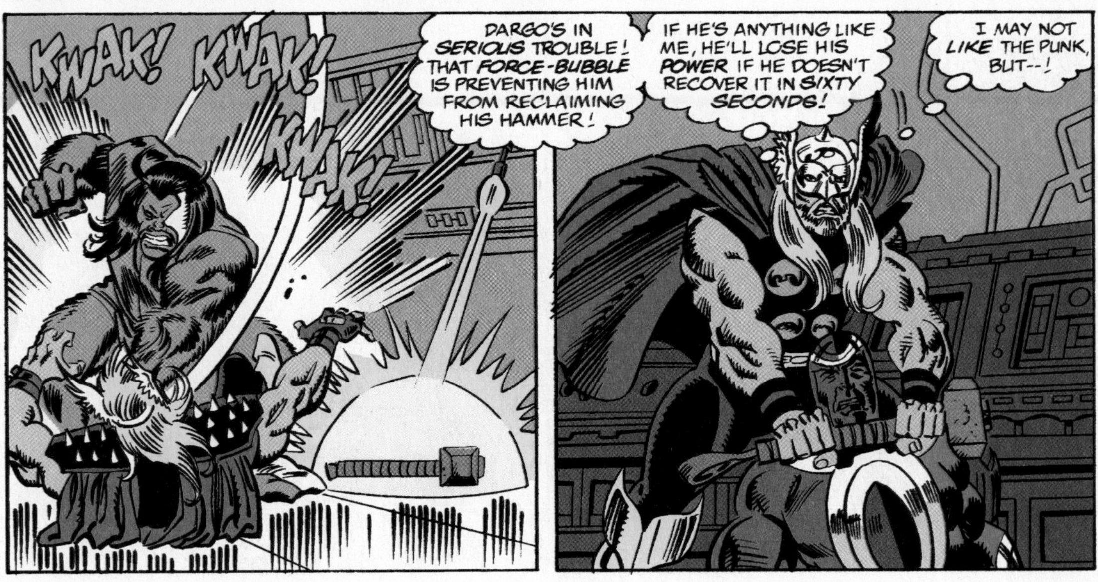
KWAK! KWAK! KWAK!
DARGO'S IN SERIOUS TROUBLE! THAT FORCE-BUBBLE IS PREVENTING HIM FROM RECLAIMING HIS HAMMER!
IF HE'S ANYTHING LIKE ME, HE'LL LOSE HIS POWER IF HE DOESN'T RECOVER IT IN SIXTY SECONDS!
I MAY NOT LIKE THE PUNK, BUT--!

SINCE WE BOTH WIELD THE SAME HAMMER FROM DIFFERENT ERAS, THERE'S A WILD CHANCE THIS TRICK COULD WORK--!
DARGO, CATCH--!

KA-BWOOM!

SWAK!
NICE MOVE, OLD PAL! TOO BAD IT LEFT YOU DE-FENSELESS!
A SITUATION SHATTERFIST MEANS TO EXPLOIT!

CONSIDER THIS JUSTIFIABLE PAYBACK, BUDDY BOY!
ERIC! I'M HANDING OFF--!
TALK ABOUT WEIRD! THIS GUY IS OBVIOUSLY FROM MY FUTURE--!

BUT I CAN'T WORRY ABOUT ALL OF THESE TIME PARADOXES!
HA! MY POWER GLOVES CAN EVENTUALLY CONQUER EVEN YOUR MAGIC HAMMER!
IF THAT'S THE CASE, I'D BETTER TRY ANOTHER TACTIC--!
W-WHAT ARE YOU UFFF!

THUNDER GOD--! I DO NOT KNOW HOW YOU HAVE MANAGED TO SUMMON ME TO THIS UNKNOWN PLACE--

--BUT I AM FULLY PREPARED TO RENEW OUR DESPERATE CONTEST!
DEMONSTAFF!! MY GREATEST ENEMY!
THINGS CAN'T POSSIBLY GET ANY WORSE--!

ON THE CONTRARY, THOU ARROGANT LITTLE CUR--!
THOU HAST YET TO FACE THE UNSTOPPABLE FURY OF UROC THE URU WARRIOR!

MEANWHILE...
YOU SEEN THE KID, MARCY?

IT'S TIME FOR OUR DAILY WEIGHT TRAINING, AND I CAN'T FIND HIM ANYWHERE!
THAT'S ODD! HIS TOYS WERE ON THE FLOOR OUTSIDE OUR ROOM!
COULD HE HAVE HEARD US DISCUSSING HIM?!

THIS SITE MANAGED BY
SAPRISTI
CONSTRUCTION
A SUPREMO COMPANY
I...I'M REAL CONFUSED, JERRY!

BOBBY STEELE, MY MOM'S NEW HUSBAND, WANTS TO ADOPT ME!
THE GUY'S A JOCK, AND CAN BE SUCH A FEEB AT TIMES... BUT HE MEANS WELL!
I... I WANT TO TALK TO MY REAL DAD... BUT HE'S NEVER HOME!

C'MON, KEVIN... ERIC LOVES YOU VERY MUCH!
THAT'S THE POINT, JERRY! YOU'RE ALWAYS STUCK MAKING SACRIFICES FOR THE PEOPLE YOU LOVE!
MY DAD'S BEEN GOING THROUGH A ROUGH TIME LATELY! HIS BUSINESS HAS GONE COLD... AND HE KEEPS DISAPPEARING ON ME!
MAYBE HE'S ALREADY SACRIFICED ENOUGH!

MAYBE HE'D JUST BE BETTER OFF WITHOUT ME!

AND, JUST THEN...
INSECTS! FLEAS! NONE CAN DEFEAT ONE WHO IS COMPOSED OF LIVING URU METAL!
FORTUNE SMILES UPON YOU, THUNDERER! WE MUST POSTPONE OUR PERSONAL CONFLICT UNTIL A LATER DATE!
I CAN HARDLY WAIT!
UROC IS GOING TOTALLY BERSERK ...BUT HE'S LASHED OUT AT THE GROUND BENEATH DARGO'S HAMMER ...AND ACCIDENTALLY FREED IT!
WAIT! WHAT'S DEMONSTAFF DOING--?!

DARGO! YOUR FRIEND JUST VANISHED IN A FLASH OF LIGHT!
THAT'S ONLY ONE OF HIS ANNOYING HABITS!
FORGET HIM! IT'S TIME TO UROC'N ROLL!
WHAT'S YOUR PLAN?
WE SMASH THE SUCKER UNTIL HE FALLS!
SUBTLE, YOU AIN'T!
WITLESS CURS! THY PUNY WEAPONS CANNOT AVAIL AGAINST ONE WHO IS INDESTRUCTIBLE!

UROC IS UNCONQUERABLE, UNDEFEATABLE, AND--
KA-ZAKK!
H-HE'S SUDDENLY BEING POUNDED BY BOLTS OF PURE ENERGY!

SCAN IT--! HE'S STREAKING UPWARD... ALMOST LIKE HE LOST HIS HOLD ON GRAVITY!
HE'S HEADING STRAIGHT FOR THE CEILING, AND--!

EEEYIII!!

WHAT'D YOU DO TO HIM?
ME?! I THOUGHT IT WAS YOU!

IT WAS I!
WHILE YOU DISTRACTED HIM, I MERELY EMPLOYED MY HAMMER TO REPEL HIM THUS!
-SHEESH- DID YOUR HAMMER COME WITH AN OWNER'S MANUAL? SOMETHING TELLS ME I AIN'T GETTING FULL USE OUT OF MINE!
DITTO!

EXPERIENCE IS THE GREATEST TEACHER... AND THERE IS A GRAVE LESSON TO BE LEARNED HERE!
EASE UP ON THE FORTUNE COOKIE PHILOSOPHY, MR. ED!
I JUST WANNA KNOW HOW MANY MORE YO-YOS ZARRKO INTENDS TO THROW AT US!

FAR MORE THAN THOU WOULDST E'ER DREAM OF DEFEATING--!
KWOMPH!

OHMIGOSH--! IT'S SKURGE THE EXECUTIONER!
I'LL TRY TO HOLD HIM BACK, DARGO-- WHILE YOU GET BILL TO SAFETY!
WHAT TRAVESTY IS THIS?!

TWAPP!
MERE MORTALS DRESSED IN THE RAIMENT OF MIGHTY THOR?
SUCH SACRILEGE CANNOT GO UNPUNISHED!

HEY, ERIC--! MAYBE YOU SHOULD RETHINK YOUR "SMASH THE SUCKER" ROUTINE!
IT ISN'T WORKING IN A BIGGGG WAY!
THINK YOU COULD DO BETTER, SPARKY?
"SPARKY"--?!
PRIVATE JOKE!

SAVE THE JOKES UNTIL AFTER I'VE SLAGGED THIS SLACKER!
THIS MASQUERADE IS MOST IMPERTINENT!
THOUGH I WOULD GLADLY DISPATCH THE SON OF ODIN TO VALHALLA'S GATE, NE'ER WOULD I SHOW SUCH CRAVEN DISRESPECT TO A FELLOW WARRIOR-BORN!

BWAKK!
NOR WILL I CONDONE IT IN ANOTHER!

THIS GROTESQUE CREATURE IS THE GREATEST AFFRONT OF ALL!

AN ABERRATION OF NATURE ART THOU!
AN UNSEEMLY MOCKERY OF THE TRUE THUNDER GOD!

AN UNRESISTING COWARD WHO I WILL NOT SUFFER TO LIVE!
FTAMM!

BILL IS BEING SLAUGHTERED! HE MUST BE STUNNED! HELPLESS!
WE MUST LEAP TO HIS DEFENSE!
NO!

W-WHAT DO YOU MEAN "NO"?!
BILL'S LESSON, YOU KNOTHEAD...OR WEREN'T YOU LISTENING EARLIER?!
I'VE GOT A PLAN!
YOU CAN'T BE SERIOUS!
A NEW ONE!

A HEATED MOMENT PASSES, AND THEN...

OD'S BLOOD! THE GROUND SUDDENLY ERUPTS BENEATH ME!

FLASHING GOOD, ERIC! YOUR SHOCK WAVE MANAGED TO BOUNCE THE EXECUTIONER AWAY FROM BILL!

AND NOW, WHILE HE'S STILL REELING, IT'S MY TURN--!

SPWANG!

A PERFECT PITCH, DARGO! I THINK YOU'VE GOT A FUTURE IN THIS HERO BIZ!

BATTER UP!

TEWONK!

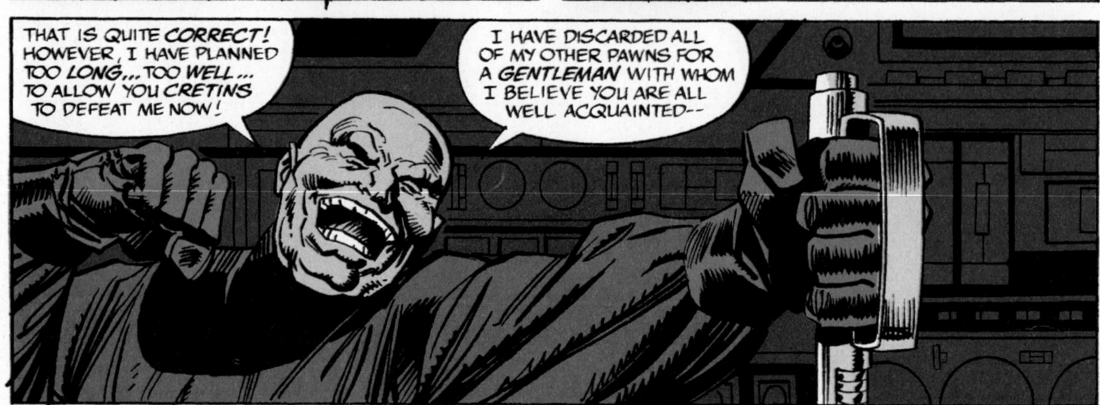

LOKI, THE GOD OF EVIL!!

TO BE CONTINUED--!

MARVEL® COMICS

THE THOR WAR! PART 4 OF 4

THE MIGHTY THOR®

TM

$1.00 US
$1.25 CAN/UK 65p
441
LATE DEC
CC 02450

APPROVED BY THE COMICS CODE AUTHORITY

LOKI'S™ BACK! (OR, IS HE?)

THE MOST OFFBEAT BATTLE OF THE YEAR!

FRENZ & MILGROM

WHEN ARCHITECT **ERIC MASTERSON** STAMPS HIS WOODEN WALKING-STICK UPON THE GROUND, HE IS TRANSFORMED INTO THE NORSE GOD OF THUNDER. ARMED WITH HIS ENCHANTED HAMMER, HE IS AT ONCE MASTER OF THE STORM, LORD OF THE LIVING LIGHTNING, HEIR TO ODIN'S THRONE IN ETERNAL ASGARD, AND ONE OF THE STRONGEST WARRIORS WHO EVER WALKED THE EARTH! STAN LEE PRESENTS . . .

THE MIGHTY THOR!

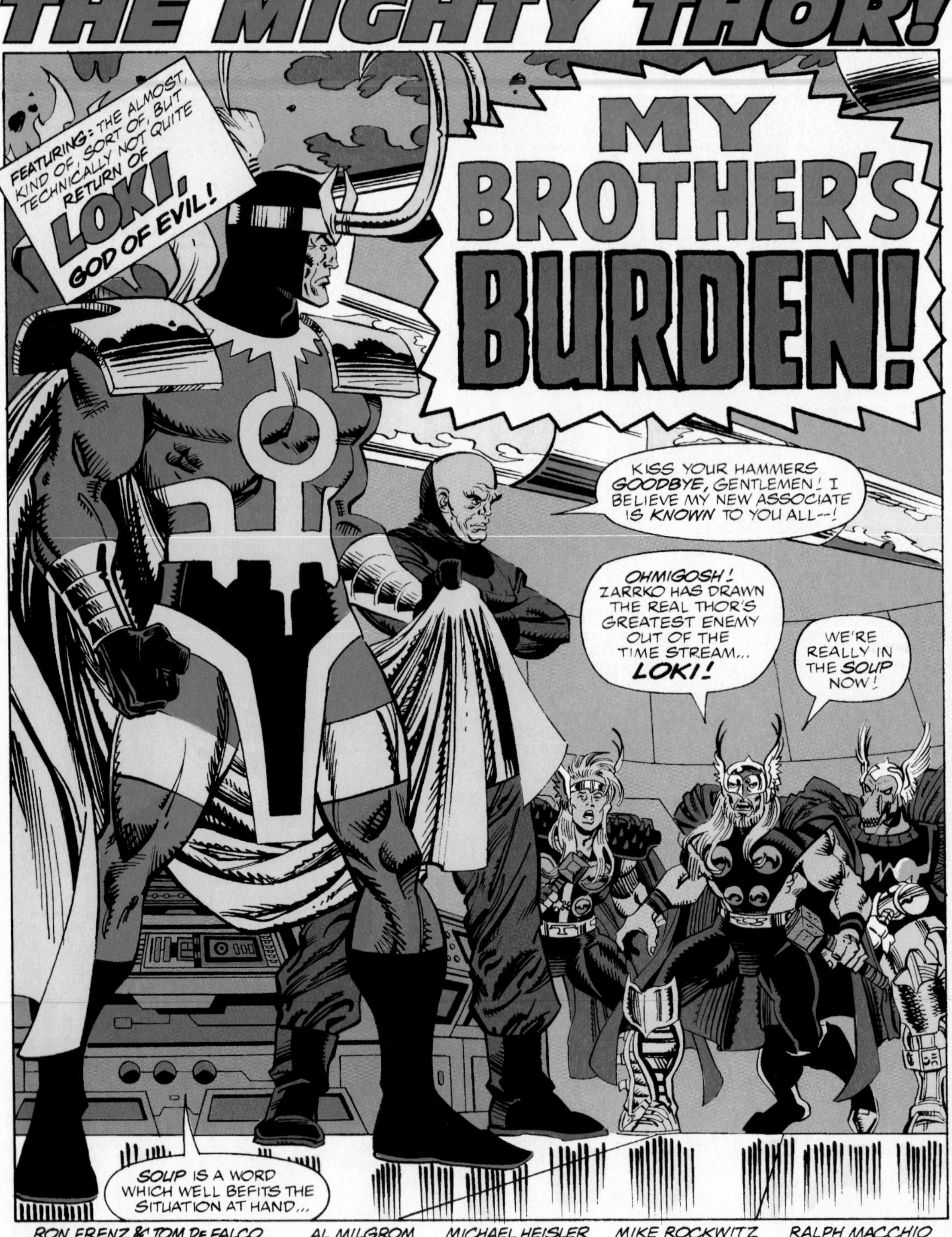

FEATURING: THE ALMOST, KIND OF, SORT OF, BUT TECHNICALLY NOT QUITE RETURN OF LOKI, GOD OF EVIL!
MY BROTHER'S BURDEN!
KISS YOUR HAMMERS GOODBYE, GENTLEMEN! I BELIEVE MY NEW ASSOCIATE IS KNOWN TO YOU ALL--!
OHMIGOSH! ZARRKO HAS DRAWN THE REAL THOR'S GREATEST ENEMY OUT OF THE TIME STREAM... LOKI!
WE'RE REALLY IN THE SOUP NOW!
SOUP IS A WORD WHICH WELL BEFITS THE SITUATION AT HAND...

RON FRENZ & TOM DeFALCO — PLOT, PENCILS & SCRIPT | AL MILGROM — FINISHED ART | MICHAEL HEISLER — LETTERER | MIKE ROCKWITZ — COLORIST | RALPH MACCHIO — EDITOR

WHILE I FAIL TO GRASP THE PURPOSE BEHIND YOUR ANNOYING RESEMBLANCE TO MY SNIVELING STEP-BROTHER...
...YOU WARRIORS THREE SHALL MOST CERTAINLY BE BOILED AND MACERATED BY MY SORCERY SUPREME!
UGNN

AWAY WITH YOU!
KA-ZAK!
OFFEND MINE EYES NO MORE WITH YOUR REPULSIVE AND IMPROPER MASQUERADE!

WHY DO YOU HESITATE? WHAT ARE YOU WAITING FOR?
FINISH THEM OFF!!

YOU WOULD BE WELL ADVISED TO LEARN THE PROPER TONE FOR ADDRESSING AN IMMORTAL OF ASGARD, MY FRIEND!
ONE DOES NOT SPEAK THUSLY TO ME!
GAKK

I... I SHOULD HAVE KNOWN BETTER THAN TO TREAT LOKI LIKE MY OTHER PAWNS!
F-FORGIVE ME, MASTER! I MEANT NO DISRESPECT!
I MERELY THOUGHT THAT YOUR PLAN WOULD BE BETTER SERVED BY THEIR DESTRUCTION!
MY PLAN--?!

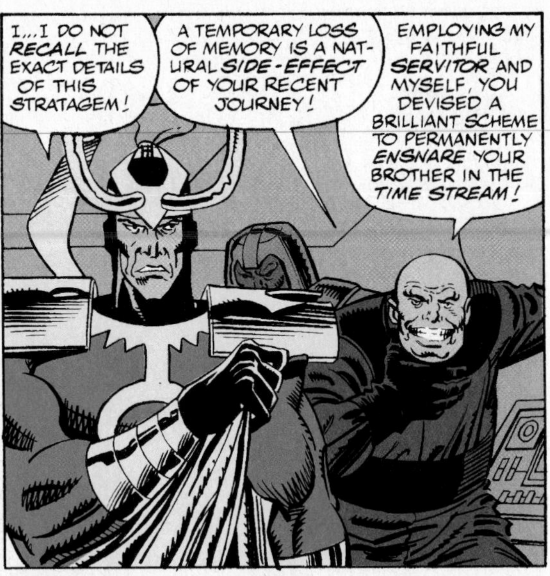
I... I DO NOT RECALL THE EXACT DETAILS OF THIS STRATAGEM!
A TEMPORARY LOSS OF MEMORY IS A NATURAL SIDE-EFFECT OF YOUR RECENT JOURNEY!
EMPLOYING MY FAITHFUL SERVITOR AND MYSELF, YOU DEVISED A BRILLIANT SCHEME TO PERMANENTLY ENSNARE YOUR BROTHER IN THE TIME STREAM!

BUT THEN, EVEN BEFORE THE CUNNING TOMORROW MAN CAN FURTHER EMBELLISH HIS TALE...
WA-BOOM!
ONE OF THE THORS HAS RECOVERED!

YOU FLASHED THAT RIGHT, GEARHEAD!
EITHER THE OTHERS TOOK THE BLAST OF THE OR WE NOW KNOW WHO'S THE TOUGHEST THUNDER GUY OF ALL!
ANYWAY YOU SCAN IT, YOU'RE SCRAP CITY!

MASTER, I CHAFE AT ALL THIS NEEDLESS BANTER AND INACTIVITY!
I WANT THE HONOR OF HUMILIATING THIS INSOLENT BOOR!
GO...ER...IN THE NAME OF THE EVER-INGENIOUS LOKI!

AT LAST, DARGO--! I AM FINALLY FREE TO PUMMEL YOU INTO OBLIVION!
I HAVE HELD YOU IN CONTEMPT EVER SINCE I FIRST EXPERIENCED YOUR SARDONIC MANNER AND CAUSTIC WIT!
AW, AND HERE I WAS PLANNING TO INVITE YOU FOR THE HOLIDAYS!

BE CAREFUL, SERVITOR! DON'T ALLOW HIM TO GOAD YOU INTO RECKLESSNESS!
THOUGH I AM ONLY AN ARTIFICIAL BEING, I SHALL FORCE HIM TO STOP TAUNTING ME IF IT IS THE LAST THING I DO!
KNOWING YOU, IT PROBABLY WILL BE!
KWA-BWAK!

THE SERVITOR IS IN SUCH A FURY THAT THEY'LL CONTINUE TO CRASH THROUGH THE TIME CUBE UNTIL THEY HIT THE FOUNDATION LEVEL!
YOU HAVE ONLY YOURSELF TO BLAME FOR HIS INADEQUACIES!
EMOTIONS ARE ONLY A BOON TO THOSE WHO POSSESS THE AUDACITY TO REVEL IN THEM!
ER...ABOUT THE OTHER THUNDER GODS?!

DO NOT DIGNIFY THOSE INCONSEQUENTIAL PRETENDERS WITH SUCH DISTINCTION! I SHALL ATTEND TO THEM FORTHWITH!
LOKI IS TOO DANGEROUS...TOO UNCONTROLLABLE!
HE MUST BE RETURNED TO HIS PROPER TIME PERIOD THE INSTANT HE'S SERVED HIS PURPOSE!
BUT NOW, I MUST CHECK ON MY RADICAL TIME STABILIZER!

EXCELLENT! IT WASN'T DAMAGED BY THE SERVITOR'S RAMPAGE!
CONTRARY TO WHAT LOKI BELIEVES, ITS TRUE FUNCTION IS TO MERGE EVERY ALTERNATE TIME LINE INTO A SINGLE ENTITY!
THE ONE IN WHICH I AM THE SUPREME MASTER OF TIME!

-URRK- NEVER KNEW I COULD HURT SO BAD! I... I FEEL ALL BUSTED INSIDE!
H-HOW'D I EVER GET MIXED UP IN THIS MESS? I...I DON'T BELONG HERE!
SH-SHOULD HAVE STAYED HOME... AND LEFT THE SUPER-HEROICS TO THE PROS! BILL AND DARGO ARE BETTER OFF WITHOUT ME, AND--
ARISE, CHARLATAN--!
FOR THE MEREST OF MOMENTS, I MISTOOK YOU FOR MY ACCURSED STEP-BROTHER!
HOW DID A MERE MORTAL COME TO POSSESS HIS SACRED HAMMER?
WHERE IS THE TRUE THUNDER GOD? WHO ARE YOU THREE THAT CARRY LIKE HAMMERS AND WEAR VARIATIONS OF HIS DISTINCTIVE COSTUME?
ANSWER ME, FOOL!
STAND ASIDE, ERIC! ALLOW ME THE PRIVILEGE OF BESTING THIS BASE VILLAIN IN SINGLE COMBAT!
I...I AIN'T GONNA ARGUE, PAL! I KNOW WHEN I'M WAY OUTTA MY LEAGUE!
HE'S ALL YOURS, BILLY BOY! GET HIM!
NOT EVEN THE FEARED LOKI CAN WITHSTAND THE CONCUSSIVE FORCE OF MIGHTY STORM BREAKER!
BUT, HOLD--! WHAT MAGIC IS THIS?!

KA-ZAK!
'TWAS ONLY A SIMPLE SPELL OF ILLUSION, MY EQUINE FRIEND!

BILL--!
H-HE STILL SEEMS TO BE BREATHING... BUT HE'S DEFINITELY OUT FOR THE COUNT!

IT'S ALL UP TO ME! I'M THE ONLY ONE LEFT--!
IF I FAIL... WE ALL DIE!
I GOTTA BRING LOKI DOWN!

DON'T BE A FOOL AS WELL AS A BUMBLING OAF!
DISCARD YOUR GROTESQUE COMRADE! FLEE WHILE YOU STILL LIVE!
NO! AS MUCH AS I FEAR YOU--! AS MUCH AS I WANT TO RUN--!
I CAN'T!
SO BE IT!

MY FIRE SWORD SHALL EXACT THE PROPER FEE FOR YOUR MOST FATAL BLUNDER!
-UGN- BARELY MANAGED TO BLOCK THAT BLOW!
MY RIBS ARE KILLING ME! I CAN HARDLY STAND--!
GOTTA TRY SOMETHING UNEXPECTED! LIKE PULPING HIS FOOT WITH MY HAMMER--!
NOT THE FAIREST WAY TO FIGHT... BUT I CAN'T BE CHOOSY!

ELSEWHERE...
WHAT A WASTE! ZARRKO WILL FREAK WHEN HE SEES THE MESS YOU'VE MADE!
I WOULDN'T BE SURPRISED IF HE DOCKED YOU THE COST OF THIS EQUIPMENT!
BRAKK!
THE JOKE IS ON YOU, DARGO! YOU'VE RACED INTO A DEAD END!
YOU'RE CORNERED! TRAPPED!
YOU CAN NO LONGER HIDE FROM THE CRUSHING POWER OF THE SERVITOR!
THOSE WIRES ABOVE ME--!
IF ONLY I CAN--
MADE IT!
NO! NO! YOU CAN'T ESCAPE ME LIKE THIS--!
YOU GOT A BETTER WAY? I'M ALWAYS OPEN TO SUGGESTION!
THE FORCE OF MY LEAP HAS WEDGED ME INTO THIS WALL, BUT I WILL SOON BE FREE!
I'M COUNTING ON IT, PAL!
IN FACT, I CAN'T WAIT FOR YOU TO EXPOSE YOUR POINTED LITTLE HEAD!
THWOK!

-TSK TSK-
SUCH SHODDY WORKMANSHIP!
THEY JUST DON'T BUILD STURDY KILLER ROBOTS, ANYMORE!

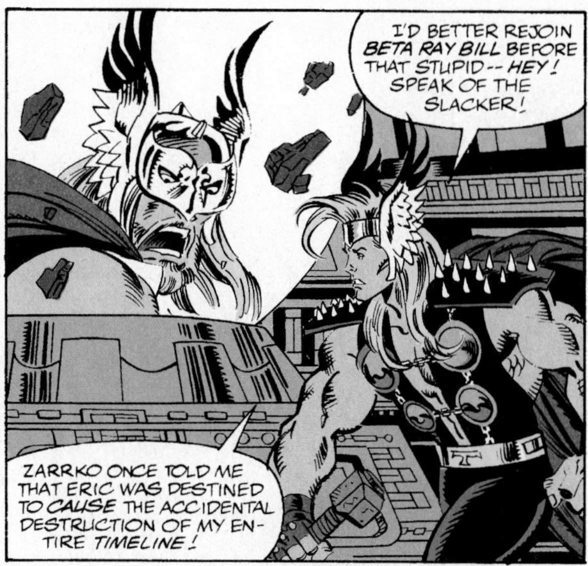
I'D BETTER REJOIN BETA RAY BILL BEFORE THAT STUPID-- HEY! SPEAK OF THE SLACKER!
ZARRKO ONCE TOLD ME THAT ERIC WAS DESTINED TO CAUSE THE ACCIDENTAL DESTRUCTION OF MY ENTIRE TIMELINE!

IT WAS PROBABLY A LIE... BUT MAYBE I SHOULD FAST FORWARD THE TIME-SCOPE THROUGH ERIC'S FUTURE... AND SEE FOR MYSELF!

WAIT! TH-THAT... CAN'T BE!
I... I NEVER REALIZED THAT I WOULD HAVE SO LITTLE TIME! THAT IT WOULD RUN OUT SO QUICKLY!

I... I GUESS I JUST DIDN'T THINK IT WOULD END LIKE THIS!

MEANTIME...
YOU IGNORANT, ARROGANT MONGREL!
DO YOU TRULY BELIEVE THAT THE GODS OF ASGARD WOULD BESTOW THE FULL POWER OF THE MIGHTY THOR ON ONE SUCH AS YOU?!
YOU BARELY WIELD A TENTH OF HIS FABLED STRENGTH!
Y-YOU'RE LYING! TRYING TO DEMORALIZE ME--!

LOKI HAS NO NEED OF SUCH SUBTERFUGE!
NOT WHEN VICTORY IS SO EASILY ACHIEVED!

NOW--WHILE YOU ARE HELPLESS --MY ENCHANTED SWORD SHALL CONTINUE HACKING AT YOUR ACCURSED HAMMER UNTIL IT HAS BEEN SHATTERED INTO A THOUSAND IRREPARABLE PIECES!
M-MY STRENGTH IS STARTING TO FAIL--! EVERYTHING'S GOING BLURRY!

B-BUT I CAN'T... I WON'T GIVE UP!
I...I'VE GOT TO FIND A WAY TO BEAT HIM!

BILL'S HAMMER--!
IF ONLY I COULD REACH IT--!

I-IT'S PURE AGONY! MY RIBS FEEL LIKE THEY'RE RIPPING THROUGH MY CHEST!
BUT I MUST FORCE MYSELF TO STRETCH EVEN FARTHER--!

I...I DID IT!

BTHAM!

KRUNCH!

M-MY LEGS FEEL ALL WOBBLY... BUT I CAN'T GIVE LOKI TIME TO RECOVER!
I'VE GOT TO KEEP POUNDING AT HIM--!
THE REAL THOR WOULD BE REVOLTED BY MY TACTICS, BUT I CAN'T AFFORD TO FIGHT BY ANY RULES!

I FIND YOUR RUTHLESSNESS MOST REFRESHING, MORTAL! YOU ARE FAR MORE PRAGMATIC THAN MY SOFT-HEARTED SIBLING!
WHAT THE--? THAT MACHINERY HAS SEIZED MY ARM!

HAVE YOU ALREADY FORGOTTEN THAT LOKI IS A MASTER OF DARK SORCERY?

SHA-RAAK!
ARRGHH!
SURELY, YOU DID NOT BELIEVE THAT I COULD BE DEFEATED BY SO SPINELESS... SO DEVIOUS A BLOW!

SLAPP!
YOU SHALL PAY FOR THAT INDIGNITY A THOUSAND TIMES A THOUSANDFOLD!
NONE MAY STRIKE THE GOD OF EVIL WITH IMPUNITY!

SLAP! SLAP! SLAP!
YOU HAVE THE UNMITIGATED GALL TO MASQUERADE AS MY ACCURSED BROTHER!
YOU DARE TO PLAY AT HIS SIMPLE-MINDED HEROICS!

IF YOUR PUNY MIND WERE CAPABLE OF CONCEIVING OF THE DARK FORCES -- THE CONSUMMATE EVILS --
-- WHICH ARE AT LOOSE IN THIS UNI-VERSE, YOU WOULD PASSIONATELY BE-SEECH ME FOR THE SANCTUARY OF MADNESS!

WHAT--?!

SO! YOU HAVE REVERTED TO YOUR TRUE FORM--!
YOU HAVE LOST THE POWER OF THE SACRED HAMMER BECAUSE IT WAS OUT OF YOUR HAND FOR MORE THAN SIXTY SECONDS!

WHAT AN IRONIC JEST--!
ODIN PLACED THAT CRUEL ENCHANTMENT UPON MJOLNIR TO TEACH THOR HUMILITY!
BUT NOW, MY BROTHER'S MOST PRIZED POSSESS-ION LIES UNPROTECT-ED!

I CAN LAY CLAIM TO IT-- AND ITS DOPPELGANGER-- FORE'ERMORE!
THE TRANSFORMATION SEEMED TO HEAL ME, BUT--
NO! YOU CAN'T--!

HAVE YOU TAKEN TOTAL LEAVE OF YOUR SENSES, MORTAL--?!
YOU WERE UNWORTHY OF MY METTLE WHEN YOU POSSESSED THE POWER OF A THUNDER GOD!
WHY RISK MY FURTHER WRATH?
THERE MUST BE A WAY TO BEAT YOU--!

THERE IS MUCH TO ADMIRE IN YOUR VALIANT TENACITY!
A PITY THAT YOU STRUGGLE IN VAIN!
I-IT DOESN'T MATTER WHAT YOU DO TO ME... BECAUSE I KNOW THAT YOU'RE DESTINED TO LOSE IN THE END!
I HAVE SEEN YOUR FUTURE!

WHAT ARE YOU SAYING, MORTAL--?
IT'S THE TRUTH--! YOU CAN SEE IT IN MY EYES!
THOR WINS!

NOOO--!

AT SOME UNKNOWN POINT IN MY FUTURE... I AM DESTINED TO BE SLAIN BY MY DETESTED HALF-BROTHER!
IT CANNOT BE--!

16

THERE IS NO TIME TO WASTE--! ZARRKO MUST DISCOVER THE EXACT INSTANT-- THE PRECISE MOMENT--SO THAT I CAN DEFEND AGAINST IT!
LOKI MUST NOT DIE!
SOME GUYS JUST CAN'T TAKE BAD NEWS!

UP AND AT 'EM, BILLY BOY!
I MANAGED TO BUY US A MOMENTARY RESPITE!
-UNNN-

HEY! HOW COME YOU DIDN'T TRANSFORM AFTER BEING SEPARATED FROM YOUR HAMMER?

STORM BREAKER HAS NO SUCH ENCHANTMENT!
-SHEESH- I'VE GOTTA TALK TO HEIMDALL ABOUT UPGRADING MY MODEL!

I...I WONDER IF IT'S SAFE FOR ME TO CHANGE--! I WAS IN PRETTY SAD SHAPE EARLIER!

YAHOO! I'M FULLY RECOVERED... AND READY FOR ACTION!
LEAD ON, ERIC--!
HEY--! WAIT FOR ME!

MEANWHILE...
YOU MUST DO AS I COMMAND, ZARRKO-- NOW!
I'M THROUGH TAKING ORDERS, LOKI! MY RADICAL TIME STABILIZER JUST ENTERED THE CRITICAL FINAL PHASE!
WITHIN MERE INSTANTS, I SHALL BECOME THE UNDISPUTED MASTER OF TIME!

STAND ASIDE, YOU UNTHINKING CLOD! THERE IS FAR MORE AT STAKE THAN YOUR PETTY LUST FOR POWER!
THE LIFE OF A GOD HANGS IN THE BALANCE!
LOOK OUT! THE CONTROL PANEL--!

YOU CARELESS FOOL! YOU'VE CAUSED AN ACCIDENTAL SHIFT IN THE STABILIZER'S POLARITY, AND BEGUN A CHAIN REACTION WHICH WILL EVENTUALLY LEAD TO--

KWA-PWOOM!

EEYII! WE'RE CAUGHT IN THE BACKLASH OF A TEMPORAL CYCLONE--!
W-WE'RE BEING SUCKED INTO THE TIMESTREAM!

IT'S... HORRIBLE! LOKI WILL PROBABLY USE SOME KIND OF SPELL TO RETURN TO HIS PROPER TIME PERIOD... BUT ZARRKO WILL SPEND THE REST OF ETERNITY IN THAT VOID!
WHAT ABOUT US--? THE ENTIRE TIME CUBE IS GETTING READY TO BLOW!
DARGO! THE CONTROLS OF THIS SHIP ARE NOT UNLIKE MY OWN SKUTTLEBUTT!
IF THE CUBE CAN CONTINUE TO REMAIN INTACT... I AM CERTAIN THAT THIS DEVICE CAN RESTORE US TO OUR DIVERSE WORLDS AND TIMES!

HURRY, BILL! THE SHIP IS CRACKING UNDER THE STRAIN!
IT CAN'T HOLD MUCH LONGER--!

THERE--! I BELIEVE THAT I HAVE FINALLY MADE THE PROPER ADJUSTMENTS!
DARGO! YOU SHALL BE THE FIRST--!
KEEP YOUR HAMMER HIGH, BUDDY!
ERIC, I...I'M SORRY FOR THE WAY I FIRST TREATED YOU!
IF I HAD KNOWN--! IF I HAD ANY IDEA--!

PROMISE THAT YOU'LL TRY TO ENJOY YOUR LIFE--AND YOUR POWER--FOR AS LONG AS IT LASTS!
THAT YOU'LL MAKE EVERY MOMENT COUNT!
YEAH...UH... SURE!
DARGO, PREPARE TO DEBARK--

NOW!!

-WHEW!- DARGO WAS ACTING REALLY WEIRD! I WONDER WHAT--AW! I CAN'T WORRY ABOUT THAT NOW!
HOW WE DOING, BILL?
BE OF GOOD CHEER, MY NOBLE BROTHER! WHAT-EVER OUR FATE, WE SHALL KNOW IT IN THE VERY NEXT--

"--INSTANT!"

-;SHEESH!- SOMEBODY'S GOT TO TALK TO BILL ABOUT HIS TIMING!
HE CUT THAT SOOOO CLOSE... ALMOST TOO CLOSE!
I JUST HOPE HE AND DARGO MADE IT HOME ALL RIGHT! THEY'RE THE ONES WITH THE LONG COMMUTES!

AFTER ALL IS SAID AND DONE, I EN-JOYED HANGING OUT WITH THOSE GUYS!
I WONDER IF WE'LL EVER BE REUNITED?!
I'M ALSO CURIOUS ABOUT LOKI...

BASED ON MY OWN EXPERIENCE, I KNOW THAT HE EVENTUALLY RETURNED TO THE PAST!
WHY DIDN'T HE USE THE KNOW-LEDGE HE GAINED TO PREVENT HIS DESTRUCTION AT THOR'S HANDS?!
MAYBE HE COULDN'T... BECAUSE THIS LOKI WAS FROM AN ALTERNATE TIMELINE!

-;WHEW!- THIS TIME TRAVEL STUFF CAN DRIVE A PERSON CRAZY! I SHOULD JUST ENJOY THE FACT THAT I FINALLY MADE IT BACK HOME, AND--
OH, NO!!

MY APARTMENT--!
I FORGOT THAT STELLARIS AND I HAD TRASHED IT DURING OUR LAST BATTLE!
WHAT AM I GONNA DO? HOW CAN I LIVE HERE? IT'S TOTALLY DEMOLISHED... AND I DON'T HAVE THE SAVINGS TO REFURBISH IT!

BRRRING!
NOW WHAT--?

THE WAY MY LUCK'S RUNNING, IT'S PROBABLY THE I.R.S. CALLING TO AUDIT ME ALL THE WAY BACK TO MY PAPER ROUTE DAYS!
HELLO--?

MR. MASTERSON--? THIS IS GARY PARETSKY... SUSAN AUSTIN'S DOCTOR!
HAS SOMETHING HAPPENED TO HER, DOCTOR?

ON THE CONTRARY... I HAVE GREAT NEWS!
REMEMBER THAT SURGEON I TOLD YOU ABOUT?

"WELL, MY PERSISTENCE HAS PAID OFF... I FOUND HIM!

"I FOUND DR. DONALD BLAKE... AND CONVINCED HIM TO TAKE MISS AUSTIN'S CASE!
DR. DONALD BLAKE MD.
"DID YOU HEAR ME, MASTERSON--?
"MASTERSON--?!"
TO BE CONTINUED--!

Loki, having learned of his imminent death via Zarrko's time travel, prepared for the day that Thor would kill him. After his death, Loki's spirit secretly entered Odin, and it was actually Loki who gave the order to banish Thor.

"Dr. Donald Blake" saved Susan's life, but was soon revealed to be a disguised Mephisto, who had posed as Thor's former alter ego to trick Eric into giving him Mjolnir. Eric journeyed to Mephisto's realm to retrieve the hammer, and while there saw that Mephisto was holding an Asgardian spirit prisoner within a soul shroud.

Teaming with Sif and Balder, who had also been searching for the true Thor, Eric learned that Mephisto's prisoner was actually Odin! The three realized Loki's scheme and soon defeated the villain, returning Odin's spirit to his body. Odin in turn revealed that Thor had been banished deep within Eric's subconscious.

Eric underwent a spiritual journey and freed Thor, who decided to remain in Asgard. Declaring that Earth still needed an Asgardian protector, Odin gave Eric an enchanted mace called Thunderstrike, which granted Eric similar powers to Thor's.

Recently, due partly to the time he spent trapped within Eric's mind, Thor developed a mental illness called "warrior's madness." Moody and paranoid, he left Asgard for outer space. Sif recruited Beta Ray Bill to help bring Thor home, but the ranting thunder god savagely attacked and defeated Bill. Ultimately, Odin would realize the cause of Thor's madness and restore his sanity.

Meanwhile, in the 26th century, Dargo's greatest enemy planned his ultimate victory...

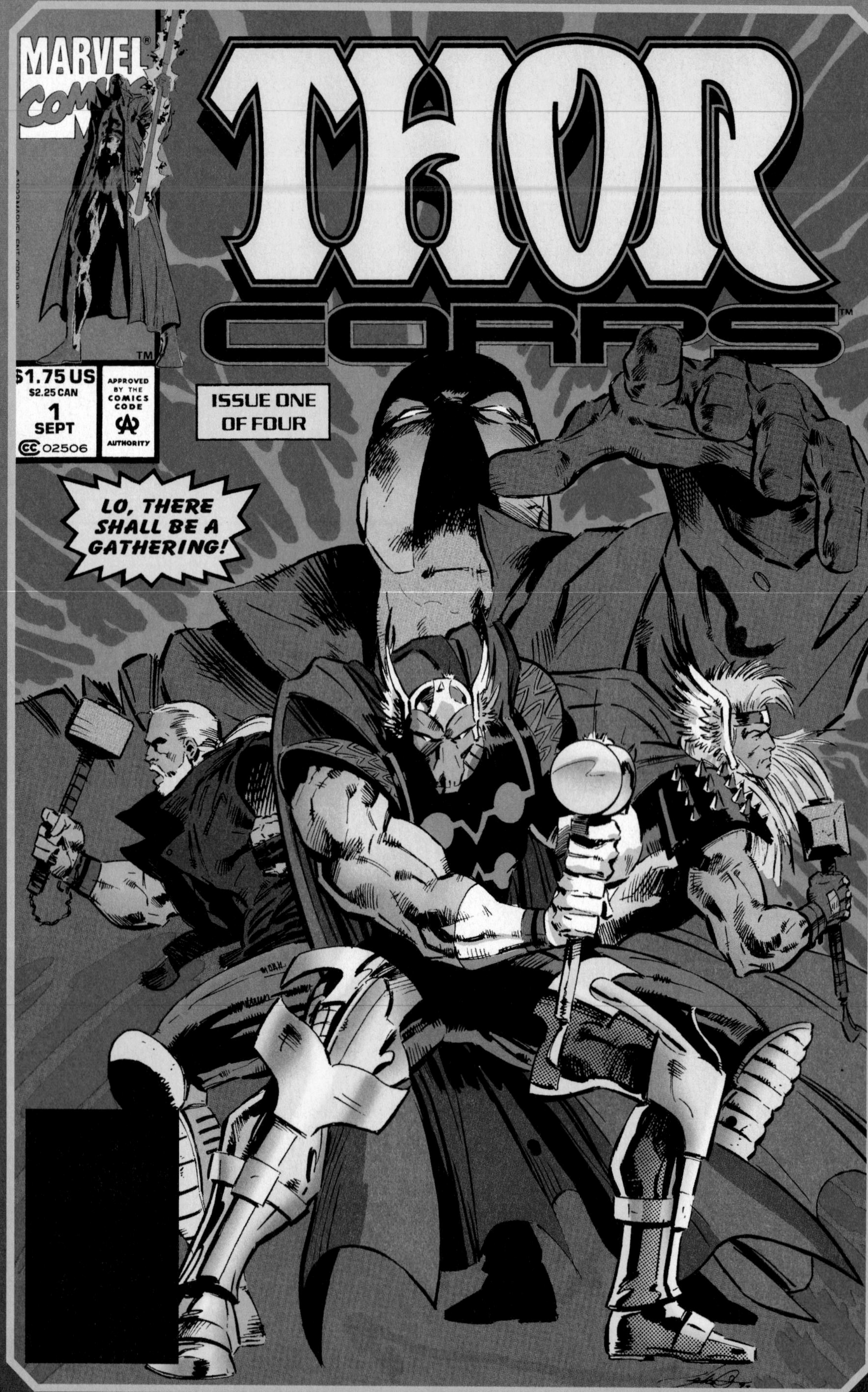
MARVEL COMICS
THOR CORPS
$1.75 US
$2.25 CAN
1
SEPT
APPROVED BY THE COMICS CODE AUTHORITY
ISSUE ONE OF FOUR
LO, THERE SHALL BE A GATHERING!

JULY 29, 2593 A.D.
TRANSIT WALKWAY 5051-B
TO SOME, NORTH AMERICAN URBAN CENTER #5 IS THE MULTI-LEVELED, MANY-WONDERED CITY OF THE FAR-DISTANT FUTURE.
TO OTHERS, IT IS A GRIM, OVER-POPULATED ALTERNATE REALITY WHERE CORPORATIONS HAVE USURPED THE ROLE OF GOVERNMENT--
--AND VIRTUALLY EVERYONE OWES HIS SOUL TO SOME COMPANY'S STORE.
BUT TO THOSE WHO LIVE HERE, IT IS--QUITE SIMPLY--HOME!
A HOME FILLED WITH THE USUAL DRUDGERIES, DISAPPOINTMENTS, JOYS, AND THRILLS.
AND, OF COURSE, THERE ARE THE OCCASIONAL SURPRISES--
--LIKE SEEING AN AUTHENTIC CAVE MAN HURLED THROUGH A PLATE-GLASS WINDOW!

FROM DIFFERENT WORLDS AND TIMES COME THREE MIGHTY WARRIORS, EACH EMPOWERED BY AN ENCHANTED ASGARDIAN WEAPON WHICH GRANTS THE ASTONISHING ABILITIES OF THE LEGENDARY GOD OF THUNDER! TOGETHER DARGO KTOR, BETA RAY BILL, AND ERIC MASTERSON JOIN TO FORM...
THE THOR CORPS!
THE LOBBY OF ADCORE, ONE OF THE LARGEST ADVERTISING AGENCIES ON THE CONTINENT...
MERE MOMENTS AGO, ALERTED BY THE NERVE-JARRING SCREAMS OF PANICKED PEDESTRIANS, DARGO KTOR, THE ONCE AND FUTURE THOR, ARRIVED TO FIND RAIDERS FROM THE DAWN OF TIME!
THESE CREATURES ARE MORE BEAST THAN MAN!
FROM THE STENCH OF THEM, I DOUBT THEY'VE EVER EXPERIENCED THE JOY OF BATHING!
THEY SUDDENLY MATERIALIZED IN THIS LOBBY AND BEGAN ATTACKING PASSERSBY AT RANDOM--BUT WHY?!
WHERE ARE THEY FROM? WHAT IS THEIR MISSION?!

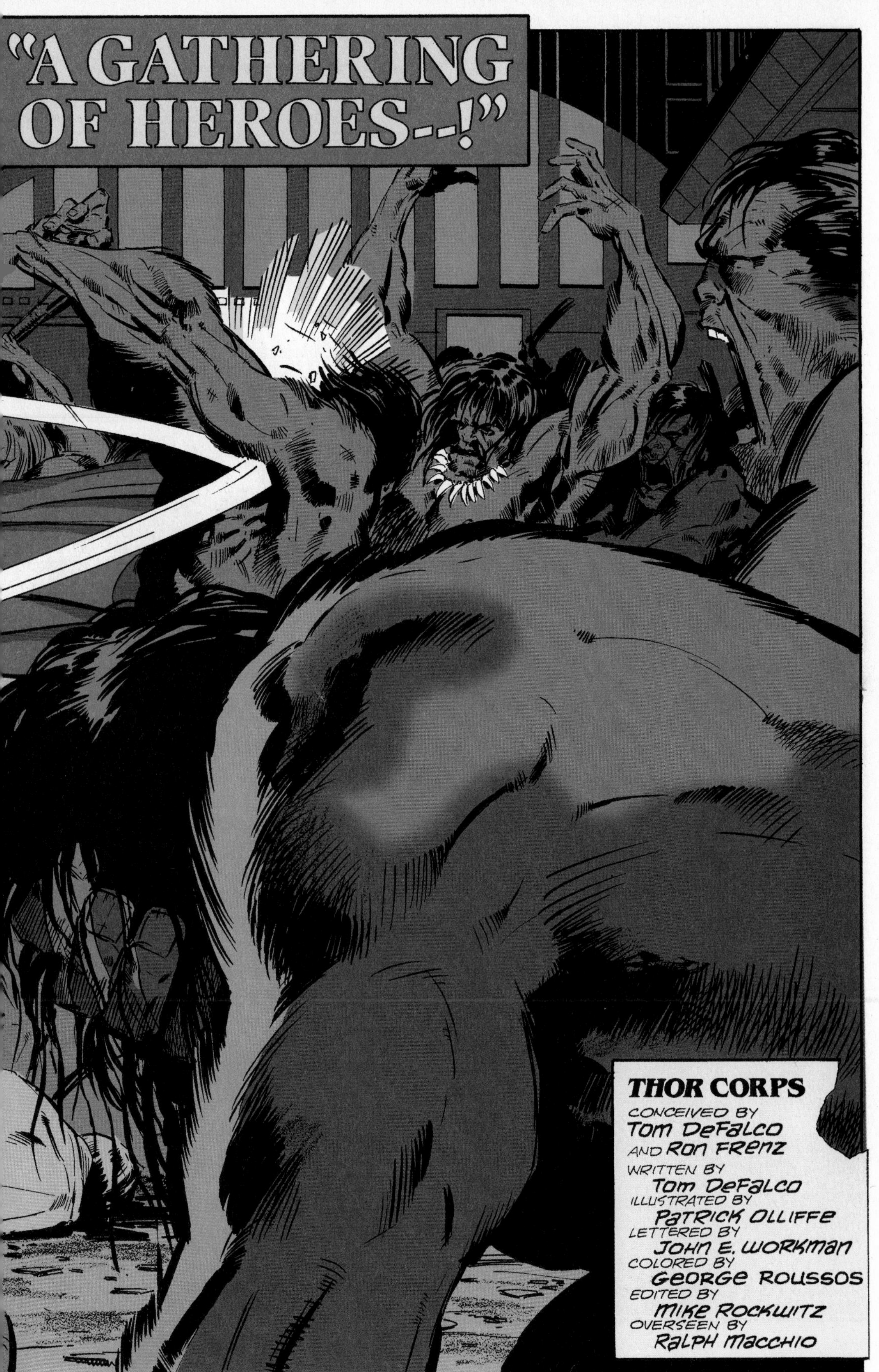
"A GATHERING OF HEROES--!"
THOR CORPS
CONCEIVED BY
Tom DeFalco
AND Ron Frenz
WRITTEN BY
Tom DeFalco
ILLUSTRATED BY
Patrick Olliffe
LETTERED BY
John E. Workman
COLORED BY
George Roussos
EDITED BY
Mike Rockwitz
OVERSEEN BY
Ralph Macchio

THESE BRUTES SEEM TO BE INSTINCTIVELY LASHING OUT MORE BECAUSE OF THEIR OWN FEAR THAN FROM ANY TRUE MALICIOUSNESS!
AND THEY APPEAR TO LACK THE NECESSARY INTELLIGENCE TO HAVE PURPOSELY ENGINEERED THIS SCENARIO!
SOMEONE IS OBVIOUSLY USING THEM AS A DISTRACTION AND ONE NAME IMMEDIATELY LEAPS TO MIND--
--DEMONSTAFF, MY GREATEST ENEMY!
CAN'T WASTE ANY MORE TIME WITH THESE SLACKERS WHILE A REAL MONSTER IS ON THE LOOSE!
A LITTLE LIGHTNING DISPLAY SHOULD--
WAIT! THEY'RE SUDDENLY PULLING A FADE!
DISAPPEARING BEFORE MY VERY EYES!
THE CAVE MEN ARE ALL ...GONE!
LIKE THEY WERE NEVER HERE!
EITHER DEMONSTAFF HAS ALREADY ACHIEVED HIS GOAL--
--OR I'M IN LUCK...AND IT'S TAKING HIM LONGER THAN ANTICIPATED!

TWENTY-SEVEN FLOORS SKYWARD, ON THE PENT-HOUSE LEVEL OF THE ADCORE BUILDING...
IT IS REFRESHING TO SEE A CHIEF OPERATING OFFICER WHO TRULY KNOWS HIS PLACE, DUNBAR!
ON HIS KNEES BEFORE HIS MOST VALUED EMPLOYEE!
HOWEVER-- NOW THAT MY STAFF HAS BLASTED AWAY THIS FALSE WALL TO REVEAL YOUR PRIVATE SAFE--THE TIME FOR SUCH PETTY TRIUMPHS IS PASSED!
I KNOW WHAT YOU WANT, GORKO...AND I BEG YOU TO RECONSIDER!
THE MAN WHO WAS HALLAN GORKO IS DEAD... THANKS TO YOU!
ONLY DEMONSTAFF REMAINS!
OPEN THAT SAFE-- NOW!
I UNDERSTAND THAT IT REQUIRES YOUR HAND-PRINT...AS WELL AS A LIVING DNA SAMPLE!
AND I AM PERFECTLY WILLING TO SEAR OFF YOUR ENTIRE LEFT ARM IF YOU REFUSE TO COOPERATE!
FOR THE SHADOW OF AN INSTANT, THE GAUNT EXECUTIVE HESITATES--WEIGHING NON-EXISTENT OPTIONS--AND THEN...
ALL RIGHT...
I'LL DO AS YOU ASK!
YOU NEEDN'T SOUND SO MAUDLIN, DUNBAR. YOU HAD NO CHOICE!
IF ANYONE DESERVES SELF-LOATHING...IT'S ME!
I NEVER EVEN QUESTIONED WHY AN ADVERTISING AGENCY WOULD FUND AN INTER-DIMENSIONAL PHYSICIST--AND JUST LOOK WHAT HAPPENED!
BUT I THINK I CAN FINALLY PUT MATTERS RIGHT!

YOU... YOU'RE GOING AFTER ELLENE ?!
YOU CAN'T BE SERIOUS! IT'S SUICIDE!
THINK OF THE RISKS... TO US ALL!
A MAN WITH NOTHING TO LOSE... IS ALSO A MAN WHO HAS NOTHING TO FEAR!
BESIDES... THIS LITTLE PIECE OF CIRCUITRY MAY HELP TIP THE ODDS IN MY FAVOR!
UNFORTUNATELY, YOU STILL PRESENT A PROBLEM TO ME--!
KRAKA-PWOOM!
WHAT THE--?!
A DISPLAY OF LIGHTNING LIKE THIS CAN ONLY MEAN GOOD NEWS AS FAR AS YOU'RE CONCERNED, MR. DUNBAR.
MY ENCHANTED HAMMER MANAGED TO TRACK YOUR DISTINCTIVE ENERGY SIGNATURE, DEMONSTAFF!
RELEASE YOUR HOSTAGE... AND GRAB AIR!
DON'T FORCE ME TO SCRAG YOU!

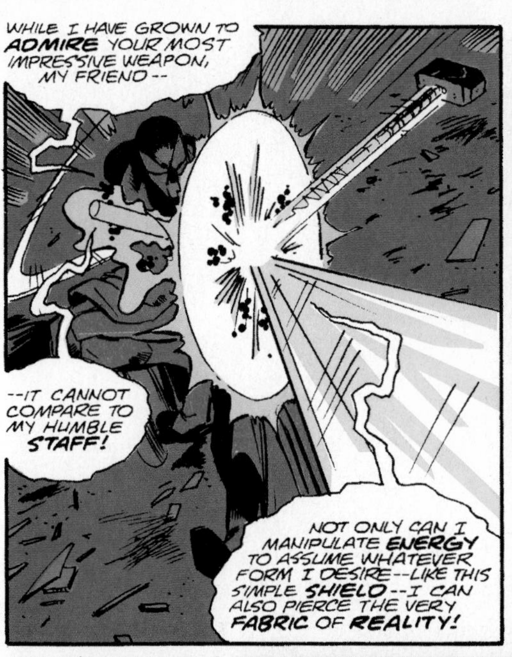
WHILE I HAVE GROWN TO ADMIRE YOUR MOST IMPRESSIVE WEAPON, MY FRIEND --
--IT CANNOT COMPARE TO MY HUMBLE STAFF!
NOT ONLY CAN I MANIPULATE ENERGY TO ASSUME WHATEVER FORM I DESIRE--LIKE THIS SIMPLE SHIELD--I CAN ALSO PIERCE THE VERY FABRIC OF REALITY!

WE HAVE NO NEED TO QUARREL, THOR! I HAVE ALREADY ACHIEVED MY GOAL!
ALLOW ME TO DEPART IN PEACE AND I WILL SPARE YOUR LIFE!

BUT THE IMPETUOUS DARGO DOES NOT HEED THE WARNING!
INSTEAD, HE LAUNCHES HIM-SELF FORWARD-- BARELY DUCKING BENEATH AN ARCING BLOW WHICH WOULD HAVE SURELY SEVERED HIS NECK!
THEN... YOU HAVE ONLY YOURSELF TO BLAME FOR WHAT FOLLOWS!
SORRY ...BUT I'M NO SLACKER!

YOUR TALK IS PURE BUZZ!
IN CASE YOU HAVEN'T NOTICED...YOU MISSED!
ON THE CONTRARY, I NEVER INTENDED TO HIT YOU...

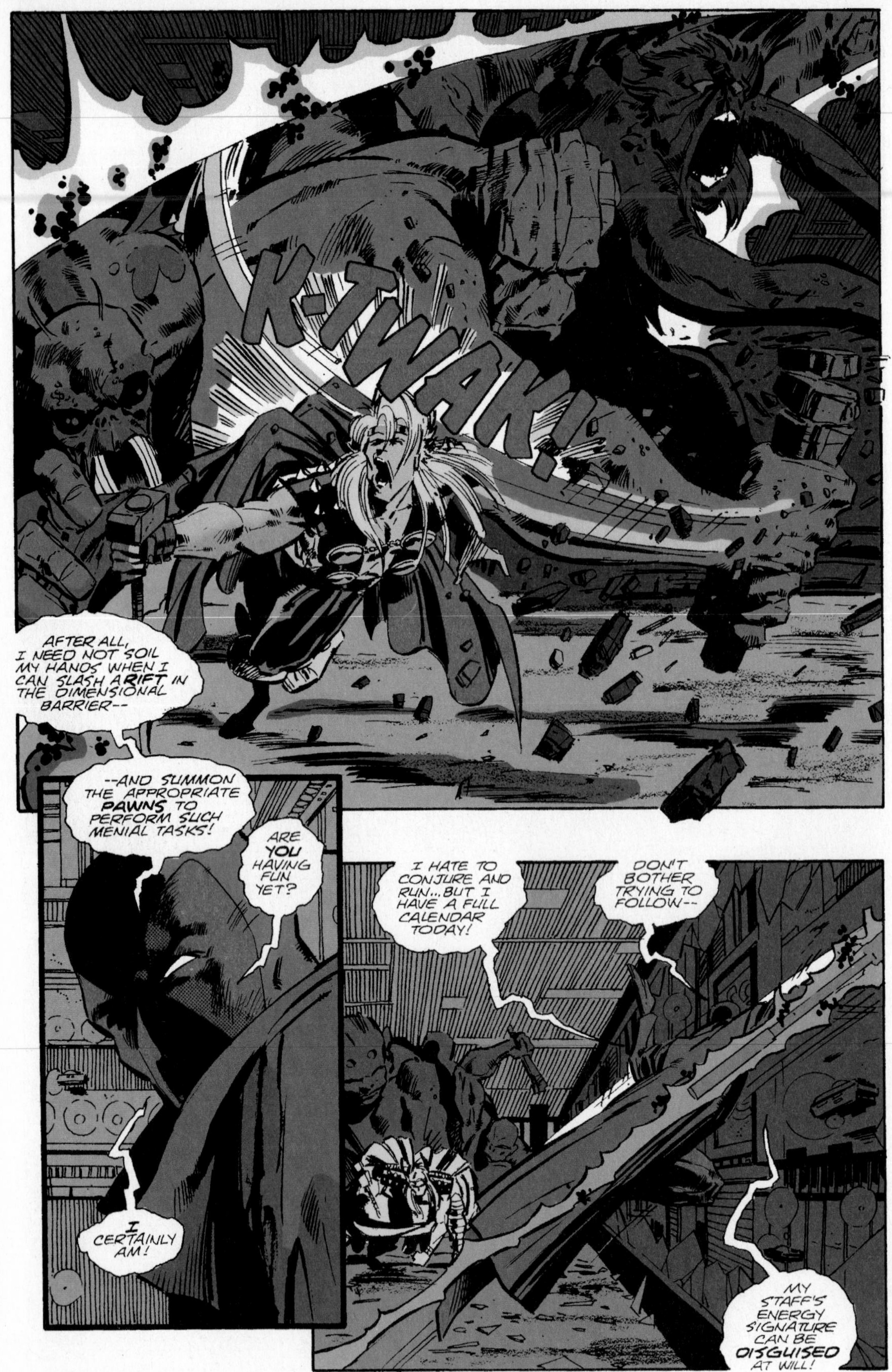
K-TWAK!!
AFTER ALL, I NEED NOT SOIL MY HANDS WHEN I CAN SLASH A RIFT IN THE DIMENSIONAL BARRIER--
--AND SUMMON THE APPROPRIATE PAWNS TO PERFORM SUCH MENIAL TASKS!
ARE YOU HAVING FUN YET?
I CERTAINLY AM!
I HATE TO CONJURE AND RUN...BUT I HAVE A FULL CALENDAR TODAY!
DON'T BOTHER TRYING TO FOLLOW--
MY STAFF'S ENERGY SIGNATURE CAN BE DISGUISED AT WILL!

SLAG THOSE MINDLESS BEASTS!
DEMONSTAFF WOULD HAVE BEEN MINE, IF ONLY THEY DIDN'T BAR MY--HO! THEY'RE ALREADY RETURNING TO THEIR OWN PLANE OF REALITY!
FORGET THOSE CREATURES! GORKO IS THE TRUE MONSTER!
HE'S TOTALLY MAD...AND MEANS TO DESTROY US ALL!
I'M SURE HE'D LIKE TO TRY!
YOU DON'T UNDERSTAND--!
HE NOW HAS THE NECESSARY POWER TO ROCK THE VERY FOUNDATIONS OF REALITY AS WE KNOW IT!
IT ALL BEGAN QUITE SOME TIME AGO...
"AS PART OF ITS SERVICE TO THE COMMUNITY, ADCORE FUNDS CERTAIN... UH... WORTHWHILE SCIENTIFIC ENTERPRISES!
"HALLAN GORKO WAS A BRILLIANT SCIENTIST IN THOSE DAYS!
"HE WAS A TRUE VISIONARY WITH AN INTEREST IN EXPLORING THE VERY NATURE OF REALITY!
"LIKE A LATTER-DAY CHRISTOPHER COLUMBUS, HE WAS CONVINCED WE COULD EXPLORE ALTERNATE WORLDS AND PARALLEL REALITIES!
"UNFORTUNATELY, HIS FIRST ATTEMPT TO OPEN A DIMENSIONAL RIFT NEARLY PROVED FATAL!
"UNWILLING TO RISK HUMAN LIVES, I WAS DETERMINED TO CANCEL THE PROJECT!
"BUT GORKO'S WIFE WAS ALSO A SCIENTIST...
"AND EVENTUALLY, ELLENE CONVINCED ME THAT HER HUSBAND'S WORK WAS TOO IMPORTANT TO ABANDON!

"SO PERSUASIVE WAS ELLENE THAT I TOOK A PERSONAL INTEREST IN THE PROJECT.
"USING GORKO'S NOTES FOR A BASIS, WE EXPANDED UPON HIS THEORIES... AND TOOK THEM IN STARTLING NEW DIRECTIONS!
"EVENTUALLY, AFTER COUNTLESS FALSE STARTS AND GRUELING WORK SHIFTS, WE COBBLED TOGETHER THE DIMENSIONIZER --A DEVICE CAPABLE OF PIERCING THE DIMENSIONAL BARRIERS.

"BLINDED BY OUR INITIAL SUCCESSES, WE RUSHED TO TEST IT--
"--BUT THAT'S WHEN TRAGEDY STRUCK!
"DURING A CRITICAL PHASE OF THE EXPERIMENT, ELLENE WAS ACCIDENTALLY SUCKED INTO A DIMENSIONAL RIFT!
"SHE MUST HAVE BEEN KILLED INSTANTLY!

"NEEDLESS TO SAY, GORKO WENT MAD WITH GRIEF!
"REFUSING TO ACCEPT HIS WIFE'S DEATH, HE BLAMED ME FOR ALL HIS TROUBLES!
"FOR HIS OWN GOOD, I HAD HIM PLACED IN A SPECIAL SANITARIUM WHERE HE COULD BE CARED FOR--
"BUT SOMEHOW HE MANAGED TO ESCAPE!"

AND NOW HE'S BACK ...WEARING SOME RIDICULOUS COSTUME!
THE MAN'S OBVIOUSLY INSANE!
HE'S OBSESSED WITH FINDING ELLENE... AND HE'S TAKEN THE DIMENSIONIZER!

THINK OF THE HAVOC HE COULD CAUSE IF HE BEGAN OPENING DIMENSIONAL RIFTS AT RANDOM!

HE COULD ENDANGER OUR ENTIRE PLANE OF REALITY!

SOMETIME LATER, AS SHIFTS CHANGE AND EVENING BEGINS TO EMBRACE THE URBAN CENTER...
MAY AS WELL CALL IT A NIGHT!
I HAVE A FULL WORK-SHIFT TOMORROW!
WHILE I MAY POSSESS THE POWER OF THOR IN THIS FORM--
--I'M STILL GOING TO NEED A FULL MEAL AND GOOD NIGHT'S SLEEP...
...IF I EXPECT TO EARN MY DAILY QUOTA!
CAN'T HELP WONDERING ABOUT DUNBAR'S STORY!
CORP CHIEFS AREN'T EXACTLY PRIZED FOR HONESTY!
BUT... WHAT'S HIS PROFIT IN LYING?
SALLA ?!
YOU HOME --?
DEMON-STAFF WASN'T JUST BUZZING ME!
I'VE BEEN FLASHING ACROSS THE CITY FOR HOURS NOW AND CAN'T SEEM TO LIGHT HIM!
WHERE ELSE WOULD I BE, DARGO DEAR?
LAST TIME I CHECKED, ONLY ONE MEMBER OF THIS FAMILY SPENT HIS OFF-HOURS REGULARLY RISKING HIS NECK OUT OF SOME ARCANE SENSE OF RESPONSIBILITY!
THE LESS INTELLIGENT MEMBER, IF I RECALL CORRECTLY!

YOU ONLY HAVE YOURSELF TO BLAME! YOU COULD HAVE CHOSEN A **SMART** SLACKER ...INSTEAD OF A GOOD-LOOKING ONE!
REALLY? LOOKS LIKE I DREW A **CRASHED DISK** ON BOTH PROGRAMS!
LUCKY FOR YOU, YOU'RE SO **HUGGABLE!**
HUNGRY, TOO!
THAT CAN BE FIXED!
THIS DEMONSTAFF SOUNDS **FAMILIAR...** BUT ALL OF THOSE COSTUMED LUNATICS YOU FIGHT HAVE THE MOST **OUTLANDISH** NAMES!
WE'VE BATTLED QUITE A FEW TIMES, BUT HE'S ALWAYS MANAGED TO ESCAPE!
NEVER KNEW WHY HE JAMMED ON HIGH-TECH COMPONENTS UNTIL NOW...

TO TELL YOU THE TRUTH, I FEEL **SORRY** FOR THE POOR MAN...

SO DO I...NOW THAT I KNOW HIS STORY!
I CAN ONLY IMAGINE WHAT HE'S BEEN GOING THROUGH... NOT KNOWING IF HIS WIFE IS DEAD OR ALIVE!
SALLA, IF **ANYTHING** LIKE THAT EVER--
DON'T EVEN **THINK** IT, DARGO!
YOU AND I MADE A SOLEMN PACT ...LONG AGO... THAT PART OF YOUR LIFE STAYS OUTSIDE! IT DOESN'T ENTER OUR APARTMENT!

WE'RE BOTH **SAFE** HERE!

HOW SICKENINGLY SWEET--!

I NEVER WOULD HAVE BELIEVED THAT THE MIGHTY THOR-- OR SHOULD I CALL HIM DARGO--WOULD LEAD SUCH A DULL AND MUNDANE LIFE!

HE APPEARS TO BE LITTLE MORE THAN A COMMON WAGE SLAVE!

JUST GOES TO SHOW HOW REALITY CAN RUIN THE BEST OF ILLUSIONS... BUT I INTEND TO FIX THAT BEFORE I AM THROUGH!

I DO NOT KNOW WHAT ANNOYS ME MORE... WATCHING HIM WITH HIS PRETTY YOUNG WIFE... WHILE I AM STILL DENIED MY LONG-AWAITED REUNION WITH ELLENE... OR KNOWING THAT HE PITIES ME?!

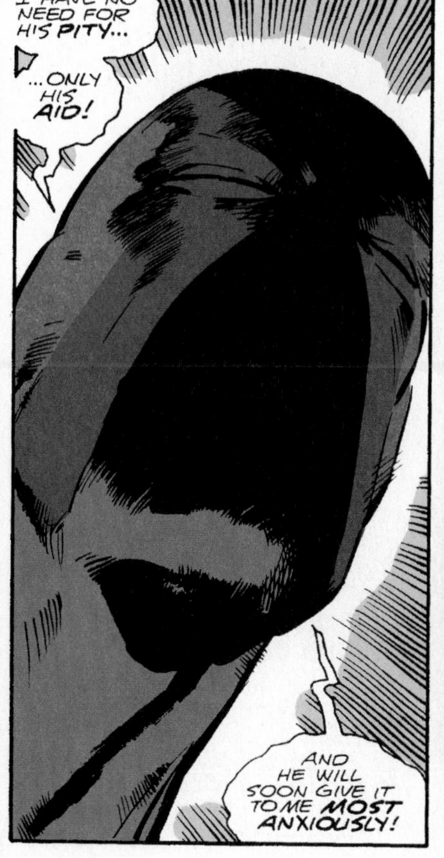

I HAVE NO NEED FOR HIS PITY...
...ONLY HIS AID!
AND HE WILL SOON GIVE IT TO ME MOST ANXIOUSLY!

EARLY THE NEXT MORNING, THE FIRST-SHIFT BELL SOUNDS AS DAWN STRETCHES ITS FINGERS ACROSS THE STILL-SLUMBERING CITY...

SEE YOU AT SHIFT-END, SWEETHEART!
IT'S A SHAME THAT DARGO HAS TO LEAVE EARLIER THAN I DO BECAUSE HE HAS MUCH FARTHER TO COMMUTE!

I'D BETTER FINISH GETTING READY AND -- WHAT'S THAT?!
KWAK!
KWAK!
KWAK!
KWAK!

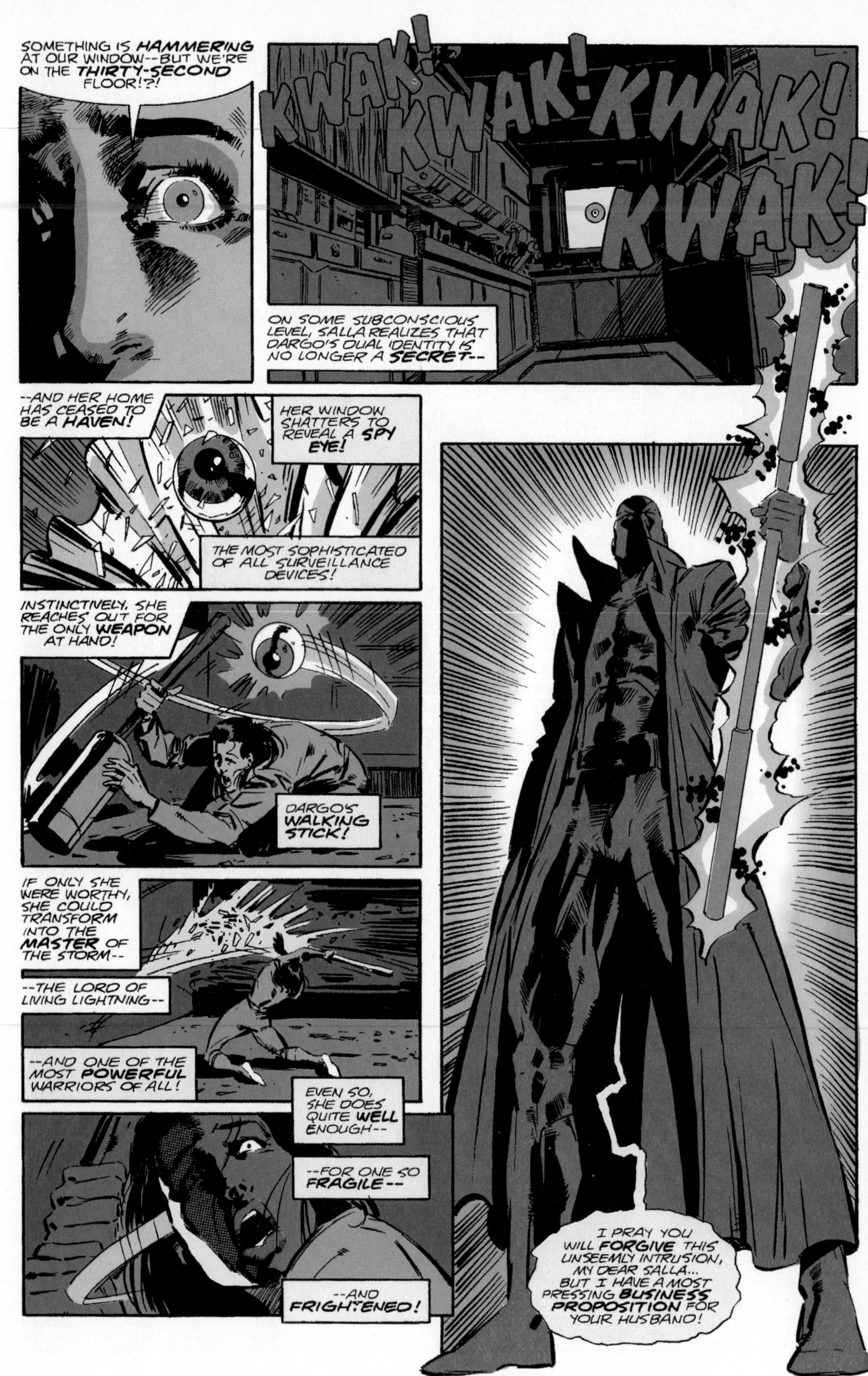
SOMETHING IS HAMMERING AT OUR WINDOW--BUT WE'RE ON THE THIRTY-SECOND FLOOR!?!
KWAK! KWAK! KWAK! KWAK!
ON SOME SUBCONSCIOUS LEVEL, SALLA REALIZES THAT DARGO'S DUAL IDENTITY IS NO LONGER A SECRET--
--AND HER HOME HAS CEASED TO BE A HAVEN!
HER WINDOW SHATTERS TO REVEAL A SPY EYE!
THE MOST SOPHISTICATED OF ALL SURVEILLANCE DEVICES!
INSTINCTIVELY, SHE REACHES OUT FOR THE ONLY WEAPON AT HAND!
DARGO'S WALKING STICK!
IF ONLY SHE WERE WORTHY, SHE COULD TRANSFORM INTO THE MASTER OF THE STORM--
--THE LORD OF LIVING LIGHTNING--
--AND ONE OF THE MOST POWERFUL WARRIORS OF ALL!
EVEN SO, SHE DOES QUITE WELL ENOUGH--
--FOR ONE SO FRAGILE--
--AND FRIGHTENED!
I PRAY YOU WILL FORGIVE THIS UNSEEMLY INTRUSION, MY DEAR SALLA... BUT I HAVE A MOST PRESSING BUSINESS PROPOSITION FOR YOUR HUSBAND!

SOMETIME LATER, EVEN AS THIRD BELL SOUNDS FOR THE SECOND-SHIFTERS...
SALLA ?!
YOU--
--HOME?!?
FEAR--COLD AND BITTER--SUDDENLY SEIZES DARGO IN AN ALL-ENVELOPING VISE!
BUT THEN, EVEN BEFORE A COHERENT THOUGHT CAN FORM--!
A HOLO-FAX--!
IF ANYTHING HAS HAPPENED TO SALLA--!
NO NEED TO PANIC, OLD FRIEND!
PLEASE! IT'S EMBARRASSING ENOUGH THAT I HAD TO RESORT TO THE OLD DAMSEL-IN-DISTRESS PLOY!
I WAS HOPING WE COULD BYPASS THE CUSTOMARY MELODRAMATIC THREATS!
I ASSUME THAT EVEN A MUSCLE-BOUND OAF SUCH AS YOURSELF WAS NOT FOOLED BY DUNBAR'S COMPANY LINE!
THE SCRAG DELIBERATELY SABOTAGED MY WORK--
--AND ATTEMPTED TO STEAL MY WIFE!
BUT OUR FRIENDLY NEIGHBORHOOD CORP RAIDER ACCIDENTALLY UNLEASHED FORCES FAR BEYOND THE SCOPE OF HIS SEVERELY LIMITED INTELLIGENCE!
OF COURSE, I AM ALSO TO BLAME!
I ACCEPTED ADCORE'S MONEY...

I WILLINGLY ALLOWED THEM TO **FUND** MY EXPERIMENTS IN INTER-DIMENSIONAL PHYSICS UNTIL I STUMBLED UPON THEIR **TRUE GOAL!**

NOT CONTENT WITH CALLOUSLY MANIPULATING THE PUBLIC'S **FANTASIES** LIKE ANY OTHER ADVERTISING AGENCY, ADCORE SOUGHT TO CONTROL **REALITY** ITSELF!

JUST IMAGINE WHAT THE **UNIVERSE** WOULD BE LIKE IF IT WERE SUBJECT TO THE **WHIMS** OF A COTERIE OF CRAZED AD EXECS.

OH, WELL... ONE MAN'S **REALITY** IS ANOTHER'S **NIGHTMARE!**

BUT YOU HAVE AN EVEN MORE PRESSING PROBLEM NOW!

AFTER CEASELESSLY SCOURING THE MYRIAD PLANES OF REALITY WITH THE MINIATURE **DIMENSIONIZER** WHICH POWERS MY STAFF... I HAVE FINALLY MANAGED TO **LOCATE** MY ERRANT WIFE!

AFTER A RECENT ADVENTURE IN DEEP SPACE THAT BEGAN WHEN THE LADY SIF ASKED HIS AID IN FINDING THE MIGHTY THOR*--
--BETA RAY BILL HAS FINALLY RETURNED TO HARMONY, BUT ALL IS NOT WELL ON THE NEW HOMEWORLD OF HIS PEOPLE!
WONDER OF WONDERS! THIS MONSTROUS PLANT IS GROWING AT A GEOMETRIC RATE--
--AND THREATENS TO ENGULF THIS ENTIRE SETTLEMENT!
*SEE THOR #461 AND SILVER SURFER #82--FACT-MINDED MIKE!
BEHOLD--!
WE ARE SAVED! OUR CYBORG WARRIOR STREAKS TO OUR RESCUE!
AS WELL HE SHOULD. THAT GROTESQUE MOCKERY WAS BIO-ENGINEERED TO DEFEND US!
AYE, BUT THOUGH I AM SWORN TO PROTECT YOU--
--I CANNOT IGNORE YOUR FEAR... OR CONSTANT DISDAIN!
BUT I CANNOT WORRY ABOUT THAT WHEN LIVES ARE ENDANGERED!
INSTEAD, I MUST SEEK THE VERY HEART OF THIS PLANT'S ROOT SYSTEM!
HERE! I SHALL SUMMON A SINGLE, SEARING BOLT OF LIGHTNING TO STRIKE HERE!
I ONLY PRAY THAT NO LIVES ARE LOST BEFORE I CAN--
SOMETHING IS AMISS!
I AM SUDDENLY GROWING INSUBSTANTIAL... I'M FADING... BEFORE MY VERY EYES!

AT THAT SELF-SAME MOMENT, ON THE PLANET EARTH...
NICE WORKOUT, KEVIN!
YEAH... BOBBY'S BEEN PRACTICING WITH ME LATELY!
DIVORCED FROM KEVIN'S MOTHER, WHO HAS CUSTODY OF THE BOY, ERIC MASTERSON RARELY ENJOYS AN ENTIRE DAY WITH HIS SON.
I SHOULD BE HAPPY KEVIN GETS ALONG WITH HIS NEW STEP-DAD, BUT THERE'S SOMETHING ABOUT BOBBY STEELE THAT I JUST CAN'T STOMACH! MAYBE IT'S ONLY PETTY JEALOUSY, BUT--
HEY, POP--ICE CREAM!
WHAT DO YOU SAY TO A QUICK CONE BEFORE WE HEAD HOME?
ICE CREAM
C'MON--! I'LL RACE YOU!
SCRE-EECH!
KEVIN--!
HOW MANY TIMES HAVE I WARNED YOU AGAINST-- WHAT THE--?!

KEVIN--?!

NICE ENTRANCE, MASTERSON! YOU'RE AS HEROIC AS EVER!

WHA--?

WHAT THE HECK ARE YOU DOING HERE?!

WHERE IS HERE, FOR THAT MATTER?

AND WHAT'S HAPPENED TO MY SON?!

GREETINGS, FRIEND ERIC! MY HEART IS GLADDENED BY YOUR UNEXPECTED PRESENCE!

LIKE YOURSELF, I AM ALSO NEWLY ARRIVED!

OUR HAMMER-BROTHER SURELY HOLDS THE ANSWERS WE SEEK!

DEMONSTAFF REALLY SCAGGED ME!

WITH ALL OF TIME AND SPACE TO CHOOSE FROM, I CAN'T BELIEVE HE TAGGED YOU TWO!

AND I MEAN NOW!
MAKE WITH THE MAGIC, LAUGHING BOY --SEND ME HOME-- AND JUST PRAY THAT NOTHING HAS HAPPENED TO MY SON IN THE MEANWHILE!
YOU DON'T HAVE THE ONLY LOVED ONE IN DANGER, MISTER!
HEY! WHAT'S WITH THE SCRAGGLY NEW LOOK--AND WHY IS A LIGHTNING BOLT DANGLING FROM YOUR EAR?
IT'S... UH...
A FASHION STATEMENT!
YOU'RE KIDDING, RIGHT? THAT WAS YOUR IDEA!
NEVER MIND!
WHAT'S IMPORTANT IS SAVING MY SON!
STAY YOUR WRATH, RASH ONE!
I, TOO, HAVE GRAVE RESPONSIBILITIES ELSEWHERE... BUT WE OWE DARGO HIS SAY!
YEAH, I GUESS WE'RE ALL IN THIS TOGETHER-- WHETHER WE LIKE IT OR NOT--SO I'D BETTER FILL YOU IN...

BUT EVEN AS DARGO KTOR BEGINS TO SPEAK...
BEHOLD, ELLENE--!
THESE WARRIORS ARE NEWLY ARRIVED WITHIN THE CHOSEN REALITIES--
--AND I BELIEVE THAT THEY HAVE JOURNEYED TO OUR HIDDEN WORLD OF ELSE-WHEN AS EMISSARIES OF YOUR INSIDIOUS HUSBAND!
I AM HONESTLY SURPRISED THAT IT HAS TAKEN HIM SO LONG TO MOUNT A RESCUE OPERATION!
WARLORD KARGUL, PLEASE--!
SILENCE, MY DEAR! I HAVE ALREADY BEGUN A'CONJURING!
WITH THE WHOLE OF REALITY AT STAKE, I SHALL DEPOSIT THESE INTERLOPERS IN A TIME AND WORLD WHERE WE WOULD BE WELL RID OF THEM!
GET REAL, DARGO! I DON'T CARE HOW POWERFUL THIS DEMONSTAFF CHARACTER IS! ONE MAN CAN'T POSSIBLY THREATEN THE ENTIRE--
WE APPEAR TO BE VANISHING FROM THIS PLANE OF REALITY!
-WHEW!- THAT DIDN'T LAST LONG!
I WONDER WHERE WE--

OKAY, AXIS! HERE WE COME--!
MY FLAME-COVERED FRIEND SPEAKS TRUE! YOU SPIES HAVE JUST CHOSEN THE WRONG DESTROYER TO SABOTAGE!
YOU'RE FACING THE INVADERS NOW!
UH... GUYS...
...THERE'S AN OLD CLICHÉ ABOUT NOT BEING IN KANSAS THAT'S TOO CORNY FOR EVEN ME TO USE, BUT IT SEEMS LIKE WE'VE LANDED SMACK IN THE MIDDLE OF WORLD WAR II!
BUT...HOW ARE WE EVER SUPPOSED TO RETURN HOME?!
NEXT ISSUE: REALITY BEGINS TO BE TWISTED EVEN FURTHER OUT OF WHACK AS MACHINE MAN 2020 AND THE ALL-NEW TEENAGE FRANKLIN RICHARDS JOIN THE FUN! DON'T MISS...
GATHER CHAOS!

MARVEL COMICS

THOR CORPS

$1.75 US
$2.25 CAN
2
OCT
02506

APPROVED BY THE COMICS CODE AUTHORITY

PART TWO OF FOUR

GUEST STARRING THE INVADERS

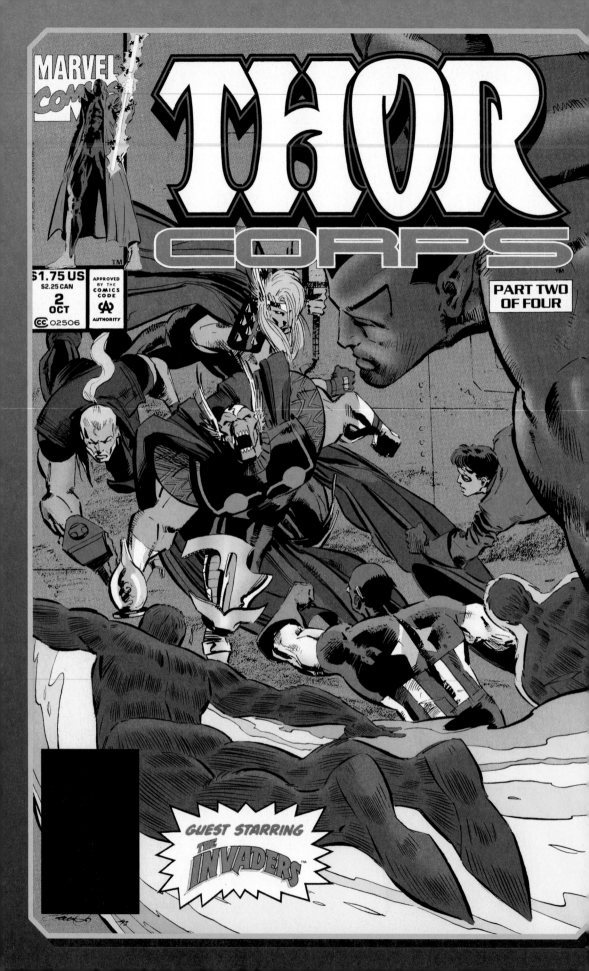

FROM DIFFERENT WORLDS AND TIMES COME THREE MIGHTY WARRIORS, EACH EMPOWERED BY AN ENCHANTED **ASGARDIAN WEAPON** WHICH GRANTS THE ASTONISHING ABILITIES OF THE LEGENDARY **GOD OF THUNDER!** TOGETHER, **DARGO, BETA RAY BILL,** AND **ERIC MASTERSON** JOIN TO FORM...

Stan Lee presents

THE THOR CORPS!

WRITTEN BY TOM DeFALCO | ILLUSTRATED BY PATRICK OLLIFFE | LETTERED BY JOHN E. WORKMAN | COLORED BY GEORGE ROUSSOS | EDITED BY MIKE ROCKWITZ | OVERSEEN BY RALPH MACCHIO

--THEY SUDDENLY FIND THEMSELVES ON A BATTLESHIP IN THE BROOKLYN NAVY YARD!
THE YEAR IS 1942 AND THEIR FOES... THE LEGENDARY INVADERS!
COWARDLY CRETINS! YOU SHALL NOT ESCAPE THE VENGEANCE OF PRINCE NAMOR OF ATLANTIS.
BETA RAY BILL HAS BEEN CALLED MANY TAUNTING INSULTS, BUT COWARD--?! NEVER!
WHO ARE THESE JOKERS, TORCH?
NO IDEA, TORO... BUT THEIR COSTUMES REMIND ME OF THAT NORDIC GOD WE ONCE BATTLED!
I'M CERTAIN THEY'RE HERE TO SABOTAGE THIS SHIP!
TORCH?! ONE FLAMING BEING CALLED THE OTHER TORCH! COULD THIS BE THE HUMAN TORCH OF LEGEND?
BUT THEN, WHERE ARE HIS ILLUSTRIOUS TEAMMATES--THE GRIMM, MISTER ELASTIC, AND THE INVISIBLE WITCH?!
OH, NO! WHILE ATTEMPTING TO DODGE CAP'S SHIELD, I BUMBLED RIGHT INTO HIS YOUNG PARTNER'S ARMS!
LOOK WHAT I CAUGHT! CAN I KEEP HIM?
PROBABLY NOT, LITTLE CHUM! THESE AGENTS OF THE MASTER RACE DON'T THRIVE WELL IN A FREE COUNTRY.
POUR ON THE FLAME, TORO!
CAP AND BUCKY ALREADY HAVE THEIR MAN! LET'S NOT COME IN THIRD BEHIND THE SUB-MARINER!
EVEN IF THESE ARE THE ILLUSTRIOUS HEROES OF THE PAST. I CAN'T LET THAT INHIBIT ME--NOT WHILE DEMONSTAFF STILL HOLDS MY SALLA HOSTAGE!
I MUST STRIKE MY ENCHANTED HAMMER ON THE GROUND--
--AND SUMMON A SUDDEN RAIN-STORM!
TORO, LOOK OUT--!

WHOA, CAP! THERE'S NO NEED FOR US TO FIGHT! IT'S ME... ERIC!
NICE TO MAKE YOUR ACQUAINTANCE, ERIC ...BUT I PREFER THAT NAZIS USE MY FULL NAME AND CALL ME CAPTAIN AMERICA!
THIS CLOWN ACTS LIKE HE KNOWS YOU, CAP.
MAYBE SO, BUCKY... BUT I'VE NEVER LAID EYES ON HIM BEFORE!
WHAT WAS I THINKING? EVEN IF THIS IS MY CAP--AND NOT SOME ALTERNATE VERSION--WE'RE NOT SLATED TO MEET UP FOR ANOTHER FIFTY YEARS!

AHHHH! WHILE THE TORCHES ARE PLAGUED BY THIS UNEXPECTED SHOWER--
--ITS LIFE-GIVING WATER ALREADY RENEWS MY STRENGTH!

I GROW STRONGER!
STRONGER!
YUNNGH!

FAR BEYOND THE EVER-EVOLVING BORDERS OF TIME AND SPACE, ON A WORLD KNOWN AS ELSEWHEN...
MAY THE CURSES OF EVERY KNOWN REALITY FALL UPON YOUR SHORTSIGHTED SPOUSE, ELLENE!
NOT ONLY HAS HE SENT THESE INEFFECTUAL PAWNS TO ALMOST CERTAIN DEATH--
--BUT HE CONTINUES TO DABBLE WITH FORCES FAR BEYOND HIS CONTROL!
TEMPER! TEMPER!
YOU REALLY SHOULD LEARN TO MIND YOUR TONGUE, WARLORD KARGUL!
YOU NEVER KNOW WHO MIGHT BE LISTENING IN!
DEMON-STAFF--!
I JUST WANTED TO WARN YOU THAT REPORTS OF MY MENTAL DETERIORATION ARE HARDLY EXAGGERATED!
I AM, IN FACT, SUFFICIENTLY CRAZY TO COME AFTER YOU... AND MY BEAUTIFUL ELLENE!
NOT EVEN A MADMAN LIKE YOU WOULD WILLINGLY RISK COUNTLESS LIVES--AND THE CHOSEN REALITIES THEMSELVES--IN A MAD QUEST FOR VENGEANCE!
TRUST ME, KARGUL! I WILL MAKE A TRUE BELIEVER OUT OF YOU YET!
'NUFF SAID!

HA! HA! YOU SHOULD HAVE SEEN THE EXPRESSION ON THAT BARBARIAN BUFFOON'S FACE WHEN I CAUSED HIS IMAGING POOL TO ERUPT!
PRECIOUS TIME WILL PASS BEFORE HE CAN REPAIR THE DAMAGE --AND AGAIN PEER ACROSS THE MYRIAD DIMENSIONS!
PAY ATTENTION, MY DEAR SALLA! SOMEONE HAS TO TAKE NOTES!
I'D LIKE TO LEAVE SOMETHING TO POSTERITY --EVEN IF IT'S ONLY A FEW WILD RAVINGS--ON THE OFF CHANCE THERE IS A POSTERITY WHEN I'M FINISHED!
KARGUL FEARS THAT I CANNOT CONTROL THE POWER EMPLOYED BY MY STAFF--
--THE BARRIER FORCE-- WHICH ALLOWS ALTERNATE DIMENSIONS TO STAND SEPARATE FROM EACH OTHER!
ALAS, HE'S RIGHT... BUT I HAVE ABSOLUTELY NO INTENTION OF EVEN ATTEMPTING TO CONTROL IT!
I MERELY WISH TO UNLEASH IT!
ACROSS TOWN, IN A SHIELDED SUBBASEMENT OF ADCORE, A MAJOR PLAYER IN THE ADVERTISING GAME...
HALLAN GORKO, A FORMER EMPLOYEE, MUST BE NEUTRALIZED AT ANY COST!
DO NOT ALLOW THE FACT THAT HE IS RUNNING AROUND IN A RIDICULOUS COSTUME--AND HAS ADOPTED THE LUDICROUS NAME OF DEMONSTAFF --CAUSE YOU TO UNDERESTIMATE THE VERY REAL DANGER HE REPRESENTS!
THIS MAN HAS THE ABILITY TO UNDERMINE THE VERY FOUNDATIONS OF REALITY AS WE KNOW IT!
WE UNDERSTAND, CITIZEN DUNBAR!
WE WILL NOT FAIL!
H315

MEANWHILE...
YOU OKAY, BILL? SUBBY REALLY CLOCKED YOU!
I HAVE SUFFERED FAR WORSE!
MOST RECENTLY, AT THE HANDS OF THE MIGHTY THOR HIMSELF!*
*SEE THOR # 461. --MIKE
STAND FAST, MY FRIENDS! THIS BATTLE ONLY SERVES TO DELAY OUR TRUE MISSION!
I SHALL ATTEMPT TO OPEN A DIMENSIONAL PORTAL WHICH CAN RETURN US TO ELSEWHEN!
THERE--! I BELIEVE THAT MY ENCHANTED HAMMER SUCCESSFULLY DUPLICATED THE ENERGY PATTERN THAT TRANSPORTED US HERE!
HOWEVER, IF I AM MISTAKEN... WE COULD BE LOST IN ANOTHER ALTERNATE DIMENSION!
SWELL!
HOW DO WE CHOOSE WHO GOES FIRST?!
CAP! THEY'RE ESCAPING--!
NOT IF I CAN HELP IT!
UNFORTUNATELY FOR ERIC MASTERSON, THE ANSWER TO HIS LAST QUESTION COMES IN THE FORM OF A HASTILY-THROWN SHIELD--!
PWANG!
-UFFF-
ERIC WAS STANDING TOO NEAR THE PORTAL! HE IS BEING PROPELLED INTO THE GAP!

AND, EVEN AS BETA RAY BILL'S WORDS ECHO BEHIND HIM, ERIC CROSSES INTO A TERRIFYING **ALTERNATE WORLD** OF THE **NEAR FUTURE**--

--THE WORLD OF **MACHINE MAN 2020!**

WHAT THE--?!

MORE **IRONBOTS** ARE CLOSING IN ON US, AND **--SWIFT!** BEHIND YOU!

THAT MAN SUDDENLY **MATERIALIZED** OUT OF THIN AIR!

THANKS FOR THE SCAN, **MM...** BUT MY CLIP IS ALREADY TARGETED!

BRAIN! SLICK! TAKE THE FLYERS! I'LL RACK THE NEW BO!

GO FOR IT, **HASSLE!**

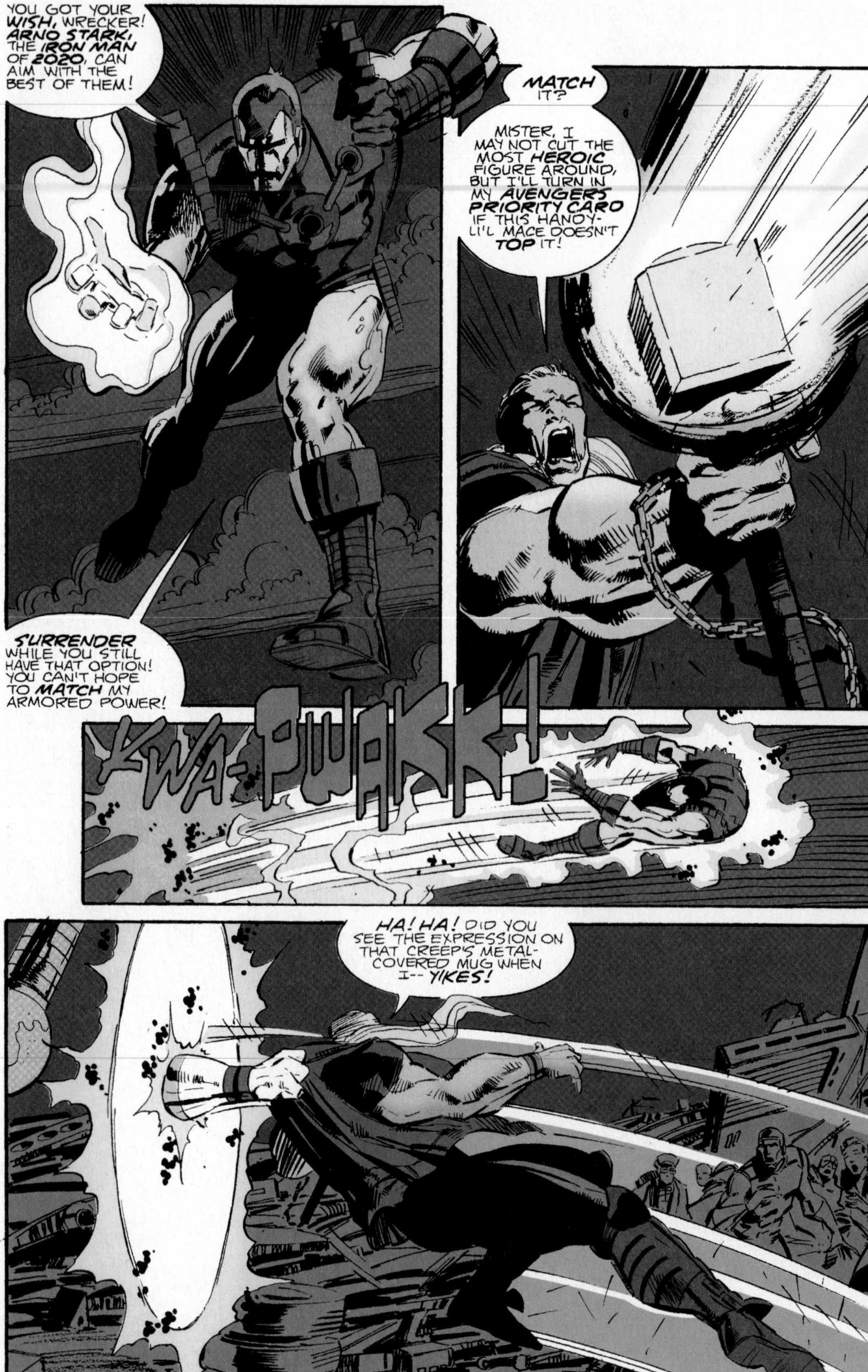

YOU GOT YOUR **WISH**, WRECKER! **ARNO STARK**, THE **IRON MAN** OF **2020**, CAN AIM WITH THE BEST OF THEM!

SURRENDER WHILE YOU STILL HAVE THAT OPTION! YOU CAN'T HOPE TO **MATCH** MY ARMORED POWER!

MATCH IT?

MISTER, I MAY NOT CUT THE MOST **HEROIC** FIGURE AROUND, BUT I'LL TURN IN MY **AVENGERS PRIORITY CARD** IF THIS HANDY LI'L MACE DOESN'T **TOP** IT!

KWA-PWAKK!

AT LAST! I HAVE RETRIEVED OUR ERRANT HAMMER-BROTHER!
WHY YOU EVEN BOTHERED... IS ANYONE'S GUESS!
NICE TO SEE YOU, TOO, DARGO!
TRY TO KEEP UP WITH THE REST OF THE TEAM, MASTERSON! IF MY WIFE IS HARMED BECAUSE OF YOUR CLUMSINESS--!
YOU THINK I FELL INTO THAT DIMENSION ON PURPOSE?
LISTEN UP, PRETTY BOY... MY SON... KEVIN... IS ALSO IN DANGER!
HE WAS ABOUT TO BE HIT BY A SPEEDING CAR WHEN I WAS SUDDENLY WHISKED AWAY AGAINST MY WILL!

RIGHT... AND I'M GUESSING THAT YOU THREE ARE RESPONSIBLE!

AN ARMORED WARRIOR!

ERIC, IS THIS THE ONE YOU BATTLED EARLIER?

NOPE! THAT'S A WHOLE NEW METAL-PLATED MANIAC!

DEFLECT HIS PLASMA BOLTS, MY FRIENDS... WHILE I AGAIN ATTEMPT TO PIERCE THE DIMENSIONAL FABRIC!

CHECK A COMPASS THIS TIME! I COULD DO WITHOUT ANOTHER WACKY DETOUR!

ANY SLACK CAN JAW ANOTHER'S WORK, ERIC!

REALITY SHIFTS, TIME PASSES, AND THEN...
GATHER YE MOST FEARSOME WEAPONS, MY WARRIORS!
REALITY IS CRUMBLING AROUND US!
WE MUST FIND THE ONE WHO CALLS HIMSELF DEMONSTAFF... AND SEIZE THE SOURCE OF HIS POWER... BEFORE FURTHER DAMAGE CAN BE DONE!
BILL SCORED! WE MADE IT BACK TO ELSEWHEN!
YEAH, BUT WHAT ARE WE GOING TO DO ABOUT THIS ANGRY HORDE?
IF THIS DEMON GUY IS STILL ON EARTH, THOUSANDS OF INNOCENT PEOPLE WILL BE EN-DANGERED!
WE'RE ON THE VERGE OF INTER-DIMEN-SIONAL WAR!
DARGO! ERIC! I HAVE LOCATED THE WOMAN WE SEEK!
I HAVE FOUND ELLENE!
IF ONLY SHE CAN BE RETURNED TO HER HUSBAND IN TIME... WE COULD SCRAG THIS BUZZ!
AND IF NOT... WHAT OF MY SALLA... AND ERIC'S KEVIN?!
OTHERWISE, IT'S THE KIDS FOR MY SALLA... AND ERIC'S KEVIN!

MEANTIME, BACK ON EARTH...
EVEN IF MY SANITATION SQUAD MANAGES TO NEUTRALIZE GORKO, MY CAREER IS RUINED!
THE BOARD OF DIRECTORS WILL NEVER FORGIVE ME FOR FUNDING THAT LUNATIC'S EXPERIMENTS!
THOSE SENILE OLD FOOLS LACK THE NECESSARY VISION TO APPRECIATE MY TRUE GENIUS!
OTHER ADVERTISING AGENCIES MERELY EXPLOIT THE PUBLIC'S FANTASIES... BUT AOCORE WOULD HAVE MANIPULATED REALITY ITSELF!
YOUR PLAN WAS SIMPLY MARVELOUS, MR. DUNBAR!
IT REALLY IS A PITY THAT I ACCIDENTALLY STUMBLED UPON IT!
GORKO--!
NOW, NOW, MR. DUNBAR... WE'VE ALREADY BEEN THROUGH ALL THAT... AND A GOOD CHIEF OPERATING OFFICER LISTENS TO HIS EMPLOYEES!
HALLAN GORKO IS DEAD! YOU KILLED ME!
HOWEVER, THOUGH I FOUND THE EXPERIENCE QUITE UNPLEASANT, I HARBOR NO MALICE... I BEAR NO GRUDGE!
IN FACT, I HAVE A LITTLE TREAT IN STORE FOR YOU!

AND, IN A PALATIAL SITTING ROOM ON ELSEWHEN...
I TRUST YOU WILL FIND THESE SWEETS TO YOUR LIKING, MILADY!
THANK YOU, SHARI. YOUR KINDNESS IS GREATLY APPRECIATED, BUT WHAT I DESIRE MOST...IS PRIVACY!
WHY CAN'T THE GUARDS WAIT OUTSIDE?
THEY MERELY OBEY THE ORDERS OF THEIR MIGHTY WARLORD!
SURELY KARGUL DOESN'T BELIEVE THAT EVEN HALLAN WOULD DARE TO --WAIT!
WHAT IS CAUSING THOSE TREMORS?
THE OUTER HALLWAY IS ABLAZE WITH THE SOUNDS OF FURIOUS BATTLE!
STAND READY! IT'S OBVIOUSLY HEADED THIS WAY!
SUDDENLY, BEFORE THE STARTLED EYES OF ELLENE GORKO'S GUARDS, THREE ENCHANTED WEAPONS INSTANTLY REDUCE THE CHAMBER WALLS TO TINY SHARDS!
HAMMERS HIGH, AMIGOS!
I WAS UNDER THE IMPRESSION YOUR WEAPON WAS A MACE, MY FRIEND!
PICKY! PICKY!

THE GIRL, DARGO!
YOU'RE CLOSEST TO HER!
BILL AND I WILL KEEP THIS RABBLE AMUSED!
I'D PREFER TO STAY... AND HELP, ERIC!
BUT... MAYBE FOR THE FIRST TIME IN YOUR LIFE... YOU MAKE SENSE!
SURROUND THEM!
WE ARE MANY AND THEY ARE ONLY THREE! WE CANNOT FAIL OUR MIGHTY WARL--UGGN!
MY HUSBAND--?!
COME WITH ME, CITIZEN ELLENE! HURRY!
YOU HAVE NOTHING TO FEAR! YOUR HUSBAND SENT US TO RESCUE YOU!
WHY WOULD I EVER CHOOSE TO RETURN TO THAT MADMAN?!
BWA-ZAK!
-UNNK- SHE SCRAGGED ME... COMPLETELY BY SURPRISE!

STRIKE, MY SISTERS! STRIKE IN DEFENSE OF OUR BELOVED ELLENE!
WE WILL ALLOW NO HARM TO BEFALL HER, SISTER SHARI!

BEWARE, ERIC! THOSE SERVANTS SEEK TO DESTROY US WITH DEADLY MYSTICAL ENERGIES!
THIS IS GETTING NUTTIER BY THE MOMENT! IF I DIDN'T KNOW BETTER, I'D THINK WE ACCIDENTALLY STUMBLED INTO ONE OF MY KID'S CRAZY COMIC BOOKS!
BUT WHY DID THAT WOMAN BLAST DARGO? DOESN'T SHE REALIZE THAT WE'RE ONLY HERE TO HELP HER?!
WHY IS SHE FLEEING US?!

HAVEN'T YOU YET GUESSED THE TRUTH?!
I WAS NO PRISONER! I AM MERELY A FUGITIVE... A RUNAWAY SEEKING SANCTUARY... FROM HALLAN GORKO!
MY CUNNING HUSBAND HAS NO INTENTION OF LIBERATING ME!
HIS SOLE DESIRE IS TO SEE ME DEAD!

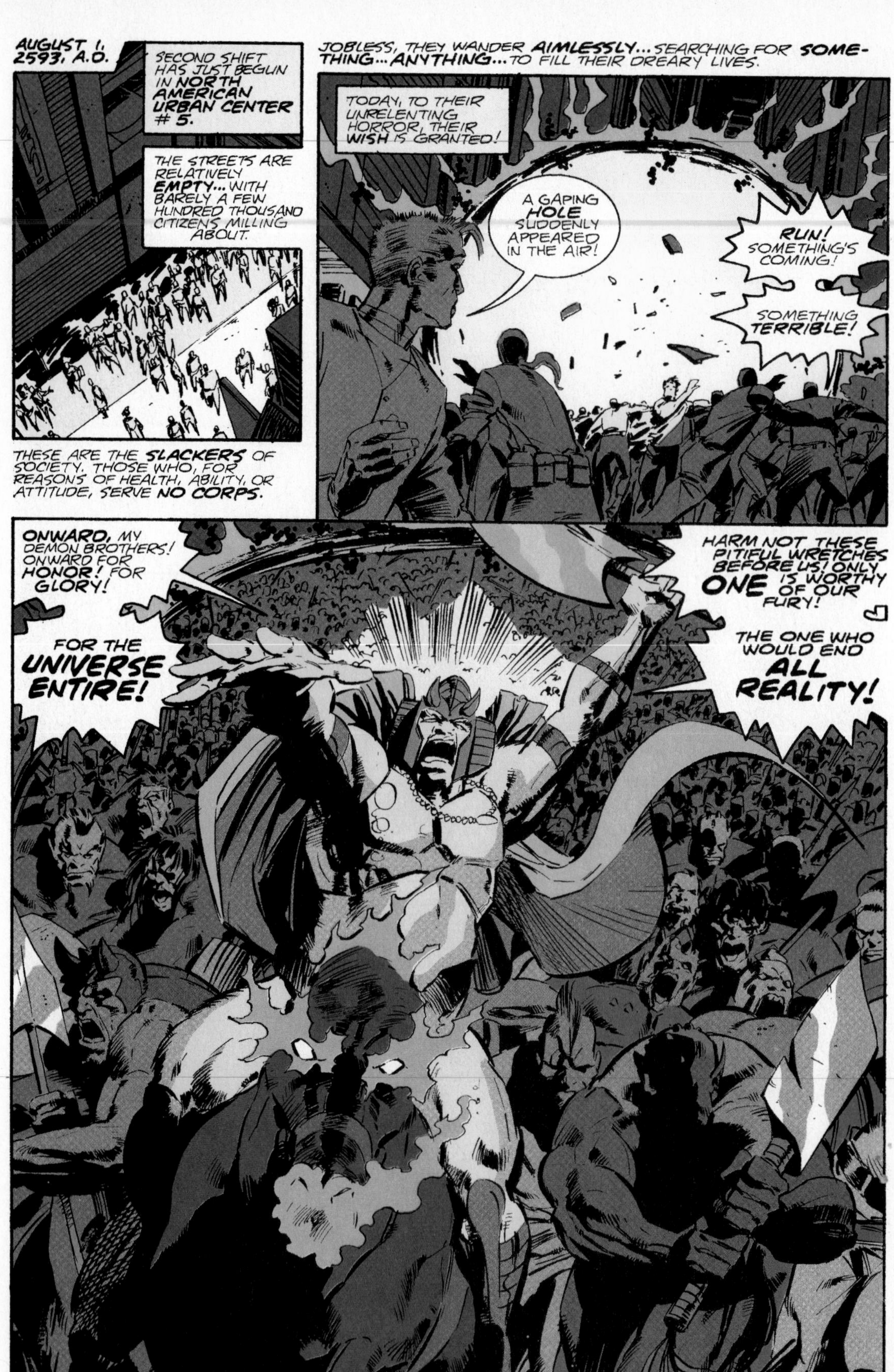
AUGUST 1, 2593, A.D.
SECOND SHIFT HAS JUST BEGUN IN NORTH AMERICAN URBAN CENTER # 5.
THE STREETS ARE RELATIVELY EMPTY... WITH BARELY A FEW HUNDRED THOUSAND CITIZENS MILLING ABOUT.
THESE ARE THE SLACKERS OF SOCIETY. THOSE WHO, FOR REASONS OF HEALTH, ABILITY, OR ATTITUDE, SERVE NO CORPS.
JOBLESS, THEY WANDER AIMLESSLY... SEARCHING FOR SOMETHING... ANYTHING... TO FILL THEIR DREARY LIVES.
TODAY, TO THEIR UNRELENTING HORROR, THEIR WISH IS GRANTED!
A GAPING HOLE SUDDENLY APPEARED IN THE AIR!
RUN! SOMETHING'S COMING!
SOMETHING TERRIBLE!
ONWARD, MY DEMON BROTHERS! ONWARD FOR HONOR! FOR GLORY!
FOR THE UNIVERSE ENTIRE!
HARM NOT THESE PITIFUL WRETCHES BEFORE US! ONLY ONE IS WORTHY OF OUR FURY!
THE ONE WHO WOULD END ALL REALITY!

AT THAT PRECISE INSTANT, IN THE PUTRID SEWERS BELOW--
--WEAPONS AT THE READY, CITIZEN DUNBAR'S SANITATION SQUAD IS GIVEN SUDDEN PAUSE!
SOUNDS LIKE A RIOT UP THERE!
GOOD! MORE WORK FOR US!
I COULD USE THE OVERTIME! MY WIFE'S BEEN SKRAGGING ME FOR A NEW FOOD SYNTHESIZER!
LOWER THE VOLUME, PEOPLE...AND PAY ATTENTION TO THE JOB AT HAND!
ADCORE IS A MAJOR CLIENT OF SANICORP! WE'RE ALL ON LINE FOR A SIGNIFICANT COMPLETION BONUS!

GREETINGS, MADMAN!
I TRUST YOU HAVE BEEN EXPECTING ME... AND HAVE PREPARED THE APPROPRIATE SNARES!
DO YOUR WORST! UNLEASH YOUR MOST TERRIBLE WEAPONS!
THIS BATTLE SHALL SURELY DECIDE THE FATE OF THE CHOSEN REALITIES AND THE UNIVERSE ENTIRE!
WAIT! THERE'S BEEN A COLOSSAL MISTAKE!

HOW RIGHT YOU ARE, CITIZEN GORKO ...AND WE ARE HERE TO CORRECT IT!

MOVE IT, MEN! MOVE IT!
THOSE WEIRD FREAKS ARE TRYING TO POACH OUR GAME!
WE ONLY GET PAID IF WE CAN CONFIRM THE KILL!
FIRE! FIRE!

NO! STOP! THIS CAN'T BE HAPPENING! NOT TO ME!
NOOOO!
BRA-TA-TA-TA-TA

THE LAST OF ELLENE'S GUARDS HAVE FINALLY DIMMED OUT!
YEAH, AND IT LOOKED LIKE YOU REALLY ENJOYED CLOBBERING THEM!
PLEASE DON'T HIT ME!
RELAX, MISTER! I GENERALLY AVOID VIOLENCE WHENEVER POSSIBLE!
ERIC! DARGO! WE MUST SECURE THE WOMAN!
SHE IS STILL KEY!
MAYBE SO... BUT I'M NOT SO ANXIOUS TO RETURN HER TO HUBBY ANYMORE!
WHY NOT? SHE COULD BE LYING ABOUT DEMONSTAFF'S INTENTIONS!
YEAH... ...AS IF YOU CARED!
STOP BICKERING, YOU TWO! WE WILL GUARANTEE HER SAFETY!
BE CAUTIOUS, MY BROTHERS! WE ARE ON UNFAMILIAR GROUND!
THIS CASTLE COULD CONTAIN DEADLY PITFALLS!
IT COULD... AND... DOES!
AND I HAVE JUST ACTIVATED...
...THE MOST PERILOUS OF ALL!
THE FLOOR IS OPENING BENEATH US--!
NOT THE FLOOR, ERIC! THESE ARE RIFTS IN THE DIMENSIONAL FABRIC!
SHE'S SEPARATING US!
CASTING US ADRIFT IN TIME AND SPACE!

THE HUMAN ASSASSINS ARE FLEEING INTO THE TUNNELS! MY DEVILISH HORDE HAS DRIVEN THEM OFF!
DEMONSTAFF LIES DEAD AT MY FEET... BUT ...WHERE IS HIS ACCURSED WEAPON?
THE STAFF WHICH IS THE SOURCE OF BOTH HIS RIDICULOUS NAME AND HIS STAGGERING POWER!
THE DIMENSIONIZER WHICH HE INVENTED --AND PLACED WITHIN HIS STAFF-- HAS BEEN SIPHONING VAST POWER FROM THE BARRIER FORCE!
UNCHECKED, HE WOULD HAVE EVENTUALLY WEAKENED THE DIMENSIONAL BARRIERS BEYOND REPAIR AND-- WAIT!
THIS MAN IS NOT HALLAN GORKO!

I ALMOST FEEL SORRY FOR WARLORD KARGUL!
IT MUST BE QUITE STRESSFUL TO RIDE HERD ON THIS UNRULY BARBARIAN RABBLE!
JUST LOOK AT THE WAY THEY'RE DISRUPTING TRAFFIC FLOW!
THE POOR SECURITY DRONES CERTAINLY HAVE THEIR CIRCUITS FULL!
YOU ARE MAD! INSANE!
OF COURSE I AM, MY DEAR! ONLY A TRUE CRAZOID WOULD DISGUISE HIMSELF IN A BRIGHTLY-COLORED COSTUME AND SEEK A TOTAL BREAKDOWN IN PHYSICAL REALITY!
BUT... WHY? WHY?
SADLY, THE ANSWER IS RATHER MUNDANE!
MY ENTIRE WORLD WAS DESTROYED WHEN MY BEAUTIFUL WIFE BETRAYED ME!
SHE WAS THE CENTER OF LIFE... AND YET SHE CONSPIRED WITH DUNBAR TO DESTROY ME... AND STEAL MY WORK!
IF I CAN'T BE HAPPY... WHY SHOULD ANYONE ELSE?!
THINK OF THE BIG BANG WE'LL HAVE WHEN ALL OF THE ALTERNATE DIMENSIONS COLLAPSE UPON EACH OTHER!
WON'T THAT BE FUN?!

NEXT ISSUE: REALITY GOES TOTAL WACKO AS--
--DARGO KTOR MEETS UP WITH THE SPIDER-MAN OF 2099--

--BETA RAY BILL IS CONFRONTED BY THE GUARDIANS OF THE GALAXY--

--AND ERIC MASTERSON SADDLES UP WITH KID COLT, THE RAWHIDE KID, AND THE TWO-GUN KID!

PLUS, WE'LL HAVE A FEW SURPRISE GUEST-STARS... INCLUDING A CERTAIN GOLDEN-HAIRED ASGARDIAN! DON'T MISS... "RAVAGED BY REALITY!"

MARVEL COMICS
$1.75 US
$2.25 CAN
3
NOV
APPROVED BY THE COMICS CODE AUTHORITY
02506
THOR
CORPS
FEATURING:
SPIDER-MAN 2099
GUARDIANS OF THE GALAXY
KID COLT
RAWHIDE KID
IF YOU WANT WACKY ENTERTAINMENT, THEN YOU MUST PICK UP THIS ISSUE!!

FROM DIFFERENT WORLDS AND TIMES COME THREE MIGHTY WARRIORS, EACH EMPOWERED BY AN ENCHANTED **ASGARDIAN WEAPON** WHICH GRANTS THE ASTONISHING ABILITIES OF THE LEGENDARY **GOD OF THUNDER!** TOGETHER, **DARGO, BETA RAY BILL,** AND **ERIC MASTERSON** JOIN TO FORM...

STAN LEE PRESENTS:

THE *THOR* CORPS!

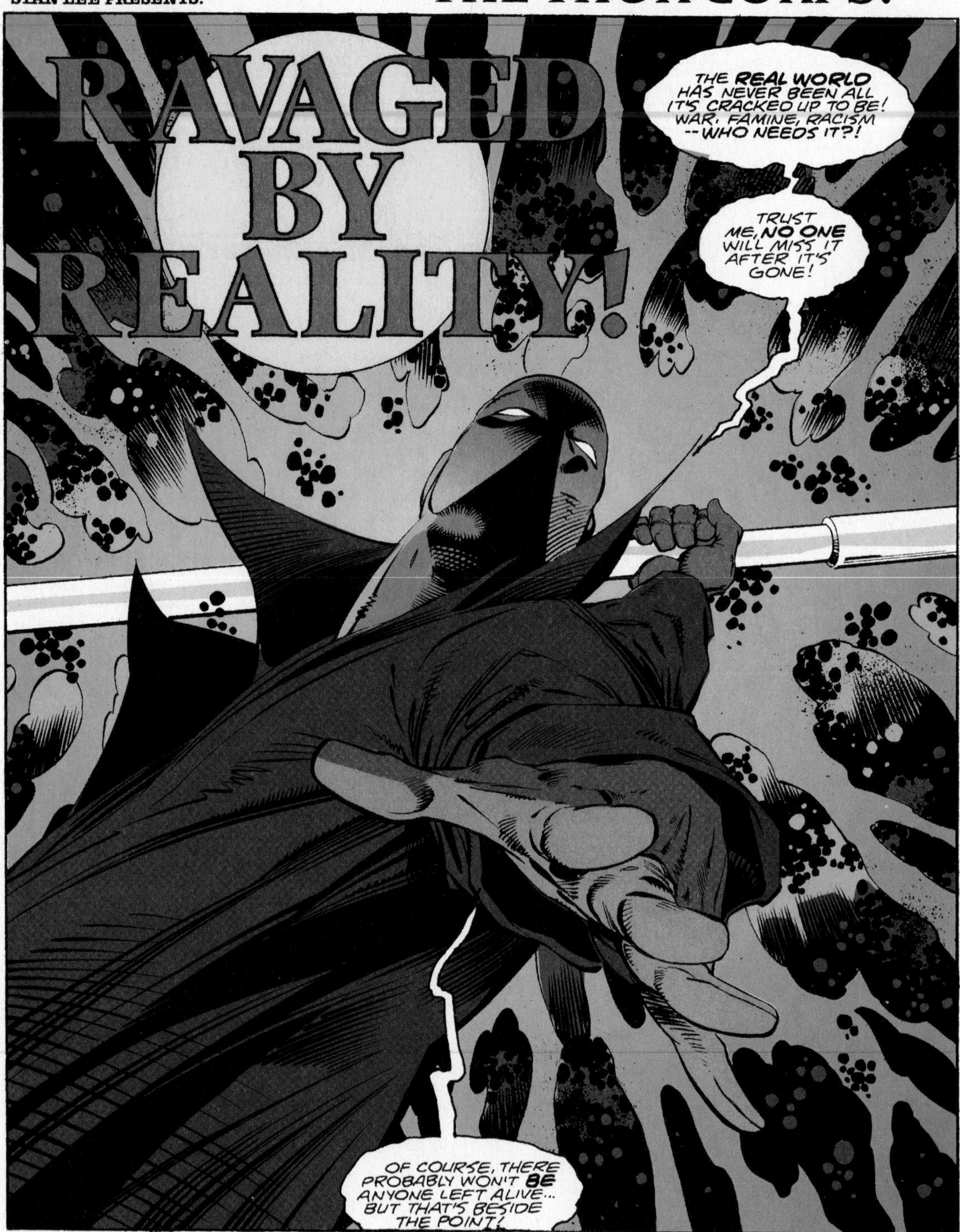

WRITTEN BY TOM DeFALCO · PENCILED BY PATRICK OLLIFFE · INKED BY ROMEO TANGHAL
LETTERED BY JOHN WORKMAN · COLORED BY GEORGE ROUSSOS · EDITED BY MIKE ROCKWITZ
OVERSEEN BY RALPH MACCHIO

BEING A MAJOR SUPER-VILLAIN IS REALLY QUITE **EXHILARATING.**
YOU CAN'T IMAGINE THE EGO-BOOST OF SEEING PEOPLE **QUAKE** WHENEVER YOU APPEAR ON THE SCENE!
STOP THIS **INSANITY** AT ONCE, DEMON-STAFF!
IS SOMETHING **WRONG,** MY DEAR SALLA?
AM I TO ASSUME THAT YOU ARE NOT **AMUSED** BY THIS SEA OF FLAMES?

NO PROBLEM!
NOW THAT I HAVE FULLY INTEGRATED MY NEW AND IMPROVED DIMENSIONIZER INTO MY TRUSTY STAFF, **REALITY** CAN EASILY BE TWISTED AND MANIPULATED AT WILL!

MY WILL!
IF THAT'S TRUE...
WHY DO YOU STILL NEED TO HOLD ME **HOSTAGE?**
YOUR HUSBAND--AND HIS HAMMER-SWINGING ASSOCIATES ARE FOOLISH TO BELIEVE THAT THE **MULTIVERSE** CAN STILL BE SAVED!

BARELY A MOMENT AGO-- OR SO IT SEEMED TO BETA RAY BILL, THE EVER-ELUSIVE ELLENE SEPARATED HIM FROM HIS COMPANIONS AND SENT THEM ALL SPIRALING THROUGH TIME AND SPACE. AND NOW...
WHERE AND--MORE TO THE POINT-- WHEN AM I?
I AM CERTAIN THAT I HAVE MATERIALIZED WITHIN A SPACE-CRAFT, BUT--
GUARDIANS GATHER--!
WE APPEAR TO HAVE A STOWAWAY ABOARD!
A MILD PSI-BLAST SHOULD HOLD HIM UNTIL WE CAN DETERMINE HIS INTENTIONS!
BASED ON THE ALL-TOO-FAMILIAR VIBRATIONS SURROUNDING ME...
UNNG! I CANNOT BE DELAYED HERE! NOT WHILE ERIC AND DARGO COULD BE IN GREAT DANGER!
YOU MUST BE SLIPPING, VANCE... OR HORSEFACE HARRY IS A LOT TOUGHER THAN HE LOOKS!
HE MANAGED TO SHRUG OFF YOUR JOLT, BUT I DOUBT HE'LL DO AS WELL AGAINST MINE!
PWAK!

CAREFUL, YELLOWJACKET! THIS CHARACTER IS DRESSED A LOT LIKE THOSE ASGARDIANS WE RECENTLY ENCOUNTERED!
HEY! I THINK I RECOGNIZE HIM, BUT I NEED A CLOSER LOOK!
STAND BACK! I WARN YOU! WHILE I HAVE NO DESIRE TO FIGHT, NONE MAY STRIKE BETA RAY BILL WITH IMPUNITY!
KWA-PUUOOM!

POUNCE ON HIM, PEOPLE--
--BEFORE HE CAN MAKE WITH MORE SHOCKWAVES!

NO! LEAVE HIM ALONE!
WHA--?! HAVE YOU LOST YOUR MIND, ALETA?!

HIS HEART IS PURE! HE MEANS US NO HARM!
TAKE THE WORD OF ONE WHO KNOWS!

YOU DON'T KNOW WHAT IT WAS LIKE!
YOU CAN'T IMAGINE THE DEPTH OF MY FEELING FOR ELLENE!
I LOVED THAT WOMAN WITH EVERY FIBER OF MY BEING! SHE WAS THE CENTRAL FOCUS OF MY WORLD!
AND YET... SHE TURNED AGAINST ME... JOINING WITH DUNBAR TO SABOTAGE MY EXPERI-MENT... AND STEAL MY WORK!

BUT... IT... IT'S PAINFULLY OBVIOUS THAT YOU STILL CARE FOR HER!
IF YOU WERE REALLY THE MASTER OF ALL REALITY LIKE YOU CLAIM, YOU COULD SET THINGS RIGHT!
YOU COULD CORRECT THE PAST ...AND HEAL THE RIFT BETWEEN YOU.
YOU COULD GIVE YOURSELF A SECOND CHANCE!

INTRIGUED BY SALLA'S WORDS, THE MAN WHO WAS HALLAN GORKO QUICKLY CONSIDERS THEIR SIMPLE TRUTH, AND THEN...
WAIT! WHERE ARE YOU GOING --?!
PLEASE... DON'T... DON'T ABANDON ME HERE!

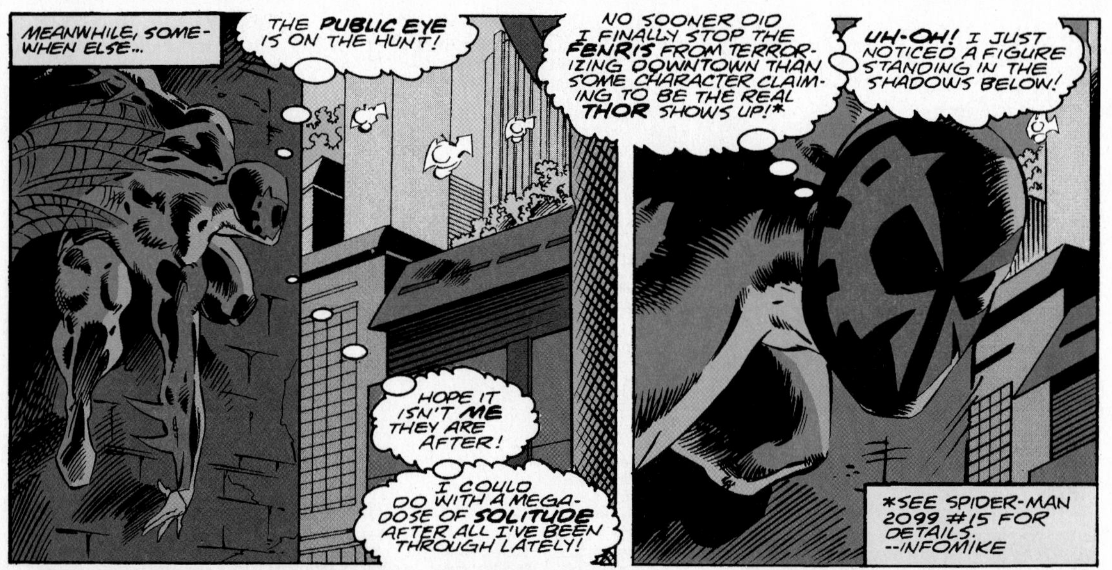
MEANWHILE, SOME-WHEN ELSE...
THE PUBLIC EYE IS ON THE HUNT!
HOPE IT ISN'T ME THEY ARE AFTER!
I COULD DO WITH A MEGA-DOSE OF SOLITUDE AFTER ALL I'VE BEEN THROUGH LATELY!
NO SOONER DID I FINALLY STOP THE FENRIS FROM TERRORIZING DOWNTOWN THAN SOME CHARACTER CLAIMING TO BE THE REAL THOR SHOWS UP!*
UH-OH! I JUST NOTICED A FIGURE STANDING IN THE SHADOWS BELOW!
*SEE SPIDER-MAN 2099 #15 FOR DETAILS. --INFOMIKE

SOMETHING ABOUT HIS SILHOUETTE DEMANDS A CLOSER INSPECTION!

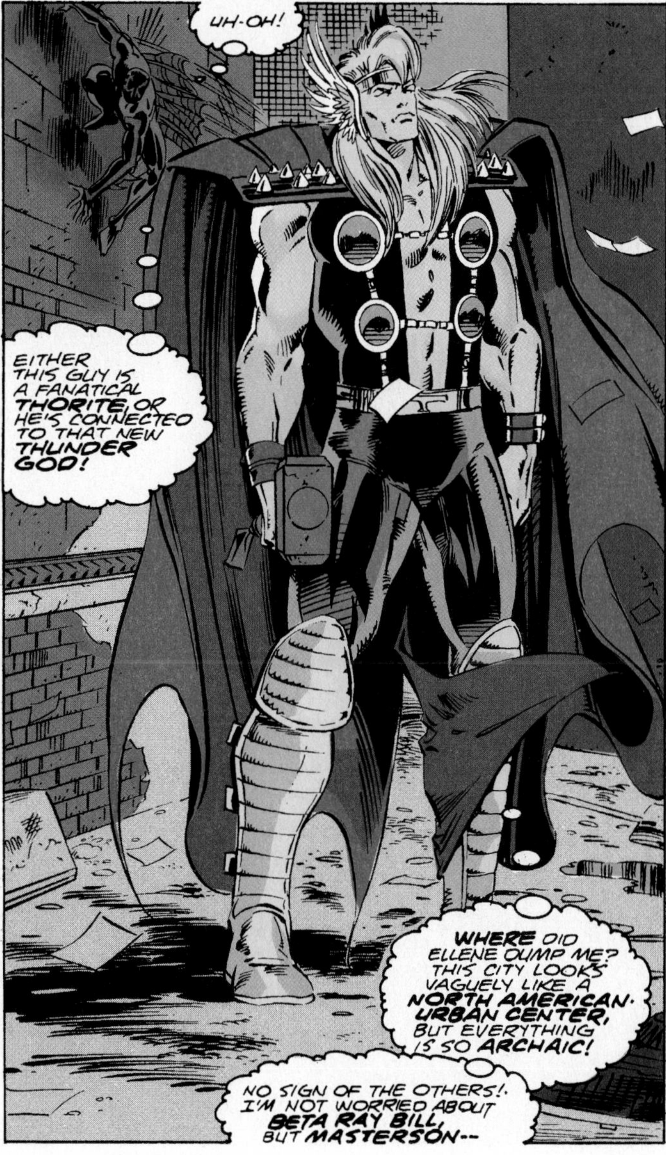
UH-OH!
EITHER THIS GUY IS A FANATICAL THORITE, OR HE'S CONNECTED TO THAT NEW THUNDER GOD!
WHERE DID ELLENE DUMP ME? THIS CITY LOOKS VAGUELY LIKE A NORTH AMERICAN URBAN CENTER, BUT EVERYTHING IS SO ARCHAIC!
NO SIGN OF THE OTHERS!. I'M NOT WORRIED ABOUT BETA RAY BILL, BUT MASTERSON--

HEY, BUDDY! I WANT TO KNOW WHAT'S GOING ON IN VALHALLA!
I'VE ALREADY SEEN YOUR SO-CALLED THOR, AND I'M LESS THAN IMPRESSED!

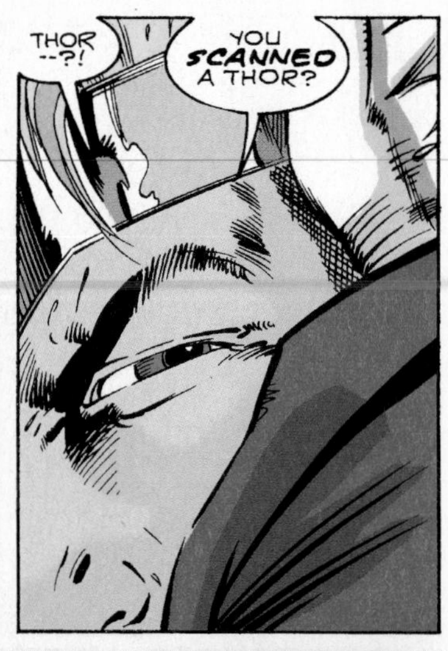
THOR --?!
YOU SCANNED A THOR?

WHERE IS HE?
WAS HE BEARDED... OR DID HE HAVE A HEAD LIKE A HORSE?
ACTUALLY, HE BORE A GREATER SIMILARITY TO A HORSE'S OTHER END!
A LOT LIKE YOU, IN FACT... BUT WITH A BETTER FEEL FOR FASHION!

LIAR!
ALL RIGHT... MAYBE HIS FASHION SENSE WASN'T THAT MUCH BETTER!

BUT YOU SHOULDN'T TAKE THAT AS A COMPLI-MENT!
EEEOWWW! YOUR JAW MUST BE MADE OF SOLID ROCK!

DITTO YOUR FISTS!
LOOKS LIKE IT'S TIME FOR ME TO CHANGE TACTICS!

AHH-- MUCH BETTER!
SO WHY DON'T YOU FILL ME IN ON WHAT YOUR BOSS IS PLANNING?
I...I DON'T KNOW WHAT YOU'RE TALKING ABOUT!
THE THOR YOU SAW ISN'T ANYONE I KNOW UNLESS...

TELL ME...DID HIS HAMMER LOOK LIKE THIS?
NO... NOT EVEN CLOSE!

WHAT THE-- WHERE IS ALL THE LIGHTNING COMING FROM?
YOU... YOU CAN'T BE DOING WHAT I THINK YOU'RE DOING!
CAN YOU?
MY WIFE AND FRIENDS ARE HEADED FOR THE BIG BUZZ! I CAN'T SCRAG ANY MORE TIME HERE!

I'M ZIPPING TO THE GREAT VOID WHICH STANDS AT THE CROSS-ROADS OF TIME AND SPACE!
YEAH...SURE... SOUNDS LIKE THE PERFECT PLACE TO GET AWAY FROM IT ALL!
THIS IS TOO CRAZY... EVEN FOR ME!

I DON'T KNOW WHY THIS NEVER OCCURRED TO ME BEFORE --!
SALLA WAS RIGHT! WITH MY DIMENSIONIZER, I CAN EASILY ALTER THE PAST AS WELL AS THE PRESENT, CORRECTING OLD MISTAKES!

I CAN ELIMINATE DUNBAR AND ACTUALLY PREVENT THE ACCIDENT WHICH FOREVER RUINED MY LIFE!

OH, NO! NO--!

IN MY HASTE... I... I MISSED MY TARGET... AND CARELESSLY STRUCK MY OWN EQUIPMENT!
IT... IT WASN'T DUNBAR WHO CAUSED THE ACCIDENT!
IT WAS ME!

AND, AT ANOTHER TIME AND PLACE...
LOWER THAT STRONG-BOX SLOW AND EASY, DRNER.
THE BARKER BROTHERS GOT A MESS OF NOTCHES ON THEIR GUNS--AND EACH ONE MARKS A DEAD MAN!
NOT MUCH OF A HAUL, ZEB! MAYBE WE SHOULD'A' STUCK TO ROBBIN' TRAINS!
OR MAYBE YOU SHOULD HAVE JUST STAYED IN BED!
HUH--?!
DROP YOUR GUNS, YOU MANGY OWL-HOOTS...AND REACH FOR THE SKY!
THERE'S A NEW LAWMAN IN TOWN!
HOO-BOY! CAN'T BELIEVE I ACTUALLY SAID THAT!
I'M ALMOST THANKFUL TO ELLENE FOR DROPPING ME IN THE OLD WEST!
I GREW UP READING ABOUT COWBOYS, AND THIS WOULD BE A REAL HOOT...IF NOT FOR DEMONSTAFF!
YOU MUST BE PLUMB LOCO, HOMBRE!
BLAM! BLAM! BLAM!
WE AIN'T BACKING DOWN FROM NO UNARMED...
...FANCY-PANTS BLACKSMITH WITH HIS HAIR TIED UP LIKE A GIRL!
BLACKSMITH--?!
YOU MUST BE REFERRING TO MY MACE!
PRETTY HANDY, HUH?
AS FOR MY HAIR, I WONDER WHAT YOU JOKERS WOULD SAY IF YOU WERE CLOSE ENOUGH TO SEE MY EARRING?
YOU WEAR AN EARRING?!

YEAH, AND I DON'T NEED FASHION TIPS FROM A PAIR OF NINETEENTH-CENTURY REPROBATES!
YEOW!
KA-WAM!
I DON'T RIGHTLY KNOW HOW YOU MANAGED TO DIS-ARM THOSE VARMINTS, MISTER ...BUT WE'RE MUCH OBLIGED!
WE'LL SEND THE SHERIFF BACK FOR THEM. ARE YOU SURE WE CAN'T GIVE YOU A RIDE INTO TOWN?
TOLD YA WE SHOULD'A' STUCK TO TRAINS, ZEB!
SHUT UP, IKE!
NO, THANKS! I...ER...I'M NOT EXACTLY HEADED IN THAT DIRECTION!
I'VE GOT TO FIND A WAY TO REJOIN THE OTHERS!
IF BILL AND DARGO CAN USE THEIR EN-CHANTED HAMMERS TO CROSS THE DIMENSIONAL PLANES, MAYBE MY MACE CAN ALSO--
RAISE 'EM HIGH, AMIGO!
DON'T MAKE ANY HASTY MOVES WITH THAT FUNNY SLEDGEHAMMER, STRANGER.
MY FRIENDS AND I HAVE BEEN TRACKING THE BARKERS FOR WEEKS AND WE SAW HOW YOU GOT THE DROP ON THEM!
I'D LISTEN TO OL' TWO-GUN IF I WERE YOU, AMIGO!
WE HAVE JUST A FEW QUESTIONS TO ASK! THERE'S NO NEED FOR US TO TRADE LEAD!
OMIGOSH! I'D RECOGNIZE THESE THREE ANYWHERE! THEY'RE EXACTLY LIKE THE HISTORY BOOKS DESCRIBED THEM!
THE TWO-GUN KID, THE RAWHIDE KID, AND KID COLT--MY CHILDHOOD HEROES!

YOU-- YOU'RE FINALLY BACK!
WHAT HAPPENED? WHERE HAVE YOU BEEN?!
I... FAILED!
...OR DID I?
MAYBE I ONLY SLAGGED AN ALTERNATE HALLAN GORKO IN A PARALLEL UNIVERSE!
I...I TOOK YOUR ADVICE, MY DEAR SALLA...
SUFFICE IT TO SAY THAT YOU WOULDN'T GET MY ENDORSEMENT FOR A CAREER IN VIDEO COUNSELING.
THAT'S THE TROUBLE WITH ALL THESE DIMENSIONS! THERE ARE JUST TOO MANY POSSIBILITIES!
TOO MANY CHOICES!
I GUESS THAT'S WHY I HAVE ALWAYS PREFERRED FICTION TO FACT!
FICTION HAS FORM AND STRUCTURE! A LOGICAL BEGINNING, A MIDDLE, AND AN END!

REALITY, ON THE OTHER HAND, IS PURE CHAOS!
WH-WHERE HAVE YOU TAKEN ME NOW?!
A PLACE BEYOND THE PHYSICAL LAWS OF NATURE --THE VOID WHICH EXISTS BETWEEN THE MYRIAD DIMENSIONS!

YOU WILL HAVE THE DISTINCTIVE PRIVILEGE OF WATCHING ME BRING TRUE ORDER TO THE UNIVERSE--
--BY DESTROYING ALL REALITY!
NO YOU CAN'T! YOU MUSTN'T!
THINK OF ELLENE! SHE LOVED YOU ONCE! SHE COULD DO IT AGAIN!

I'M AFRAID THAT'S TOTALLY OUT OF THE QUESTION, MY DEAR!

THERE ISN'T GOING TO BE A HAPPY ENDING TO THIS STORY--!
MY PRECIOUS ELLENE IS LOST TO ME FOREVER!

YOU SEE, I NEGLECTED TO MENTION A FEW DETAILS OF MY ACCIDENT!
CONTRARY TO POPULAR BELIEF, I DO NOT WEAR THIS RIDICULOUS COSTUME OUT OF CHOICE!
IT IS-- QUITE LITERALLY-- ALL THAT'S HOLDING ME TOGETHER!
NO WOMAN COULD EVER LOVE ME NOW!
NO SECOND CHANCE WAS EVER POSSIBLE!

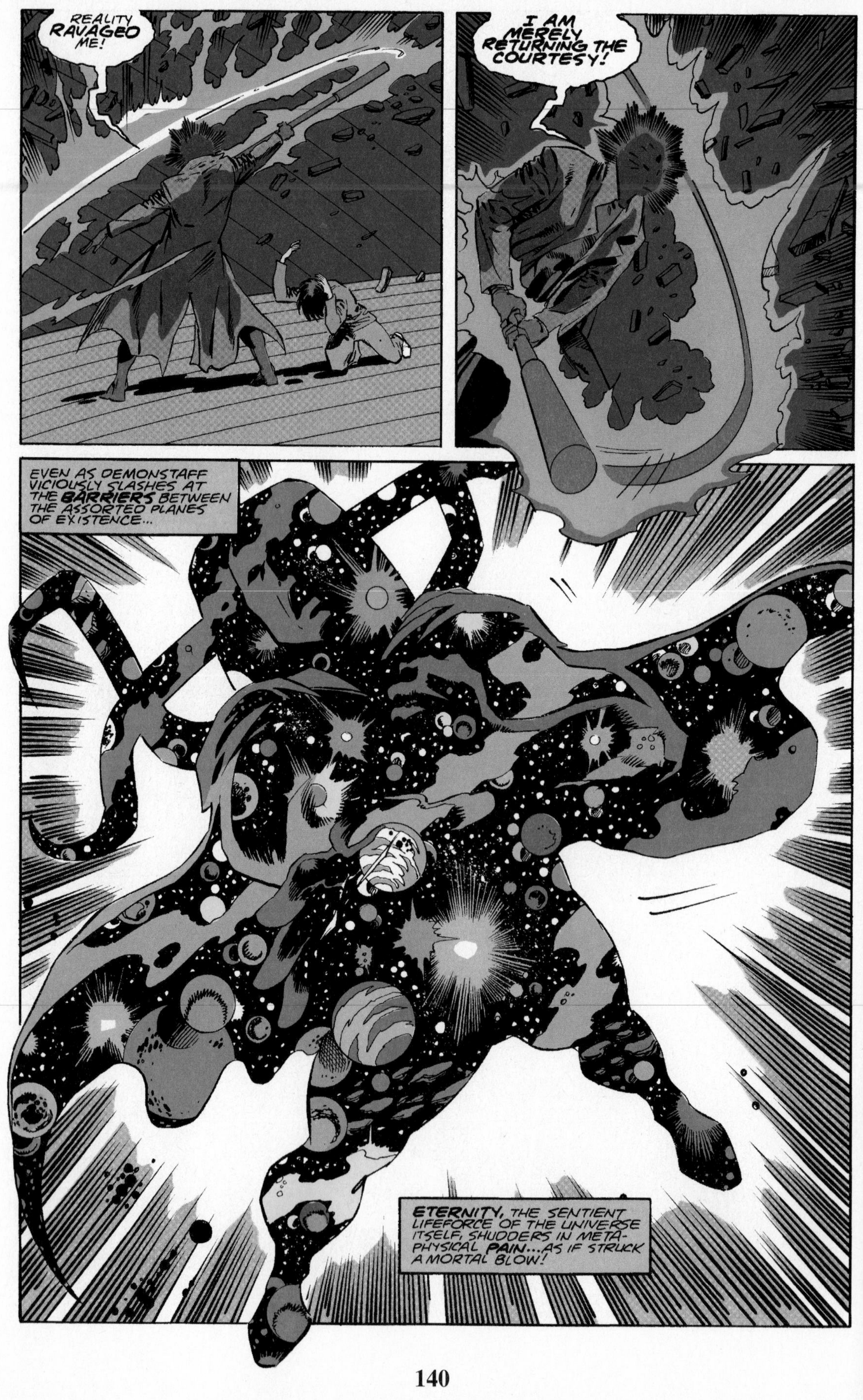
REALITY RAVAGED ME!
I AM MERELY RETURNING THE COURTESY!
EVEN AS DEMONSTAFF VICIOUSLY SLASHES AT THE BARRIERS BETWEEN THE ASSORTED PLANES OF EXISTENCE...
ETERNITY, THE SENTIENT LIFEFORCE OF THE UNIVERSE ITSELF, SHUDDERS IN META-PHYSICAL PAIN...AS IF STRUCK A MORTAL BLOW!

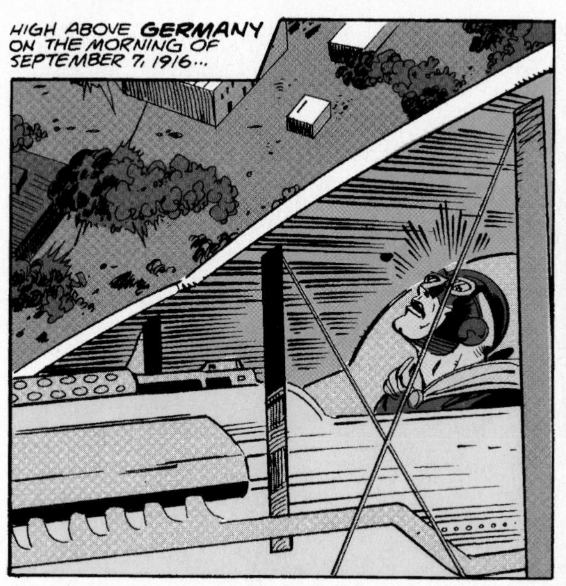
HIGH ABOVE GERMANY ON THE MORNING OF SEPTEMBER 7, 1916...

REALITY TAKES A DECIDEDLY WICKED TURN FOR PILOT KARL KAUFMAN!

IN ANCIENT HYBORIA, A BATTLE-STAINED BARBARIAN IS GIVEN SUDDEN PAUSE...

...AS HE CONFRONTS A STARTLING VISION OF THINGS TO COME!

IN A WESTCHESTER MANSION...
THAT MAN... UNEXPECTEDLY APPEARED IN OUR MIDST!
BEWARE! X-MEN! THIS IS NO TEST! I AM AS SURPRISED AS THE REST OF YOU!

DON'T WORRY, PROFESSOR! WE'LL GET TO THE BOTTOM OF THIS!
YEAH, WE CAN EASILY HANDLE THIS JOKER!
INCONTROVERTIBLY!

IN THE THIRTY-FIRST CENTURY...
WHAT THE--?!
IF I DIDN'T KNOW BETTER, I'D SWEAR THESE ARE ROMAN CENTURIONS!

DEMONS! MONSTERS! WE CLAIM THIS SHADOW-HAUNTED LAND IN THE NAME OF NOBLE CAESAR!
ANCIENT SWORDS AGAINST ADVANCED TECH-NOLOGY?
YOU'VE GOT TO BE KIDDING!

I FEAR HE IS DEADLY SERIOUS, TALON!
IT'S STARTING! THE BOUNDARIES BETWEEN TIME, SPACE, AND THE MYRIAD DIMENSIONS ARE BEGINNING TO BLUR!

EVEN I AM... CONFUSED... BY THESE EVENTS... THOUGH I DO SENSE THE DISRUPTION OF AN INDESCRIBABLE, UNEARTHLY FORCE!
I KNOW THE AUTHOR OF THIS DISRUPTION... AND MUST NOW GATHER MY COMRADES... TO FACE THE FINAL CHALLENGE!

AND, IN THE EVEN WILDER WEST...
THESE ARE THE STRANGEST DANG CREATURES I'VE EVER SEEN!
SLOW DOWN, TWO-GUN! MY MACE CAN STOP THESE MONSTERS!
RAWHIDE FELT THE SAME ABOUT HIS SIX-SHOOTER... AND LOOK WHERE IT GOT US!
YOU DON'T UNDERSTAND! MY MACE IS FROM ASGARD!
THAT ANYWHERE NEAR ABILENE? I KNOW THIS DANCE HALL GIRL WHO--
HEY! WHAT'S THAT LIGHT IN THE SKY?
UNLESS I MISS MY GUESS...
...IT'S MY TICKET HOME!
YOU... YOU CAN FLY?!
TECHNICALLY-- NO!
I JUST TOSS MY MALLET AND HANG ON FOR DEAR LIFE!
HARDLY THE MOST EFFICIENT MODE OF TRAVEL, BUT IT GETS THE JOB DONE!

HI, BOYS!
WHAT'S **NEW?**
DEMONSTAFF HAS **EMBARKED** ON HIS MAD CRUSADE!
ACTUALLY, I HAD KIND OF **NOTICED** THAT MYSELF!
DID YOU, MASTERSON?

TOGETHER WE SHALL CALL UPON THE POWER SUPREME WITHIN THEM TO SUMMON THE GREATEST WARRIOR OF ALL!
YOU MEAN THOR?!
IS THIS WISE?
I MEAN... THE WORD'S OUT THAT HE'S BEEN ACTING KIND OF WACKO LATELY!
THOR'S AN ASGARDIAN IMMORTAL... WHO HAS LIVED FOR CENTURIES!
WHO KNOWS WHEN WE'LL PLUCK HIM? WE COULD END UP WITH THE NOBLE WARRIOR--
...OR THE MAD GOD!
AYE... BUT WHAT CHOICE HAVE WE?
YOU GOT ME THERE!

WHO DARES SUMMON THE LORD OF LIGHTNING?
WHO HATH NEED OF THE NOBLE SON OF ODIN?
THE MIGHTY THOR, GOD OF THUNDER!
TAKE A WILD GUESS, CHIEF!

ERIC, MY BROTHER-IN-ARMS--
AND BETA RAY BILL!
MY HEART SOARS AT THIS UNFORESEEN REUNION!
AND... WHO IS THIS STRIPLING?
I... I...
MY NAME IS DARGO, SIR!
THOU ART WELL MET AND AMONG EQUALS, MY NEW FRIEND!
SEEING MR. ARROGANT STRUCK SPEECHLESS REALLY BRINGS HOME THE RARE PRIVILEGE I'VE HAD KNOWING SOMEONE LIKE THOR!
ARISE, YOUNG WARRIOR! THOUGH THY HUMILITY DOES THEE PROUD...
THERE IS A SACRED BOND WHICH UNITES ALL WHO HAVE E'ER HELD MIGHTY MJOLNIR!
I JUST HOPE OUR COMBINED POWER IS ENOUGH TO COP A WIN... IN TIME FOR ME TO SAVE THE ONE PERSON I LOVE THE MOST!

UNKNIT THY FURROWED BROW, ERIC! WHATE'ER THE MENACE WE FACE, WHATE'ER THE EVIL THAT THREATENS...
...WE SHALL FACE IT LIKE TRUE WARRIORS-BORN, STRIKING FOR HONOR AND GLORY!
I'M WITH YOU, PAL!
LET'S GO KICK BUTT!
YOU MAY NOT EXACTLY BE THE EPITOME OF ELOQUENCE, MASTERSON... BUT I LIKE THE WAY YOU THINK!
TO BE CONCLUDED!

MARVEL® COMICS

FEEL THE POWER OF THE

THOR CORPS™

THE LONG AWAITED CONCLUSION TO THE MOST OFF-BEAT LIMITED SERIES OF THEM ALL!

$1.75 US
$2.25 CAN
4
DEC
02506

APPROVED BY THE COMICS CODE AUTHORITY

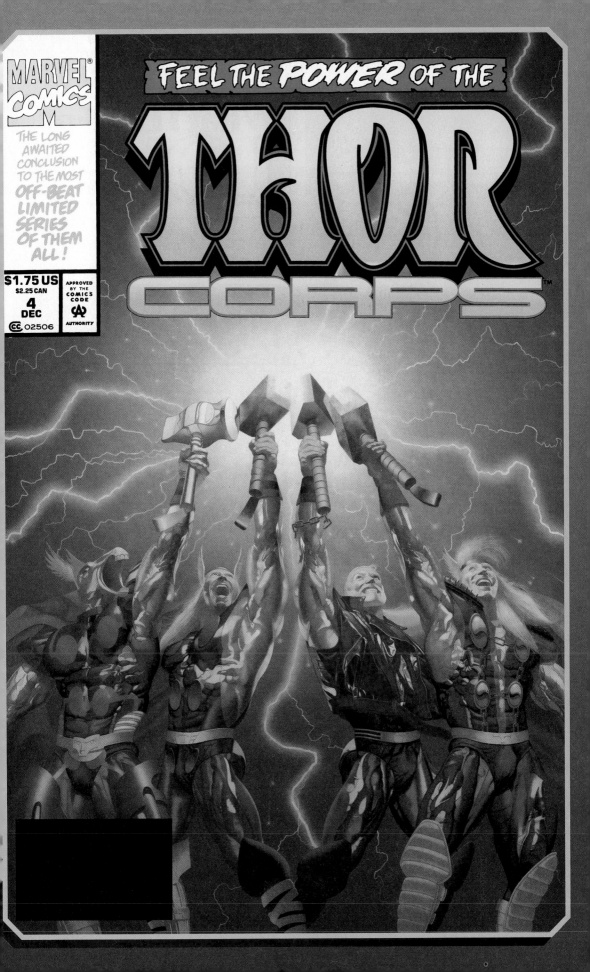

FROM DIFFERENT WORLDS AND TIMES COME THREE MIGHTY WARRIORS, EACH EMPOWERED BY AN ENCHANTED **ASGARDIAN WEAPON** WHICH GRANTS THE ASTONISHING ABILITIES OF THE LEGENDARY **GOD OF THUNDER!** TOGETHER, **DARGO, BETA RAY BILL,** AND **ERIC MASTERSON** JOIN TO FORM...

STAN LEE PRESENTS:

THE *THOR* CORPS!

What I Did For LOVE!

WARLORD KARGUL, I HAVE NEVER SEEN YOU SO *GRIM*... SO *DESPERATE!*
ELLENE, I FEAR THAT WE-- AND THE *CHOSEN REALITIES* THEM-SELVES--STAND ON THE EVE OF *ANNIHILATION!*
YOUR MAD HUSBAND HAS UNLOOSED TOTAL *ANARCHY* UPON AN UNSUSPECTING UNIVERSE!

WRITTEN BY TOM DeFALCO • PENCILED BY PATRICK OLLIFFE • INKED BY ROMEO TANGHAL
LETTERED BY JOHN E. WORKMAN, JR. • COLORED BY GEORGE ROUSSOS
EDITED BY MIKE ROCKWITZ • OVERSEEN BY RALPH MACCHIO

BEHOLD! THE SACRED TIME-LINES CAN NO LONGER HOLD!
DINOSAURS AND BIPLANES ROAM THE 31ST CENTURY!
THE DIMENSIONAL BARRIERS ARE FALLING APART! PARALLEL WORLDS ARE MELTING INTO EACH OTHER!
IT IS ONLY A MATTER OF TIME BEFORE REALITY, AS WE KNOW IT, COLLAPSES UPON ITSELF!
IS THERE NO HOPE... NONE AT ALL ?!
THERE IS ALWAYS HOPE WHILE LIFE ENDURES!
YEAH... AND YOU CAN HELP IT ENDURE A LOT LONGER BY SUPPLYING US WITH A CURRENT ADDRESS FOR DEMONSTAFF!

TRAVEL REALLY BROADENS ONE'S PERSPECTIVE, MY DEAR SALLA!
I NEVER REALIZED THAT THESE WALLS-- WHICH SEPARATE ONE DIMENSION FROM ANOTHER-- WERE SO FLIMSY AND VULNER-ABLE!
IT'S ALMOST AS IF THESE PARALLEL WORLDS WERE ONLY WISPS OF FANCY!

YOU...YOU'RE TALKING ABOUT THE CASUAL DESTRUCTION OF COUNTLESS LIVES AND CIVILIZATIONS!

THIS IS ALL A GREAT, BIG GAME TO YOU, DEMON-STAFF!
UFFFT

YOU ARE THE WORST MONSTER IMAGIN-ABLE!
...A CREATURE TOTALLY DEVOID OF CONSCIENCE OR COMPASSION!
YOU ARE TRULY EVIL INCARNATE!

I SINCERELY WISH THAT I COULD DISAGREE WITH YOU, SALLA!
ALAS... I CANNOT!

AND WHY?!
BECAUSE MY OWN WIFE-- MY PRECIOUS ELLENE-- BETRAYED MY LOVE AND SABOTAGED MY WORK!

PLEASE! PLEASE--!
I'LL DO ANYTHING... ANYTHING... TO SAVE MY DARGO!

YOU...YOU WOULD SACRIFICE YOURSELF FOR YOUR HUSBAND?!

YOU ARE AN EVEN GREATER FOOL THAN I!

IF REALITY ITSELF IS SO FRAIL AND FRAGILE...
LOVE CANNOT HAVE ANY TRUE SUBSTANCE!
YOU OFFER YOUR ALL... BUT HOW MUCH DO YOU HONESTLY BELIEVE THAT DARGO WOULD RENOUNCE FOR YOU?!

THERE WAS A TIME WHEN I WOULD HAVE EAGERLY FORSAKEN EVERYTHING FOR HALLAN GORKO!
CONTRARY TO WHAT YOU MAY HAVE ALREADY HEARD...
...MY LOVE FOR HIM WAS SO MUCH GREATER THAN HIS FOR ME!

AND YET I COULD NOT COMPETE WITH HIS TRUE MISTRESS...

"BEWITCHED WITH THE DESIRE TO EXPLORE OTHER PLANES OF REALITY, HE BECAME OBSESSED WITH HIS WORK...

"...SHUTTING ME OUT OF HIS LIFE...

"...UNTIL WE WERE LITTLE MORE THAN STRANGERS!

"I NEVER EVEN KNEW THAT HE WAS ACTUALLY PLANNING TO OPEN A DIMENSIONAL RIFT--

"--UNTIL I ACCIDENTALLY STUMBLED UPON HIS EMPLOYER, CITIZEN DUNBAR."

WHAT ARE YOU DOING WITH MY HUSBAND'S EQUIPMENT?

THERE SEEMS... TO BE A DEFECT IN THIS POWER CONDUIT!

"I IMMEDIATELY SHOUTED A WARNING--

"I STILL WONDER IF I WAS AN INSTANT TOO LATE--

"--OR, IF LIKE USUAL, HALLAN MERELY IGNORED ME!"

"TO MY HORROR, I FOUND THAT THE ACCIDENT HAD SOMEHOW **TRANSFORMED** HIM INTO SOMETHING THAT WAS NO LONGER QUITE **HUMAN**...

"BUT I... I STILL **LOVED** HIM.

"DESPERATE TO FIND A CURE, I CONVINCED **DUNBAR** TO CONTINUE FUNDING HALLAN'S WORK!

"I WAS DETERMINED TO HARNESS THE TERRIBLE ENERGIES WHICH HAD **MUTATED** MY HUSBAND...

"BUT SOMETHING WENT **WRONG**... AND I WAS ACCIDENTALLY **SUCKED** INTO A DIMENSIONAL RIFT!

"I... I DON'T KNOW HOW LONG I **DRIFTED** ... MAYBE DAYS... MAYBE WEEKS...

"EVENTUALLY I WAS RESCUED FROM THE GREAT **VOID**..."

THUS WAS **ELLENE** BROUGHT TO OUR HIDDEN WORLD OF **ELSEWHEN** WHICH LIES AT THE CENTER OF THE **CHOSEN REALITIES!**

WARLORD KARGUL GENEROUSLY VOLUNTEERED TO HELP ME RETURN HOME!

A MASSIVE TASK WHICH INVOLVED **SORTING** THROUGH COUNTLESS ALTERNATE REALITIES!

BY THE TIME WE HAD FINALLY LOCATED THE RIGHT ONE... HALLAN WAS ALREADY **CONVINCED** THAT I HAD BETRAYED HIM!

HOO BOY!
EVERY TIME WE HEAR THIS STORY, WE GET **NEW** DETAILS...
...FROM WIDLY **DIFFERENT** PERSPECTIVES!
AND **ALL** HAVE BEEN WRONGED IN THEIR OWN EYES!
YEAH, BUT... **WHO'S** TELLING THE TRUTH?!

TRUTH--?!
THERE IS NO STINKING **TRUTH!** IT'S ALL AN **ILLUSION!**

HOW CAN TRUTH POSSIBLY EXIST IN THIS UNIVERSE--
--WHEN REALITY ITSELF IS IN SUCH PURE CHAOS!
EVERY-THING IS SUBJECT TO INTERPRE-TATION!
IT'S DEMON-STAFF!
WHAT HAVE YOU DONE WITH MY WIFE?
WHERE'S SALLA?!
SHE IS MY-- GUEST!
AND IN HER NAME... I HUMBLY SEEK THE PLEASURE OF YOUR COMPANY!

NEVER SHALL WE SURRENDER OUR COMRADE TO THEE!
NOT WHEN YOU SO OBVIOUSLY PLAN HIM ILL!
B-BUT... WE'RE TALKING ABOUT THE GUY'S WIFE!

WHAT WOULD I DO IF KEVIN WAS THE HOSTAGE?
YOU THINK I SHOULD GO, ERIC?
I-IT ISN'T FOR ME TO SAY.

NO...

IT MUST BE MY DECISION!

OOOOO! YOU CERTAINLY HAVE A FLAIR FOR THE DRAMATIC!
I PRACTICALLY HAVE GOOSE BUMPS!
BLANK THE BUZZ BEFORE I CHANGE MY MIND!

PLEASE TAKE CARE OF THIS FOR ME, SIR!
I MAY NEED IT LATER.
NO NEED TO WAIT UP, EVERYONE! ONLY ONE OF US WILL BE SURVIVING--

--AND IT WON'T BE HIM!

THERE--! THAT DIDN'T TAKE LONG!
AT LEAST, I THINK IT DIDN'T! HOPPING BETWEEN PLANES OF REALITY PLAYS HAVOC WITH ONE'S SENSE OF TIME!
DON'T EXPECT ANY SYMPATHY FROM ME!

I THOUGHT YOU WERE BRINGING ME TO MY WIFE!
WHERE IS SHE?

WHILE THE YOUNG LADY IN QUESTION IS A BIT TOO OPINIONATED AND HEAD-STRONG FOR MY TASTES...
I SEEM TO HAVE GROWN RATHER ATTACHED TO HER!
SO I BROUGHT YOU HERE TO NEGOTIATE A TRADE!

YOU'RE A TOTAL MIND CRASH, MISTER!
YOU CAN SHOVE THESE PRECIOUS JEWELS AND RARE METALS IN YOUR MOST CONVENIENT ORIFICE!
I WANT SALLA!

WHOOPS! I APOLOGIZE IF I'VE OFFENDED YOU...
I SHOULD HAVE REALIZED THAT A MACHO GUY LIKE YOU WOULD VALUE RAW POWER OVER MERE WEALTH!

WHAT WOULD YOU SAY TO YOUR OWN PRIVATE KING-DOM... COMPLETE WITH THE OBLIGATORY BARBARIAN HORDE TO HEED YOUR EVERY WHIM?

SHALL I TAKE THIS AS A "NO"?

PERHAPS WE'LL TRY ANOTHER TACK...
AFTER ALL, EVERY MAN HAS HIS PRICE...AS WELL AS HIS OWN SECRET DESIRES!
SALLA IS QUITE THE BEAUTY...

BUT THERE ARE OTHERS... EVEN MORE BEAUTIFUL... AND I CAN PERSONALLY GUARANTEE THEM AGAINST ANY FUTURE NAGGING OR BLIMPING!
I STRONGLY ADVISE YOU TO STOP STRUGGLING, DARGO...
I'M BE-GINNING TO LOSE PATIENCE--

--AND THESE YOUNG LADIES REACT VERY POORLY TO REJECTION!

BEHOLD! I HAVE BUT TO WILL IT AND THEY ARE TRANSFORMED INTO A DEADLY POOL OF UNYIELDING MUCK AND MIRE!
WHY? WHY ARE YOU JAMMING ON US?
WHY ME? WHY SALLA?

DON'T EXPECT ANY RATIONAL EXPLANATIONS FROM ME!
I'M A TOTAL MIND CRASH, REMEMBER?
A MALEVOLENT CREATURE RULED BY WHIM AND FANCY WHO PRESENTLY WISHES YOU DEAD!

NO! NO! I... I CAN'T GIVE UP! I WON'T LET YOU BEAT ME!
I'LL KEEP FIGHTING! I'LL CONTINUE STRUGGLING! I WILL NOT... I MUST NOT DIE!

SO! WE'VE FINALLY FOUND SOMETHING YOU TRULY PRIZE!
A SACRIFICE EVEN YOU WON'T MAKE!

I... I CAN'T FAIL! CAN'T QUIT!
NOT WHILE SALLA...
...IS STILL...
...YOUR CAPTIVE!

YOU ARE A TERRIBLE DISAPPOINTMENT, DARGO!
YOUR GARISH DISPLAY OF NOBILITY HAS RUINED WHAT PROMISED TO BE AN OTHERWISE ENTERTAINING EXECUTION!
I'M TIRED OF TOYING WITH YOU! IF YOU ARE SO FIXATED ON YOUR WIFE...
...YOU SHALL HAVE HER!
DARGO--!

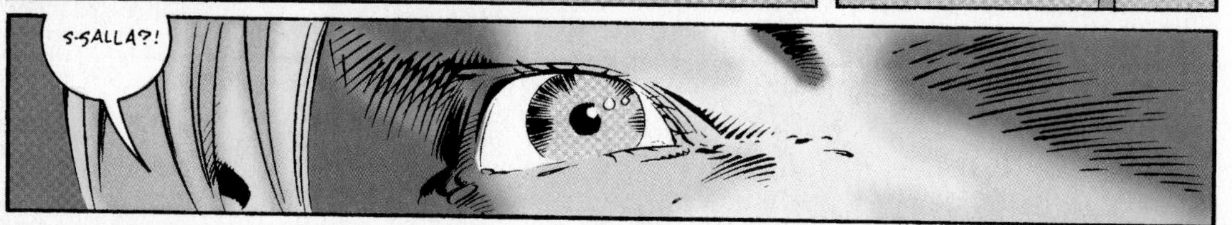
S-SALLA?!

YOU WERE MAYBE EXPECTING TO RESCUE SOME OTHER DAMSEL IN DISTRESS? SCRAG IT! YOU'RE STUCK WITH ME!
FOR LIFE, I HOPE!
I... I NEVER MEANT TO PUT YOU AT SUCH RISK!
I KNOW! I KNOW! JUST DO YOUR HERO THING AND GET US HOME!

I DON'T KNOW WHAT YOU'RE PLANNING, DEMONSTAFF... BUT I SWEAR THAT YOU'LL NEVER SEPARATE US AGAIN!

OH, REALLY?! WELL, YOU MAKE SUCH A CHARMING COUPLE...
...I'LL ONLY SLAG ONE OF YOU!
AND IN THE INTERESTS OF TRUE FAMILY DISHARMONY, EVEN ALLOW YOU TO DECIDE WHO LIVES ...AND WHO DIES!

SHOVING SALLA BEHIND HIM, DARGO TENSES FOR ACTION!
BUT THEN, EVEN BEFORE THE IMPETUOUS YOUTH CAN HURL HIMSELF FORWARD--
KRAKA-
PWOOM!
STAY THY HAND, VILLAIN!
TURN AND FACE FOES MORE WORTHY OF THY METTLE!
THOSE WHO WIELD THE SACRED WEAPONS OF ASGARD!
WOW! YOU DID IT, THOR! YOU ACTUALLY MANAGED TO USE MJOLNIR TO TRACK DEMONSTAFF TO THIS VOID WHICH EXISTS BE-TWEEN THE ALTERNATE PLANES OF REALITY!
WHY DO YOU SOUND SO SURPRISED, ERIC? WAS THAT NOT MY INTENTION?
YEAH, BUT... AW, FORGET IT! YOU'LL NEVER SEE THINGS FROM MY POINT OF VIEW!
GET BACK, SALLA! FIND WHATEVER COVER YOU CAN! I HAVE WORK TO DO!
ALL RIGHT! JUST THIS ONCE... BUT DON'T TAKE ANY NEED-LESS CHANCES!
HERE, PRETTY BOY-- CATCH!
MAYBE YOU SHOULD LISTEN TO THE LADY... AND STICK TO THE SIDELINES!
Y'KNOW, MASTERSON... FOR A MOMENT THERE, I WAS AFRAID THAT I WAS GOING TO FEEL INDEBTED TO YOU...
YOUR SMART MOUTH CON-VINCED ME OTHERWISE.
THOUGH DEMON-STAFF IS A THREAT TO THE ENTIRE MULTIVERSE, MY WIFE IS THE ONE HE TOOK HOSTAGE.
THIS IS PERSONAL!
VERY PERSONAL!

I HONESTLY HATE TO SPOIL SUCH A MELODRAMATIC SPEECH...
BUT AS YOU SEE, I CAN EASILY SUMMON ASSISTANCE FROM A VARIETY OF DIMENSIONS!

GORKO MUST BE PANICKING... IF HE'S RELYING ON THESE SLACKERS!
THEY'RE ONLY A DELAYING TACTIC!
HIS TRUE GOAL IS THE DESTRUCTION OF ALL REALITY!
STANO READY, BETA RAY BILL!
THOR SHALL CLEAR A DIRECT PATH TO YON VILLAIN!

THOR USED HIS OWN BODY AS A BATTERING RAM TO GIVE ME THE OPENING I NEED!
THAT STAFF IS SUPPOSED TO BE THE SOURCE OF ALL GORKO'S POWER!
I PRAY MY AIM BE TRUE--!

SPLAK!
OH, NO! NO--!

THE WORST IS COME!
COUNTLESS ALTERNATE DIMENSIONS WILL COLLAPSE UPON THEMSELVES UNLESS WE ACT!
I ASSUME YOU'VE GOT A PLAN! YOU USUALLY DO.
AYE! WE MUST JOIN OUR MALLETS--
--AND CALL UPON THE ENCHANTED FORCES WHICH LIE WITHIN!
TOGETHER WE SHALL BECOME ONE WITH THESE HAMMERS SUPREME!
TOGETHER WE SHALL RELEASE ENERGIES OF INCOMPARABLE AND IRRESISTIBLE INTENSITY!
TOGETHER WE SHALL BOLSTER THESE SAGGING BOUNDARIES.

I--IT'S **WORKING!**
THOR INSPIRED US ALL... BUT EVEN HE **CAN'T** KEEP THIS UP FOREVER!
WHAT'LL HAPPEN TO **KEVIN**--AND EVERYONE ELSE IN THE UNIVERSE--WHEN WE FALTER?!

AND AT THAT SELFSAME MOMENT, BACK ON **ELSEWHEN...**
RARELY HAVE I BEEN PRIVILEGED TO **WITNESS** SUCH INCREDIBLE HEROISM!
A PITY THAT IT'S ALL FOR **NAUGHT!**
I PRAY THAT THE **CHOSEN REALITIES** ARE SUFFICIENTLY BARRICADED TO WITHSTAND THE COMING DEVASTATION!
WHAT OF THE **PLANET EARTH** THAT I KNOW?

I FEAR THAT YOUR HUSBAND HAS ALREADY SEALED ITS **DOOM!**
THERE **MUST** BE A WAY--! WE MAY **LOSE!** WE MAY **FAIL!** BUT WE **CAN'T** GIVE UP!
ELLENE! HAVE YOU GONE **MAD**--?!
PERHAPS...
OUR ONLY **HOPE** MAY LIE IN AN ACT OF MADNESS!

ELLENE --?!
THIS IS A MOST UNEXPECTED-- THOUGH NOT TOTALLY UNPLEASANT-- SURPRISE!
I... I NOTICED YOU COWERING IN THE BACKGROUND EARLIER... WHEN I ...UH... BORROWED YOUNG DARGO!
HALLAN! YOU'VE GONE TOO FAR! YOU MUST END THIS MADNESS AT ONCE!

END IT--? HA! WE HAVE THE BEST SEATS IN THE HOUSE FOR THE BIGGEST BANG IN RECORDED HISTORY!
BEHOLD THE CHAOS YOU HAVE SPAWNED!
UNIVERSES WILL DIE! ENTIRE DIMENSIONS WILL CEASE TO EXIST!

STOP BLAMING ME FOR YOUR FAILINGS!
YOU WERE SO OBSESSED WITH YOUR WORK THAT YOU HAD NO ROOM IN YOUR LIFE FOR ME!
I NEVER BETRAYED YOU! IT WAS YOUR OWN INDIFFERENCE THAT DROVE ME AWAY!

EVEN IF I WERE SOMEWHAT AT FAULT, AND I'M NOT WILLING TO CONCEDE THAT I WAS...
STOP STARING AT THAT USELESS STAFF!
I HAVE LOST MY ABILITY TO WARP REALITY!
THE DIMENSIONIZER NEVER WORKED! IT WAS A FAILURE!

YOUR STAFF WAS ONLY A CRUTCH! THE POWER WAS ALWAYS WITHIN YOU!
THAT'S WHY DUNBAR NEVER EMPLOYED IT WHEN HE HAD THE CHANCE!
BUT IF WHAT YOU SAY IS TRUE...

...I STILL POSSESS THE POWER TO DESTROY YOU!

DO IT!
I'M THE ONE YOU HATE! KILL ME!
BUT PLEASE--I'M BEGGING YOU--YOU MUST REPAIR THE DAMAGE YOU'VE CAUSED!
YOU WOULD SACRIFICE YOURSELF--?!
GLADLY!
ELLENE, I HAVE NO REASON TO BELIEVE A SINGLE WORD YOU HAVE SPOKEN.
NOR DO I HAVE PROOF THAT I CAN TRUST YOU.
I ONLY KNOW THAT I...
...I STILL LOVE YOU!
HALLAN, WAIT--!
NO! THERE IS NO TIME! IF I AM TO DO WHAT MUST BE DONE...

IF I AM TO ATONE FOR MY CRIMES AGAINST THE MYRIAD REALITIES...
IT MUST BE NOW!
KAR-THROOM!

SCRE-EECH!
BARELY A MOMENT AGO, YOUNG KEVIN MASTERSON CARELESSLY DARTED INTO THE STREET IN PURSUIT OF A QUICK ICE CREAM CONE...

AND NOW...
GOT YOU!

T-THAT WAS ALL MY FAULT, DAD! I KNOW I SHOULD HAVE LOOKED! I--I'M SORRY!
TAKE IT EASY, SON! YOU'RE SAFE NOW!
ARE YOU OKAY, MISTER?
YOU LOOK LIKE YOU'RE IN SHOCK!
I'M SHOCKED, ALL RIGHT! I... I CAN'T BELIEVE THAT I'M FINALLY HOME!
HOW DID I GET HERE? WHAT HAPPENED TO THE OTHERS?

ON THE PLANET HARMONY, BETA RAY BILL HAS SIMILAR THOUGHTS...
I...I SEEM TO HAVE RETURNED TO MY WORLD... AN INSTANT OR SO AFTER I DEPARTED!
IT'S LIKE I WAS NEVER GONE!
THIS MONSTROUS PLANT STILL THREATENS A NEARBY SETTLEMENT--

--BUT A SEARING BOLT OF LIGHTNING SHALL FOREVER END THIS MENACE!
COULD IT BE THAT I IMAGINED THE ENTIRE ADVENTURE? THAT IT NEVER TRULY OCCURRED?!

TRUST ME... IT HAPPENED! THOSE POOR SLACKERS ON THE STREET ARE STILL SHAKING FROM THEIR UNEXPECTED BRUSH WITH DINOSAURS AND BIPLANES!

BUT... HOW DID WE END UP HERE? BACK IN OUR OWN APARTMENT?!

I... I CAN'T SAY FOR SURE!
MAYBE DEMONSTAFF'S COLLISION WITH OUR ENCHANTED HAMMERS MANAGED TO BRING REALITY BACK ON LINE!
OF COURSE, I'M SURE SOME ALTERNATE WORLDS SUSTAINED MORE DAMAGE THAN OTHERS!

HALLAN GORKO WAS SICK! DERANGED!
HE TERRORIZED ME AND PUT NUMEROUS OTHERS AT RISK!
AND YET I DO NOT BELIEVE THAT HE WAS INHERENTLY EVIL...

WHERE IS HE NOW? WHAT'S HAPPENED TO HIM--
--AND ELLENE?!
WE MAY NEVER KNOW...

I... I'VE BEEN EXPECTING YOU, KARGUL.
HALLAN GORKO! THE MULTIVERSE MAY NEVER RECOVER FROM YOUR ACTIONS!
YOU HAVE SPAWNED COUNTLESS CRISES ON INFINITE WORLDS!
SINCE YOUR DEATH WOULD SERVE NO PURPOSE OTHER THAN MERE VENGEANCE...

...YOU HAVE BEEN CONDEMNED TO BANISHMENT ETERNAL IN THIS TRACKLESS VOID!
A FITTING PUNISHMENT FOR ONE WHO SOUGHT AN END TO REALITY!

AND YET I AM NOT WITHOUT MERCY--!
WHAT IS SHE DOING HERE ?!
OVER MY MOST STRENUOUS OBJECTIONS, SHE HAS ELECTED TO SHARE YOUR FATE.

NO! IT ISN'T RIGHT! SHE HAS COMMITTED NO CRIMES! SHE'S DONE NOTHING WRONG!
THERE'S NO NEED TO PUNISH HER!

THE GREATEST PUNISHMENT WOULD BE TO LOSE YOU AGAIN!
I LOVE YOU, HALLAN!

ELLENE... I... I CANNOT ALLOW YOU TO SACRIFICE YOURSELF!
YOU HAVE NO CHOICE! THE DECISION IS MINE, AND --YOUR VOICE! IT SOUNDS... DIFFERENT!
DON'T TOUCH MY MASK! YOU MUSTN'T SEE MY--

--DISFIGURE-MENT?!
HALLAN-- YOUR FACE!
THE FINAL DISCHARGE OF POWER MUST HAVE RESTORED YOUR HUMANITY!
I DON'T MATTER ANYMORE, ELLENE! FORGET ME!
YOU MUST GO! IT WOULD BE MADNESS FOR YOU TO STAY!
AS YOU HAVE OFTEN SAID... LIFE, LOVE, TRUTH, AND REALITY ARE ALL DIFFERENT FORMS OF MADNESS!
SINCE WE HAVE ALREADY FAILED IN OUR ATTEMPTS TO CONTROL THEM...
...MAYBE WE SHOULD JUST LEARN TO ENJOY THEM WHILE WE STILL CAN!
END

BONUS! Witness the origins of Beta Ray Bill, Dargo Ktor and Eric Masterson in these stories from **Thor #337**, **#384** and **#433**.

STAN LEE PRESENTS: the MIGHTY THOR®

FAR BEYOND THE FIELDS WE KNOW, THE CORE OF AN ANCIENT GALAXY...
...EXPLODES!
AND A MOLTEN INGOT OF STAR-STUFF IS LEFT BEHIND...
...BUT NOT LEFT ALONE.

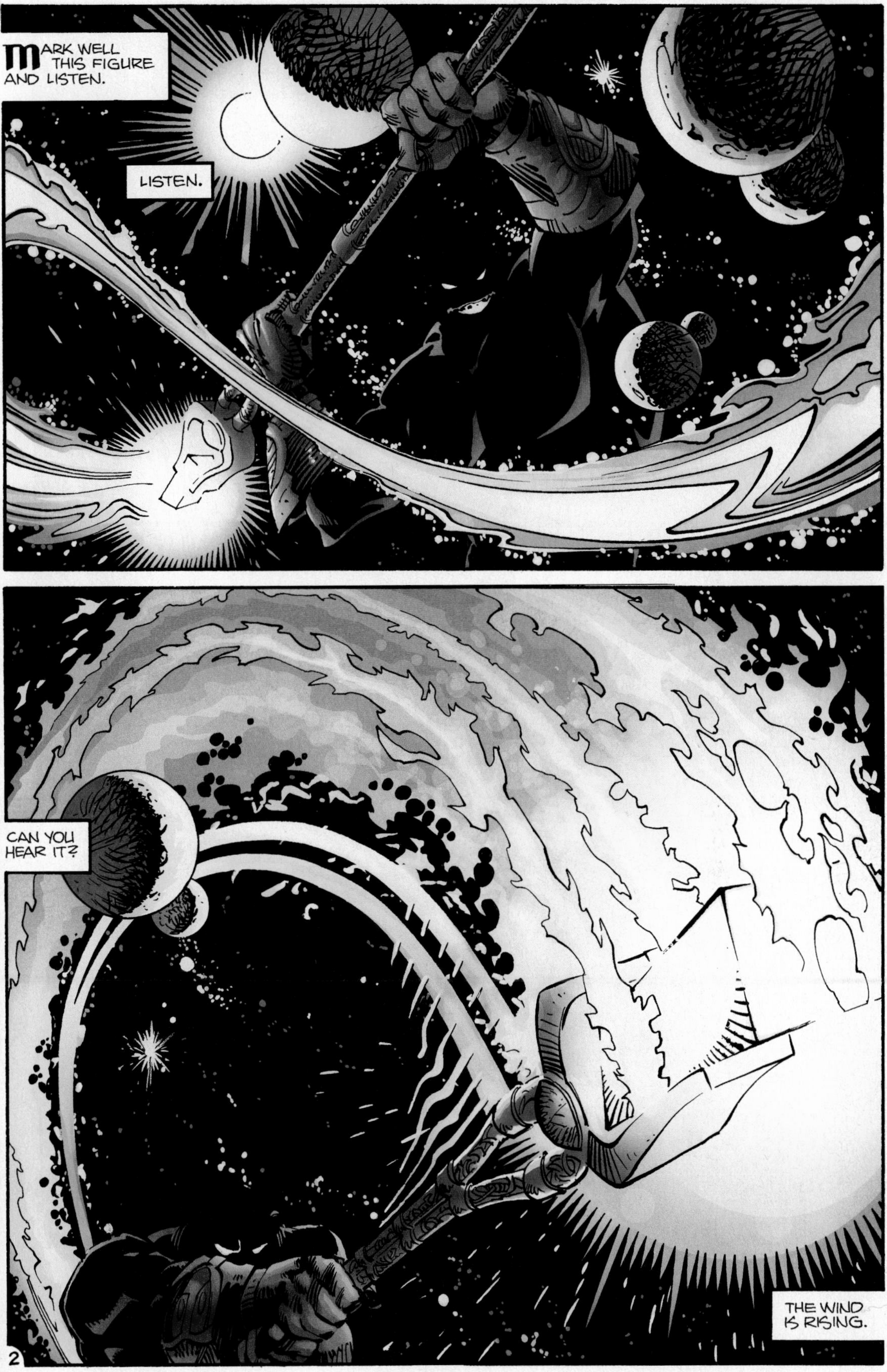

MARK WELL THIS FIGURE AND LISTEN.

LISTEN.

CAN YOU HEAR IT?

THE WIND IS RISING.

2

THE SOUND OF THUNDER REVERBERATES THROUGH-OUT A BILLION BILLION WORLDS.
DOOOM!

YET HERE ON EARTH, THE ECHOES ARE BURIED BENEATH THE SOUNDS OF THE CITY, AS CHICAGO BASKS IN A SUMMER AFTERNOON, AND DR. DONALD BLAKE STROLLS THROUGH GRANT PARK...
ON A BEAUTIFUL DAY LIKE TODAY, I ALMOST ENVY EVERY MORTAL I SEE.
FOR WHO COULD GUESS THAT WITHIN MY FRAIL BODY LIES THE SOUL AND POWER OF THE MIGHTY THOR, WAITING TO BE RELEASED BY A MERE TAP OF MY EN-CHANTED CANE.
AND WITH THAT POWER COMES A MEASURE OF RESPONSIBILITY FAR BEYOND ANYTHING AN ORDINARY MAN COULD BEAR.
SOMETIMES, THE BURDEN IS SO HEAVY, I WISH I COULD SET ASIDE MY HERITAGE EVEN FOR A DAY AND BE A MAN, JUST A MAN.
YET EACH AND EVERY ONE OF THESE PEOPLE IS TIED TO THE EARTH, WHILE I AM FREE TO ROAM THE GLORY OF THE HEAVENS IF I CHOOSE.
TO SEE THINGS NO MORTAL HAS EVER DREAMED OF.
DESPITE ALL THE RESPONSIBILITIES IT IS NO BAD THING TO BE THE SON OF LORD ODIN.
WHA--?!
IS THIS SOME NEW ATTACK?
OH, GOOD GRIEF.
GEE, MISTER, SORRY ABOUT THAT. JOHN'S A LOUSY SHOT.
NO HARM DONE, MISS.
4

WHY NOT LET US BE THE JUDGES OF THAT, MISTER. A LAME GUY LIKE YOURSELF--YOU LOOK LIKE YOU COULD USE SOME HELP.
LET ME TAKE YOUR CANE.
HEY!

NOT TOO LOUD NOW, BUB. YOU'RE JUST GOING FOR A LITTLE RIDE.
THROW THE STICK IN, TOO, BOYS.

SURE THING, COLONEL.
YOU'RE ALL SET, SIR.
SLAM!

ANY IDEA WHAT'S GO-ING ON?
BEATS ME.
VARROOOOOM!

WHAT DO YOU THINK YOU'RE--
COLONEL NICK FURY!
YOU WIN THE KEWPIE DOLL, DOCTOR BLAKE.
SORRY TA GRAB YA SO DRAMATIC-LIKE, BUT WE NEED YER HELP ...FAST!
HOLD ON TA YER HELMET.
I'M CONVERTIN' TA AERIAL MODE!

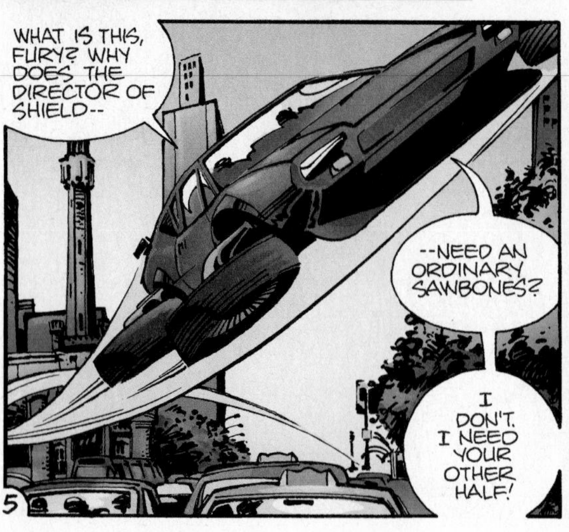
WHAT IS THIS, FURY? WHY DOES THE DIRECTOR OF SHIELD--
--NEED AN ORDINARY SAWBONES?
I DON'T. I NEED YOUR OTHER HALF!
5

WHAT DO YOU MEAN?
LOOK, DOC, I'LL LEVEL WITH YA.
WE GOT AN EMERGENCY ON OUR HANDS LIKE WE AIN'T SEEN BEFORE.
ONLY ONE GUY I KNOW OF CAN MAYBE HANDLE IT.
AND HE PACKS A HAMMER THAT MAKES OUR LATEST WEAPONS LOOK LIKE TINKERTOYS!

HOW...HOW DID YOU FIND OUT?
IT'S MY JOB, REMEMBER? I'M SUPPOSED TA KNOW STUFF.
BUT YA GOT MY WORD-- NOBODY ELSE IN OR OUT OF SHIELD KNOWS WHAT I KNOW.
SO WHAK YER MAGIC STICK THERE AND HANG ON, 'CAUSE WE'RE ALMOST HOME.

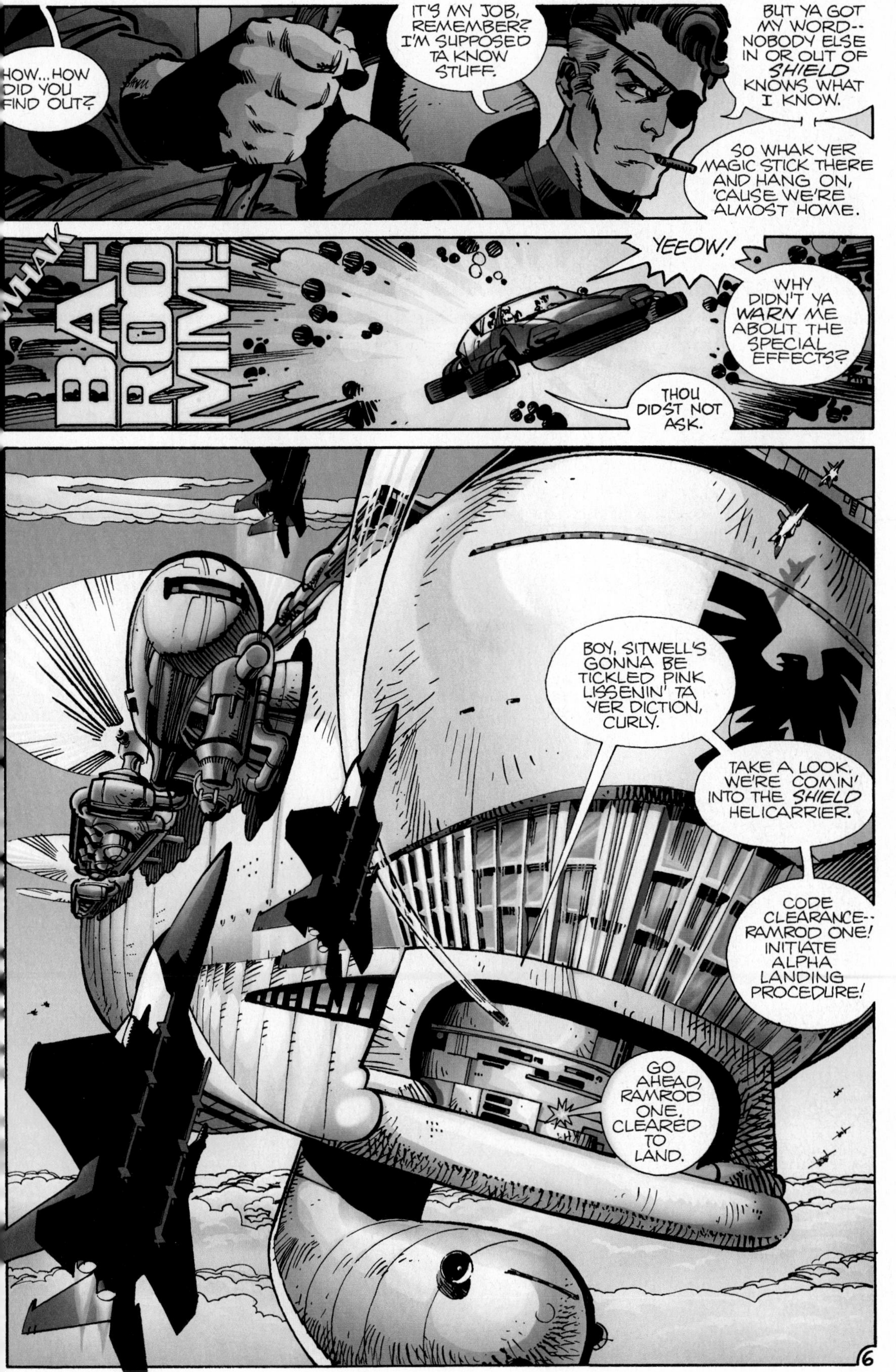

WHAK
BA-ROOM!
YEEOW!
WHY DIDN'T YA WARN ME ABOUT THE SPECIAL EFFECTS?
THOU DIDST NOT ASK.

BOY, SITWELL'S GONNA BE TICKLED PINK LISSENIN' TA YER DICTION, CURLY.
TAKE A LOOK. WE'RE COMIN' INTO THE SHIELD HELICARRIER.
CODE CLEARANCE-- RAMROD ONE! INITIATE ALPHA LANDING PROCEDURE!
GO AHEAD, RAMROD ONE. CLEARED TO LAND.
6

SHORTLY, IN A DARKENED SHIELD SCREENING ROOM...
SITWELL'S OUR LOCAL ENCYCLOPEDIA. IF HE DON'T KNOW IT, IT AIN'T A FACT!
OKAY, SITWELL, FILL IN OUR GUEST AND MAKE IT SNAPPY, HUH?

WELL, SIR, YOUR HONOR... AHEM... THIS IS THE VERY LATEST DEVELOPMENT FROM OUR TELEMETRY DIVISION.
AN EXPERIMENTAL WARP-DRIVEN PROBE CAPABLE OF COVERING UNIMAGINABLE DISTANCES AND TRANSMITTING PICTURES INSTANTANEOUSLY VIA HYPER-WAVE BACK TO A RECEIVER.
NAMELY US.
OPERATING ON AN ASSIGNED CARRIER FREQUENCY OF--
THE GUTS, SITWELL, JUST THE GUTS!

YESSIR! THESE ARE THE LAST PICTURES WE RECEIVED FROM THE PROBE. NOTE THE APPARENT VESSEL IN CENTER SCREEN.
AN ALIEN SHIP, UNLIKE ANYTHING WE'VE EVER SEEN BEFORE.

NOW WATCH THE STAR.
AS THE SHIP PASSED BY IT, THE STAR SUDDENLY FLARED TO LIFE...
...AND WAS SUCKED IN BY THE SHIP.
OUR EXPERTS THINK THE VESSEL WAS REFUELING AND DESTROYED AN ENTIRE STAR TO DO IT.

SHORTLY THEREAFTER, THE PROBE WAS DETECTED BY THE ALIEN SHIP AND ALL TRANSMISSION CEASED.
ACCORDING TO OUR BEST ESTIMATES, THE SHIP IS TRAVELING AT SEVERAL TIMES LIGHT SPEED...
...HEADING DIRECTLY FOR OUR SOLAR SYSTEM.

AND THE PROBE?
DEADER'N A DOORNAIL, THOR. BLOWN APART BY SOMETHING COMING OUR WAY.
SOMETHING REAL POWERFUL! AND DANGEROUS!
WE GOTTA FIND OUT WHAT IT IS! AND YER THE ONLY JOE WHO CAN DO IT!
WILL YA HELP US?
7

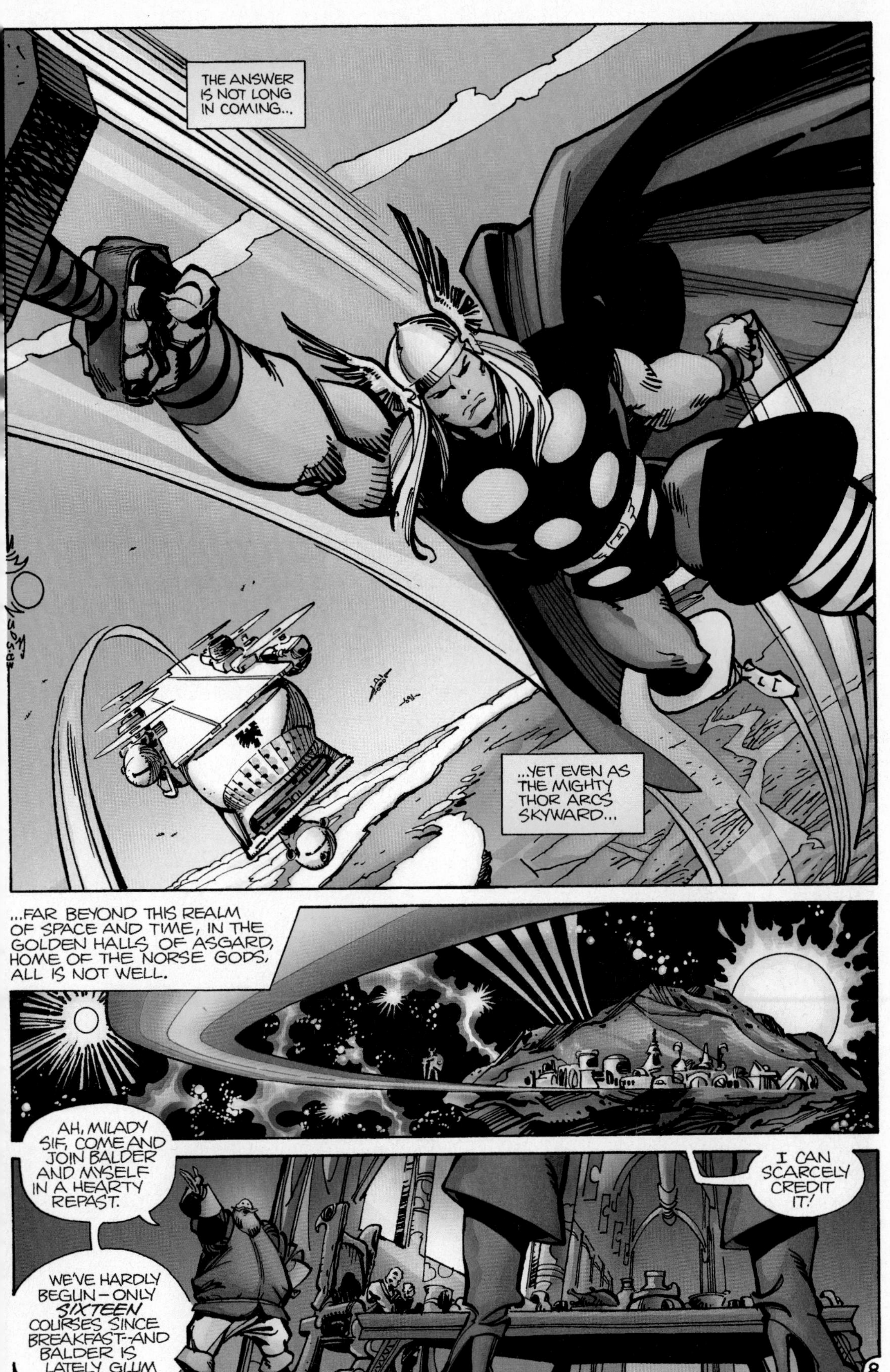
THE ANSWER IS NOT LONG IN COMING...
...YET EVEN AS THE MIGHTY THOR ARCS SKYWARD...
...FAR BEYOND THIS REALM OF SPACE AND TIME, IN THE GOLDEN HALLS OF ASGARD, HOME OF THE NORSE GODS, ALL IS NOT WELL.
AH, MILADY SIF, COME AND JOIN BALDER AND MYSELF IN A HEARTY REPAST.
WE'VE HARDLY BEGUN—ONLY SIXTEEN COURSES SINCE BREAKFAST-AND BALDER IS LATELY GLUM COMPANY!
I CAN SCARCELY CREDIT IT!
8

BRAVE BALDER, I RETURN TO ASGARD FROM EARTH ONLY TO FIND YOU IN THE MEAD HALL WITH VOLSTAGG THE ENORMOUS, FEASTING WITHOUT RESPITE!
THOR HAS FORSAKEN ME FOR MIDGARD.*
*EARTH.

MY HEART, MY SOUL ARE EMPTY.
I NEED YOUR STRENGTH, YOUR UNDER-STANDING, YOUR TENDERNESS...
THEN SEEK SOLACE ELSEWHERE, LADY. BALDER THE BRAVE IS NO MORE.
HE WHO HAS RETURNED FROM HELA'S DARK DOMAIN IS NOT FIT TO BE A MAN MUCH LESS A GOD!

I HAVE FORSWORN ALL BATTLES SAVE THIS ONE--THAT I WILL FORGET EVERYTHING I HAVE EVER CHERISHED...
...DEFEATING AT LAST THE FEARFUL CURSE OF THE MEMORY OF THE GOD I ONCE WAS.
ETERNITY IS A LONG TIME, MILADY. BALDER THE BRAVE IS A MYTH I HAVE OUTLIVED.

SOMEONE APPROACHES HEIMDALL THE WATCHER.
BY WHOSE LEAVE DO YOU TREAD UPON BIFROST, THE RAINBOW BRIDGE?

IT IS I, SIF. I HAVE COME BECAUSE I HAVE NOWHERE ELSE TO TURN.

SIF, DEAR SISTER, I HAVE HEARD YOUR TROUBLES. WHAT WOULD YOU HAVE ME DO?
I AM A SHIELD MAIDEN, MY BROTHER. YOUR EYES AND EARS SEE AND HEAR ALL THINGS.
WHITHER CAN I FIND THE CLASH OF BATTLE TO MAKE ME HAPPY AND EASE MY EMPTINESS?
MY POOR DAR-LING. MAYHAP ONLY ODIN HIMSELF CAN HELP YOU NOW.
9

MEANWHILE, A LONG WAY FROM EARTH...
THE POWER OF MY ENCHANTED MALLET TO CROSS TIME AND SPACE HAS BROUGHT ME CLOSE TO THE ALIEN VESSEL...
...AND RESTORED MY FAITH IN MY HERITAGE! WHAT MORTAL COULD DO WHAT I HAVE DONE?
'TIS GOOD TO BE THE GOD OF THUNDER!
ODIN'S BLOOD! THE SHIP OUTRACES ME AS THE HARE OUTRACES THE TORTOISE!
I MUST INCREASE MY SPEED A HUNDREDFOLD IF I AM TO OVERTAKE YON VESSEL.
BUT OVERTAKE IT I SHALL!
ITS APPEARANCE REFLECTS A GRIM AND SERIOUS PURPOSE. T'WOULD SEEM TO BE A WARSHIP!
CHIKCHIKCHIK
SENSORS DETECT UNIDENTIFIED PURSUER ON INTERCEPT COURSE. ENERGY CONFIGURATIONS SIMILAR TO DEMON BREED. PREPARE TO OPEN FIRE.
MAIN BATTERIES CHARGED AND READY.
TARGET LOCKED MAGNIFICATION THREE.
TARGET CLOSING.
10

FIRE!

BY THE GOLDEN SPIRES OF ASGARD!
AN ENERGY BOLT OF PURE FORCE!

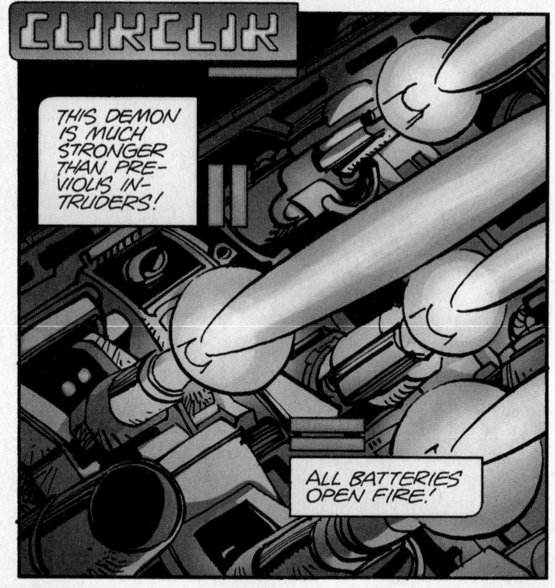
CLIKCLIK
THIS DEMON IS MUCH STRONGER THAN PRE-VIOUS IN-TRUDERS!
ALL BATTERIES OPEN FIRE!

AGAIN THE VESSEL DIRECTS AN UNPROVOKED ATTACK AT ME!

SO BE IT!
LET THE HAMMER OF THOR SPEAK FOR ME NOW!
11

THRAAKKT

AS EVER, MY HAMMER RETURNS TO ME...

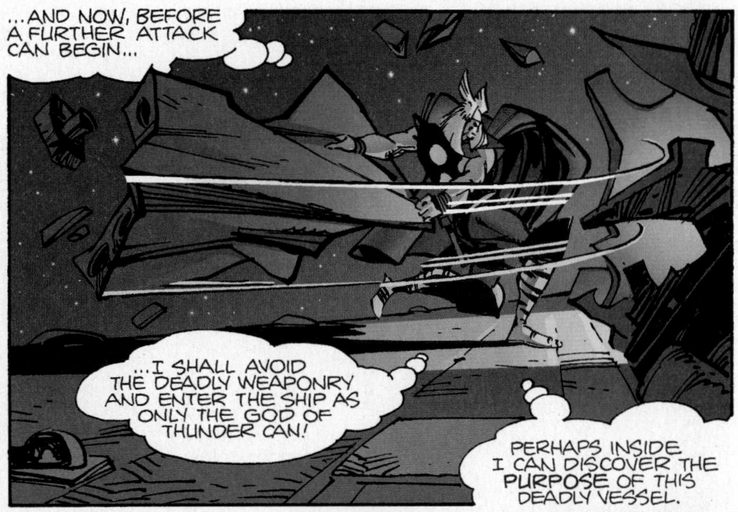
...AND NOW, BEFORE A FURTHER ATTACK CAN BEGIN...
...I SHALL AVOID THE DEADLY WEAPONRY AND ENTER THE SHIP AS ONLY THE GOD OF THUNDER CAN!
PERHAPS INSIDE I CAN DISCOVER THE PURPOSE OF THIS DEADLY VESSEL.

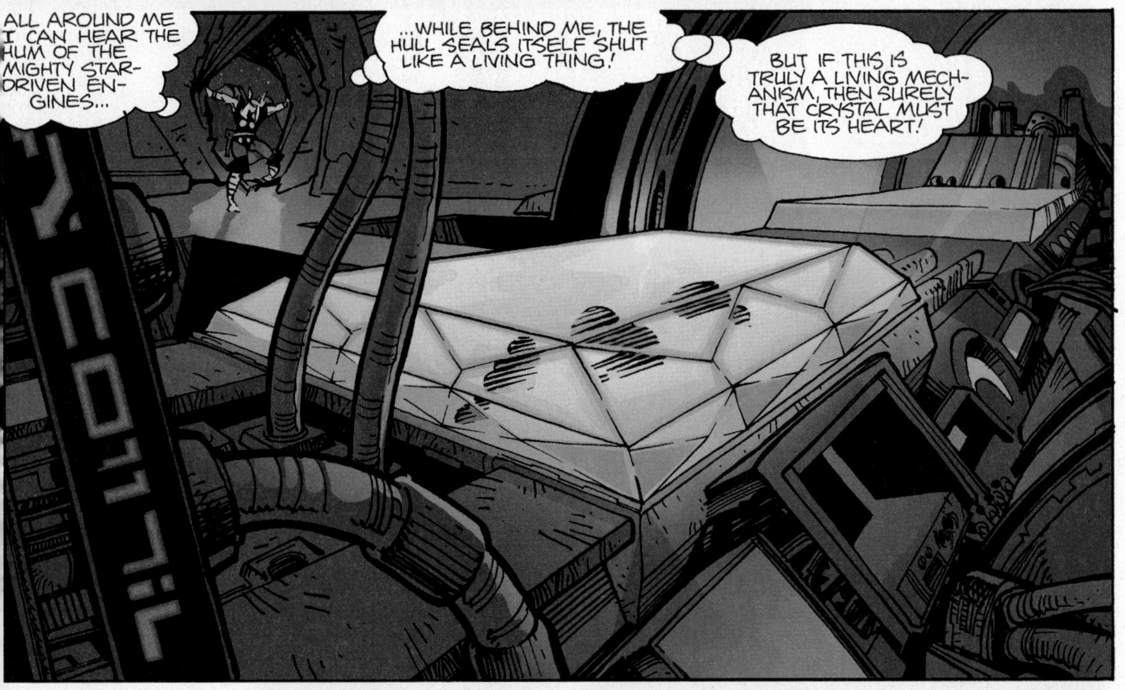
ALL AROUND ME I CAN HEAR THE HUM OF THE MIGHTY STAR-DRIVEN ENGINES...
...WHILE BEHIND ME, THE HULL SEALS ITSELF SHUT LIKE A LIVING THING!
BUT IF THIS IS TRULY A LIVING MECHANISM, THEN SURELY THAT CRYSTAL MUST BE ITS HEART!

YET WHAT LIES HERE AT ITS VERY CENTER?
A FIGURE OF SOME SIZE.
PERHAPS-- EH?
12

CHIRCHIR
DANGER! DANGER!
INTRUDER HAS BREACHED THE HULL!
ULTIMATE DEFENSE PROCEDURE!
RELEASE COLDSLEEP DEFENSE!
KRASH!
UGGH!

BUT EVEN AS THOR STRUGGLES FOR BREATH, LET US TURN TO A DESOLATE CORNER OF ASGARD TO FIND...

I AM BORED TO DEATH!

TO THINK THAT LOKI, PRINCE OF DARKNESS, SHOULD WASTE HIS TIME IN MONOTONOUS EXILE WHILE CHEER AND GOOD FELLOWSHIP ABOUND IN THE LAND.
BAH! I'VE HALF A MIND TO...

...BUT SOFTLY! WHAT'S THIS I HEAR?

WHO DARES TO PASS SO CLOSE TO LOKI'S LONELY ABODE?

"SO! A FEW LACKWIT WARRIORS VENTURE TO ENGAGE IN A FORBIDDEN TROLL HUNT!

"I BELIEVE THE END OF MY BOREDOM IS AT HAND!"
13

PUFF PUFF
MUST HIDE! MUST HIDE! OR HUNTERS SLAY ME!
DID YOU SEE?
YES, HELGI, THE TROLL'S GONE TO COVER IN THOSE THISTLES!
BY YMIR'S BEARD, WE MAY NEVER FLUSH HIM NOW!

LITTLE ONE! PSST! LITTLE ONE!

HUH?
DO NOT BE AFRAID, LITTLE TROLL. I CAN HELP YOU. I CAN HIDE YOU.
IT GIRL! SHE...SHE BEAUTIFUL!

COME. LOOK AT ME. GIVE ME YOUR HAND...
...AND FEAR NOTHING.
LOOK AT ME.
I...

WHITHER AWAY, MY LORDS?
WHA--?
IT'S LORELEI! WITH THE TROLL! SHE'S WON THE HUNT!

JUST AS I FORETOLD YOU!
INDEED, MILADY. AS NONE KNOW BETTER THAN I.
WEAPONS AND STRENGTH ARE NOT EVERYTHING, MY LORDS.
4

I THINK WE SHOULD DISCUSS THIS FURTHER. WILL YOU NOT ACCOMPANY ME BACK TO MY HUMBLE DWELLING?
PERHAPS I SHALL, MY LORD.
LORELEI, YOU'D BEST LEAVE WITH US. THE OPEN HAND OF LOKI IS NOT SAFE!

NOR WILL YOU BE SAFE IF ODIN LEARNS OF THIS HUNT! LEAVE US AND FORGET WHAT HAS HAPPENED HERE...
...OR THE NEXT HAND OF LOKI YOU SEE WILL BE FILLED WITH MENACE.

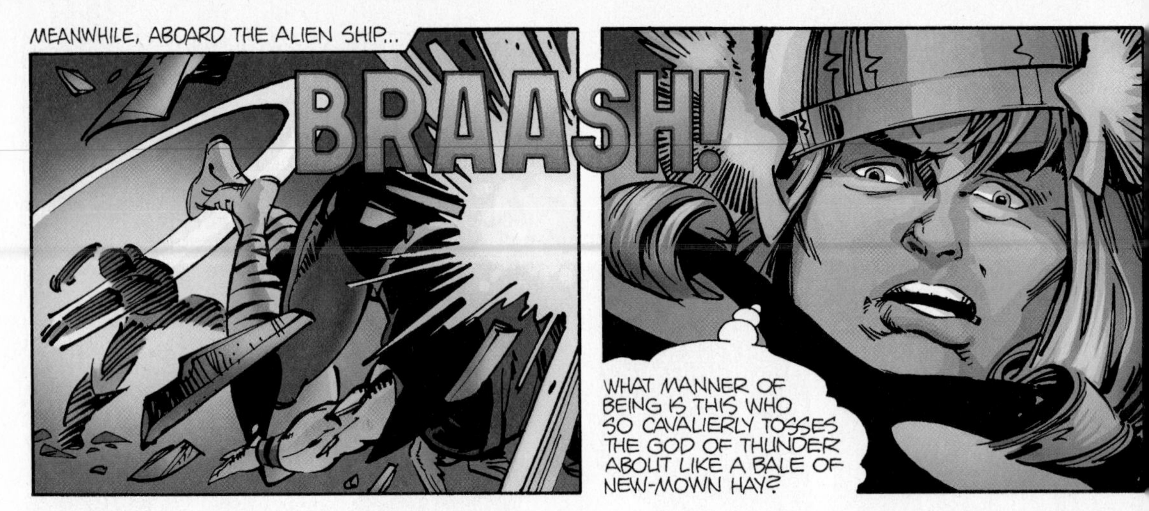

RISE UP, DEMON!

YOU HAVE PURSUED ME ONLY TO FIND DEATH!

AND WHEN I AM THROUGH WITH YOU, YOU WILL WELCOME IT!

I AM CALLED BILL--**BETA RAY BILL!**

15

BUT DO NOT TROUBLE YOURSELF TO REMEMBER IT!
YOU SHOULD HAVE WAITED FOR YOUR FELLOWS TO ARRIVE RATHER THAN FACE ME ALONE!

I DO NOT KNOW WHAT YOU MEAN, CREATURE...
...BUT NONE MAY TOUCH THE MIGHTY THOR SO WITHOUT PAYING THE PRICE!
YET HOW IS IT YOU SPEAK MY TONGUE?
AAGGH!

THE SHIP WAS RIGHT! YOU ARE MUCH STRONGER THAN YOUR PREDECESSORS!
APPARENTLY THE BREED IS IMPROVING!

BUT IT WILL NOT SAVE YOU!

KRANG!

SKUTTLEBUTT HAS DECIPHERED YOUR BARBAROUS LANGUAGE AND RELAYED IT TO ME THROUGH MY CRYSTAL CHAMBER!
THUS I SHALL ENGRAVE YOUR EPITAPH IN YOUR OWN TONGUE ON MY NEW WORLD...
...ON THE MEMORIAL CELEBRATING MY VICTORY OVER YOU AND ALL OF DEMONKIND!
16

YOU STILL SPEAK IN RIDDLES, WARRIOR...
...BUT IT IS CLEAR TO ME THAT I CAN NEVER PERMIT SUCH A DANGEROUS ENTITY TO REACH EARTH...

...EVEN IF I MUST DESTROY THIS SHIP FROM WITHIN TO STOP YOU!

CHIRCHIR
INTERNAL MONITORS INDICATE GRAVE DAMAGE TO SURVIVAL AND WEAPONS SYSTEMS.
IMMEDIATE LANDING NECESSARY TO EFFECT REPAIRS. BEGIN INSTRUMENT SEARCH FOR POTENTIAL SITES!

CURSÉD DEMON! YOUR DEATH WILL BE AN UNCLEAN ONE FOR THIS DELAY!

CHIRCHIR
SEARCH COMPLETE. ACCEPTABLE PLANETARY SYSTEM AHEAD.
PRELIMINARY SCAN INDICATES THIRD PLANET CONTAINS NECESSARY MATERIAL FOR REPAIRS.
CHANGE COURSE TO SEVEN--GAMMA--Y--SEVEN.

EVER HAVE I BEEN O WELL MATCHED BY ANY MORTAL, BUT HOUGH I RELISH HE STRUGGLE, T MUST END NOW!
WILL YOU YIELD, WARRIOR?
ONLY IN DEATH!

CHIRCHIR
ANDING MODE CONFIRMED.
SHIP NOW ENTERING THE PLANE OF THE ECLIPTIC OF THE THIRD PLANET.

OU LEAVE ME NO CHOICE. I MUST--
Y MY TROTH!
WHAT WEAKNESS SUDDENLY ASSAILS ME?

OH, NO! NOT NOW! NOT LIKE THIS!
WE MUST BE CLOSING FAST WITH EARTH AND WITHOUT MY HAM-MER IN MY HAND, I'VE REVERTED TO MY BLAKE FORM!
I'VE GOT TO--

YOU'LL DO NOTHING, DEMON!
YOU MAY HAVE CHANGED YOUR SHAPE... BUT IT CERTAINLY SEEMS ILL SUITED FOR COMBAT!
UHHH!
18

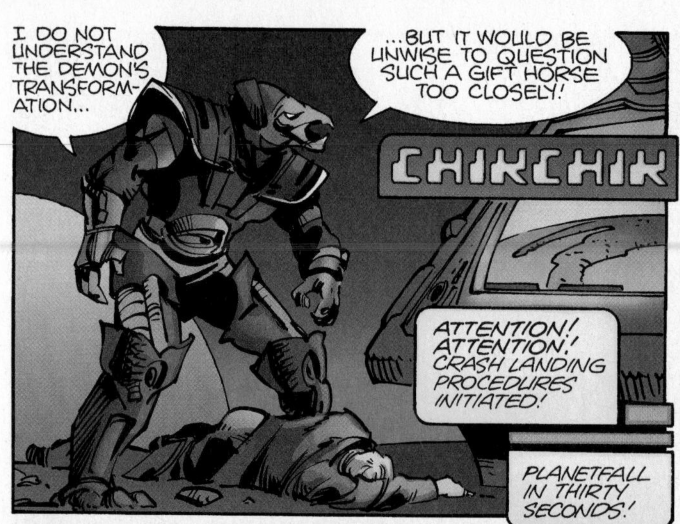
I DO NOT UNDERSTAND THE DEMON'S TRANSFORM-ATION...
...BUT IT WOULD BE UNWISE TO QUESTION SUCH A GIFT HORSE TOO CLOSELY!
CHIRCHIR
ATTENTION! ATTENTION! CRASH LANDING PROCEDURES INITIATED!
PLANETFALL IN THIRTY SECONDS!

QUICKLY, SKUTTLEBUTT.
NOW!

MOMENTS LATER, THE FURIOUS FLIGHT OF THE ALIEN SHIP THUNDERS TO A FIERY END...
AND INSIDE...

THE STASIS FIELD HELD. I AM ALIVE AND UNHARMED.
AND IT WOULD SEEM THAT THE DEMON HAS SURVIVED WITH-IN THE FIELD AS WELL.
SOMETHING I WILL ATTEND TO IN A MOMENT.
SKUTTLE-BUTT, REPORT STATUS.

CHIRCHIR
WEAPONS CAPABILITY DOWN TO 5%--REPAIR TIME IS 40 HOURS TO LIFTOFF. SCANNERS DETECT APPROACHING VEHICLES WITH CLASS 3 LIFE FORMS.
IN OUR CURRENT STATE, THEY COULD DESTROY US.
I AM ALSO RECEIVING A BROAD-CAST FROM ONE OF THE VEHICLES IN A VARIANT OF THE DEMON'S LANGUAGE.

HEADS UP IN THE SHIP! THIS IS NICK FURY, DIRECTOR OF SHIELD TALKIN' AT YA!
WE GOT YA SURROUNDED! WADDYA SAY YOU COME OUT PEACE-ABLE AND WE'LL TALK!

THE DEMON'S WEAPON! THE HAMMER HE WIELD-ED SO POWERFULLY!
IT COULD BE MY ONLY CHANCE TO SAVE MY MISSION!
BUT WHERE...?

WHAT'S THIS? A STICK?
THE HAMMER HAS VANISHED!
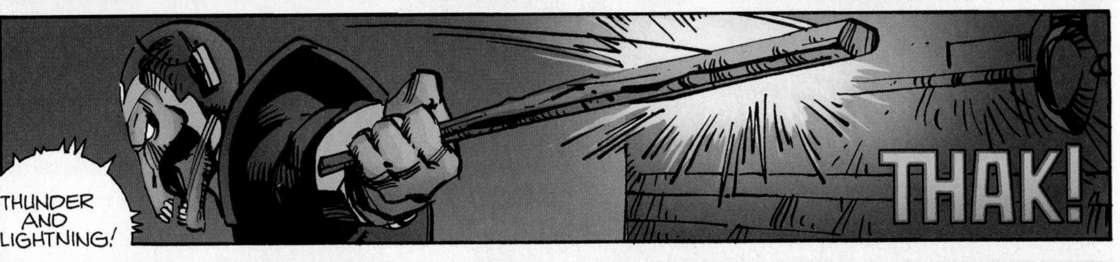
THUNDER AND LIGHTNING!
THAK!

WHA--?!

I...I HAVE THE POWER! THE STICK WAS THE HAMMER!
AND NOW I...I CAN FEEL THE POWER OF THE DEMON HIM-SELF ADDED TO MY OWN!
POWER ENOUGH TO SHAKE THIS PLANET TO ITS FOUNDATIONS!
20

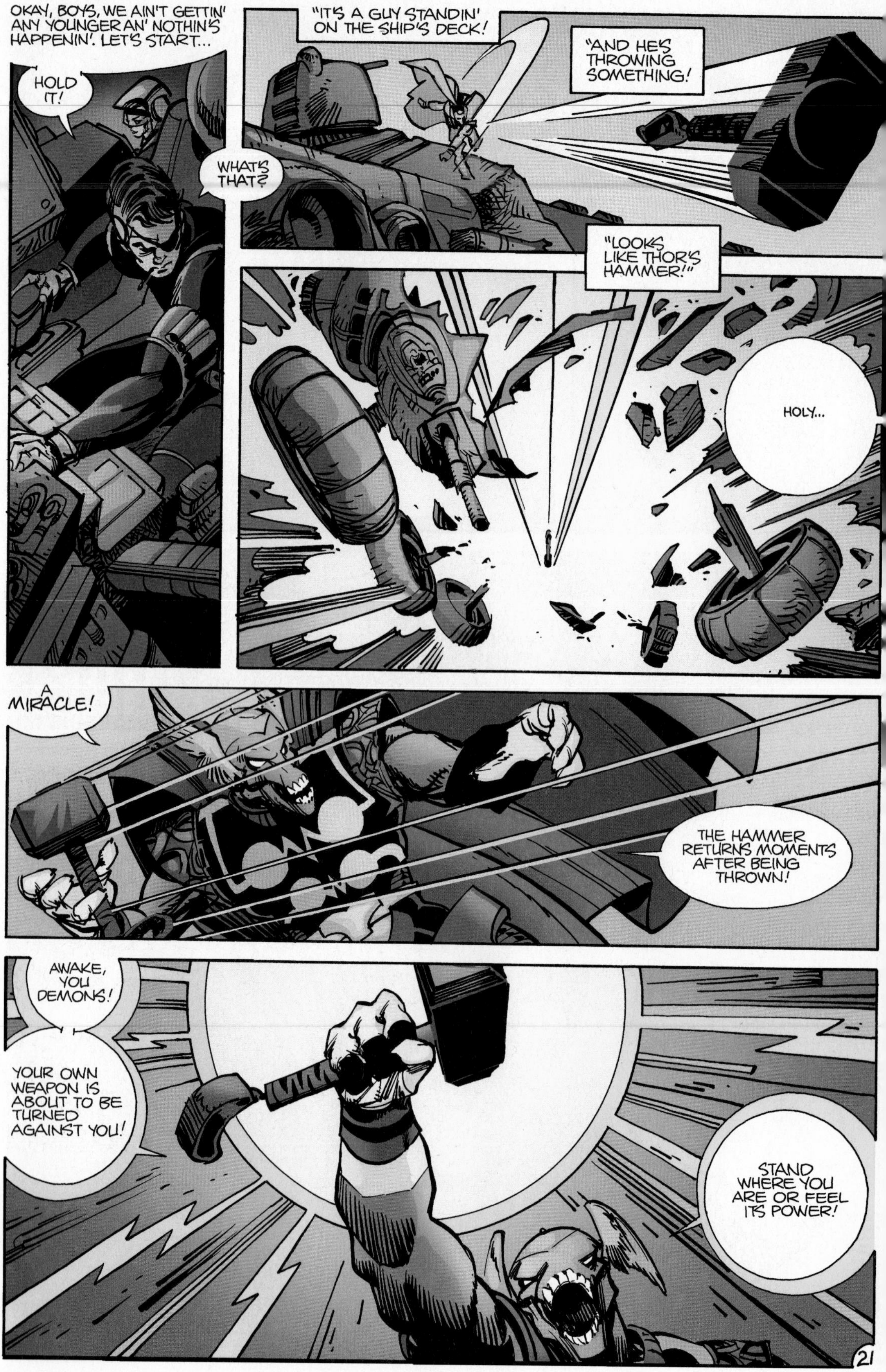

OKAY, BOYS, WE AIN'T GETTIN' ANY YOUNGER AN' NOTHIN'S HAPPENIN'. LET'S START...

HOLD IT!

WHAT'S THAT?

"IT'S A GUY STANDIN' ON THE SHIP'S DECK!

"AND HE'S THROWING SOMETHING!

"LOOKS LIKE THOR'S HAMMER!"

HOLY...

A MIRACLE!

THE HAMMER RETURNS MOMENTS AFTER BEING THROWN!

WHAT THE HECK IS GOIN' ON? THAT'S THOR'S HAMMER ALL RIGHT BUT THAT SURE ISN'T THOR!

WE'LL FIGURE IT OUT LATER AFTER WE NAIL HIM! OPEN UP, BOYS!

BEYOW!

BEYOW!

VERY WELL, DEMONS! YOU WERE WARNED!

COLONEL FURY, I'M REGISTERING SOME SORT OF ATMOSPHERIC DISTURBANCE!

AND I'M GETTING AN AUDIO SIGNAL, TOO.

IT'S CENTERED AROUND THAT GUY WITH THE HAMMER!

MAYBE HE'S BREWING UP ONE OF HIS STORMS!

I DON'T THINK SO, COLONEL!

THOR, MY SON! WE HAVE URGENT NEED OF THEE IN ASGARD.

I MUST CALL THEE HOME!

22

BARROOOOM!
HE'S GONE! THEY'RE BOTH GONE!

AND I GOT A FEELIN' SOMEBODY'S GETTIN' THE SURPRISE OF THEIR LIFE RIGHT ABOUT NOW!

BUT THAT SHIP'S STILL HERE...
...AND IT COULD STILL BE DANGEROUS!
SIGNAL EVERYBODY TA ADVANCE... REAL CAREFUL LIKE.

LOOK, SIR! THERE'S SOME-BODY ELSE CRAWL-ING OUT OF THE SHIP!
HOLD YER FIRE! IF THAT'S WHO I THINK IT IS, WE COULD ALL BE IN BIG TROUBLE!

MY CANE IS GONE! AND SOMEHOW I KNOW THAT THAT ALIEN IS RESPONSI-BLE.
BUT THE ATMOSPHERE, THE STORM! ODIN WAS HERE!
HIS PRESENCE STILL LINGERS! AND HE DID NOT TAKE ME!
ONLY A FEW HOURS AGO, I NEARLY ENVIED THE MORTALS AROUND ME!

AND NOW, I MAY HAVE TO JOIN THEM... FOREVER!
FATHER! HEAR ME!
DO NOT FORSAKE ME HERE!
23

FATHER!
BUT THE LASHING STORM DOES NOT LISTEN.
AND ONLY THE WIND AND RAIN REPLY.

ART AND STORY: WALTER SIMONSON · LETTERING: JOHN WORKMAN, JR. · COLORS: GEORGE ROUSSOS · EDITING: MARK GRUENWALD · EDITOR-IN-CHIEF: JIM SHOOTER

NEXT--A FOOL AND HIS HAMMER...

BE HERE! 'CAUSE WE'LL MISS YOU IF YOU'RE NOT AROUND.

Thor #337 was recolored by Steve Oliff for **Thor by Walter Simonson Vol. 1 TPB**

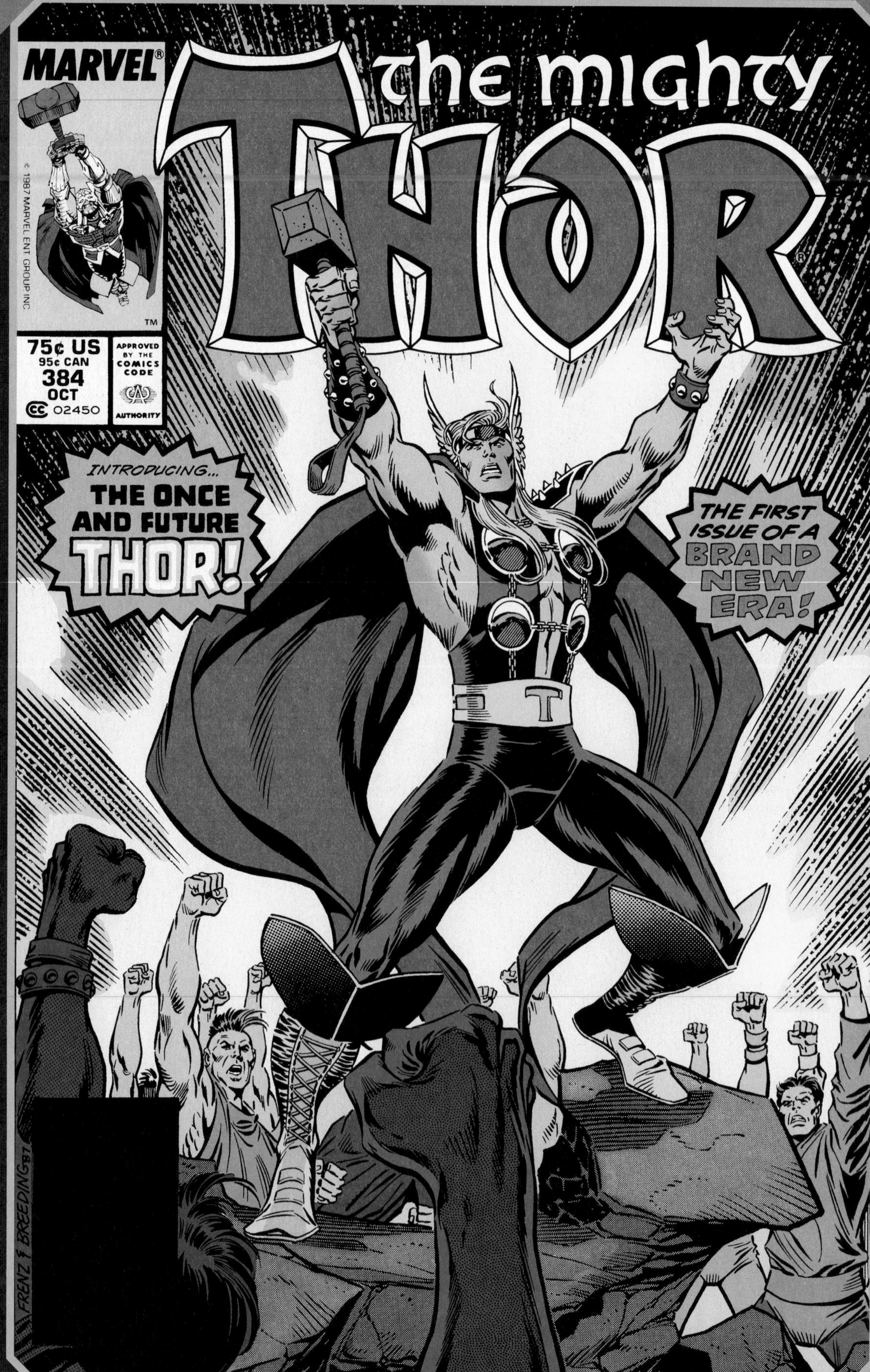
MARVEL
the mighty
THOR
© 1987 MARVEL ENT GROUP INC
75¢ US
95¢ CAN
384
OCT
02450
APPROVED BY THE COMICS CODE AUTHORITY
INTRODUCING...
THE ONCE AND FUTURE THOR!
THE FIRST ISSUE OF A BRAND NEW ERA!
FRENZ & BREEDING 87

"WHO SHALL BE WORTHY?"
A STUNNING SAGA STARRING THE MIGHTY THOR!
SEPTEMBER 4, 2537, QUEENS, NEW YORK...
GET BACK, SALLA! STAY SHADOWED.!!
CAN'T LET THAT CORP TRACKER SCOPE US.!
THAT'S THE FIFTH ONE TONIGHT.!
WHAT'S THE SCAN, DARGO?
WHY IS THE CORP OUT IN SUCH FORCE?!
STAN LEE PROUDLY PRESENTS:
TOM DeFALCO WRITER
RON FRENZ PENCILER
BRETT BREEDING INKER
DIANA ALBERS LETTERER
"MAX" SCHEELE COLORIST
RALPH MACCHIO EDITOR
JIM SHOOTER EDITOR IN CHIEF

HAVEN'T YOU FLASHED, YET? THE CORP HAS DECLARED WAR ON CURFEW CUTTERS LIKE US.!
CAN'T WORRY THAT NOW.!
SPEED IT.! THE CEREMONY'S ABOUT TO START.!

MOVING QUICKLY, THE TWO FURTIVE FIGURES RACE INTO THE SEEMINGLY ABANDONED SUBWAY ENTRANCE, AND THEN...
WHO DARES ENTER MY DANK DOMAIN?

ER...TWO WHO WOULD BE WORTHY.!
PASS, AND MAY THE GODS GRANT YOU WORTHINESS.!
KEEP DREAMING.!

LOOK.! WE'RE LATER THAN I THOUGHT.!
THE OTHERS HAVE ALREADY GEARED UP.!
THEY'RE HEADED FOR THE MAIN PLATFORM.!

HURRY.! I DON'T WANT TO MISS ANYTHING.!
WE MAY HAVE ACTUALLY FOUND SOMEONE WHO IS WORTHY--AND HE'S GOING TO TRY TO PROVE IT TONIGHT.!
HE'LL FAIL... LIKE ALL THE OTHERS.!
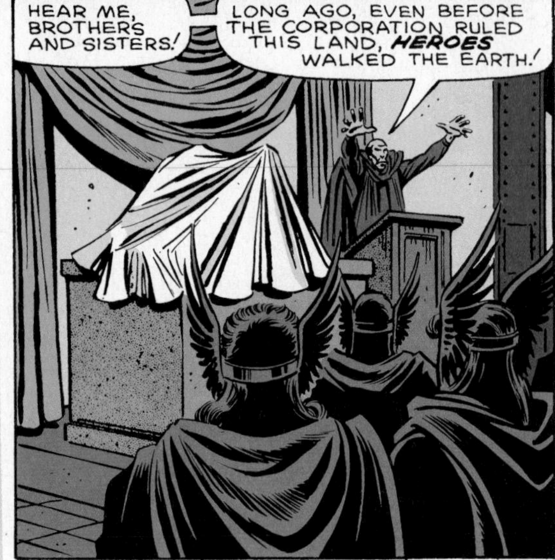
HEAR ME, BROTHERS AND SISTERS.!
LONG AGO, EVEN BEFORE THE CORPORATION RULED THIS LAND, HEROES WALKED THE EARTH.!

GREAT AND POWERFUL WERE THESE NOBLE HEROES WHO DEFENDED THE COMMON MAN, BUT THE GREATEST AND MOST POWERFUL OF ALL WAS...
THE MIGHTY THOR!!

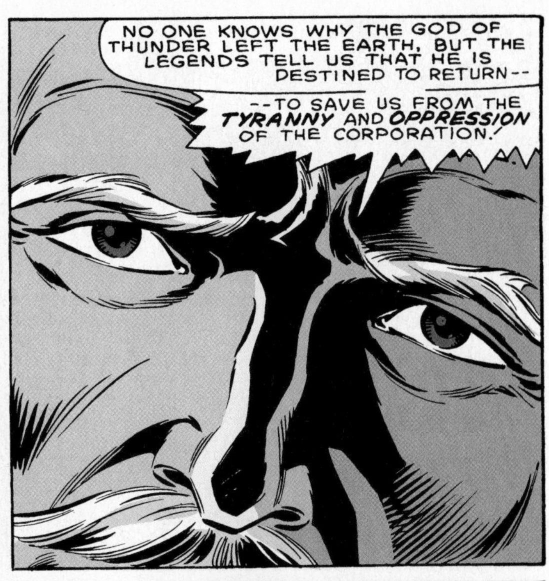
NO ONE KNOWS WHY THE GOD OF THUNDER LEFT THE EARTH, BUT THE LEGENDS TELL US THAT HE IS DESTINED TO RETURN--
--TO SAVE US FROM THE TYRANNY AND OPPRESSION OF THE CORPORATION!

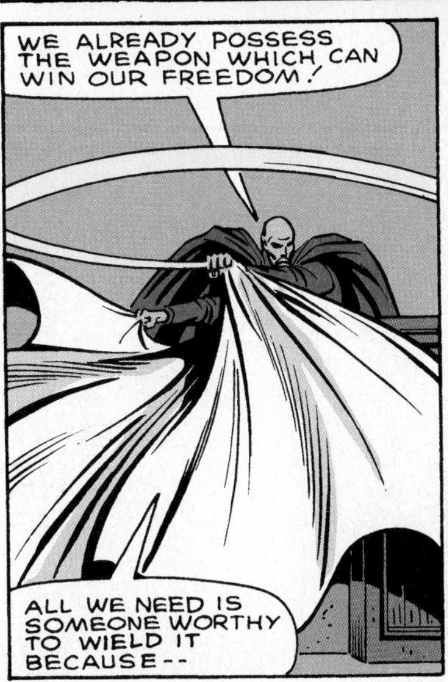
WE ALREADY POSSESS THE WEAPON WHICH CAN WIN OUR FREEDOM!
ALL WE NEED IS SOMEONE WORTHY TO WIELD IT BECAUSE--

--WHOSOEVER HOLDS THIS HAMMER, IF HE BE WORTHY, SHALL POSSESS THE POWER OF... THOR!

IS THERE ANY AMONG YOU WHO CLAIMS TO BE WORTHY?!

I DO!
I'M THE STRONGEST MAN IN MY DORM-BLOCK!
TAKE THE HAMMER, BROTHER, AND MAY THE GODS GRANT YOU WORTHINESS!

EVERYONE'S HOPING, PRAYING THAT THIS ONE WILL SUCCEED!
WHY CAN'T THEY SEE IT'S ALL A MONUMENTAL WASTE OF TIME?!

UGGG
I-IT'S NO USE!
C-CAN'T BUDGE IT!

A FAILURE! ANOTHER FAILURE!
HOW MUCH LONGER MUST WE WAIT?
WHAT'S WRONG WITH THESE PEOPLE?
HOW CAN THEY PUT SO MUCH FAITH INTO SOME STUPID OLD HAMMER?!

SOME TIME LATER...
I WAS SO CERTAIN, SO SURE THAT THIS TIME--
GET A FLASH, SALLA!
EVEN IF SOME SLACKER DOES MANAGE TO SHAKE THAT HAMMER LOOSE, NOTHING'S GOING TO CHANGE!

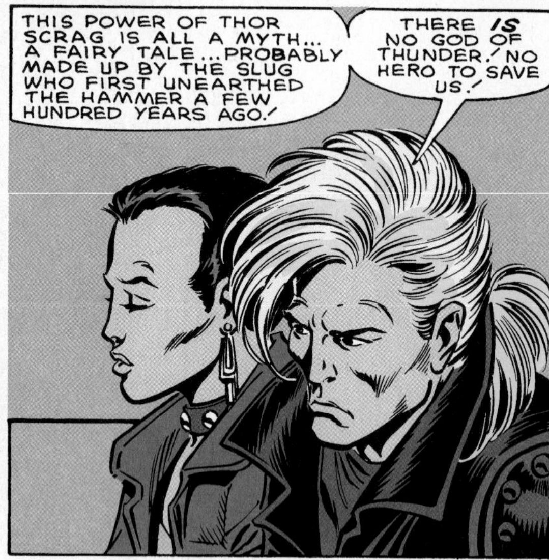
THIS POWER OF THOR SCRAG IS ALL A MYTH... A FAIRY TALE...PROBABLY MADE UP BY THE SLUG WHO FIRST UNEARTHED THE HAMMER A FEW HUNDRED YEARS AGO!
THERE IS NO GOD OF THUNDER! NO HERO TO SAVE US!

IF THE PEOPLE WANT THEIR FREEDOM FROM THE CORP, THEY'LL HAVE TO FIGHT FOR IT THEMSELVES!
OH, DARGO, I WISH YOU HAD MORE FAITH.
THEY SAY IT CAN MOVE MOUNTAINS...

...ALL WE'RE ASKING FOR IS A SIMPLE HAMMER!
SEE YOU AT FIRST SHIFT.
YEAH, RIGHT...

EARLY THE NEXT MORNING...
THESE CULTISTS ARE REBELS!
THEY UNDERMINE THE PEACE AND SECURITY OF THE ENTIRE CORPORATE STRUCTURE!
THEY VIOLATE CURFEW, DON'T GET THEIR REQUIRED FIVE HOURS REST, AND CONSEQUENTLY CAN'T WORK AT PEAK EFFICIENCY!

THEY'RE COSTING THE CORPORATION MONEY!
FIND THESE SLACKERS, AND EXTERMINATE THEM BEFORE THEY TOTALLY ERODE OUR BOTTOM LINE!

HMPH
INEFFICIENT BAND OF BUMBLERS!
MS. COHEN, PLEASE SEND IN MY NINE-FIFTEEN APPOINTMENT.
YES, MR. CHAIRMAN!

LET'S GET RIGHT DOWN TO BUSINESS, SHALL WE? I HAVE A CULT PROBLEM, AND I HEAR THAT YOU ARE A SPECIALIST IN THE ART OF THEIR REMOVAL.
I CAN ABSOLUTELY GUARANTEE SUCCESS.
HOW MUCH WILL THIS COST ME?
NOTHING. I AM WILLING TO FOREGO MY USUAL FEE!

WHAT?! ARE YOU SERIOUS?
DEADLY SERIOUS!
LET'S JUST SAY THAT I AM WILLING TO TOTALLY ELIMINATE THIS PARTICULAR CULT FOR MY OWN PERSONAL REASONS!

MEANWHILE, AT A NEARBY FACTORY COMPLEX...
TONIGHT, WE GATHER!

SO SOON?
THINK OF THE DANGER, SALLA! THE CORP TRACKERS WILL BE OUT IN FULL FORCE!
YOU MAY NOT BE A TRUE BELIEVER, DARGO, BUT I AM!
MY FAITH WILL PROTECT ME!
ALL RIGHT, I'LL COME...JUST IN CASE YOUR FAITH NEEDS HELP!

HOURS LATER, AS NIGHT CARESSES THE CITY, STRANGE, SAVAGE CREATURES STALK THE SHADOWS, SEARCHING, EVER-SEARCHING...

THAT MORTAL FOOL DIDN'T REALIZE THE HORROR HE WAS UNLEASHING WHEN HE HIRED ME!

I WOULD CHEERFULLY EXTERMINATE HIS TROUBLESOME CULT--AND THE ENTIRE HUMAN RACE, IF NEED BE--TO FIND THAT WHICH I SEEK!

THE HAMMER IS NEAR, FAITHFUL TYRUS! I CAN ALMOST SENSE IT!

AT LAST, LOKI! OUR CENTURIES-LONG QUEST IS OVER!

AYE, 'TIS TIME TO LOOSE OUR DEMON HORDE--!

SOON! SOON ALL WHO LIVE WILL TREMBLE BEFORE--
--THE POWER OF LOKI!!

MERE MOMENTS LATER, AT THE SECRET CEREMONY HONORING THE LONG-VANISHED THUNDER GOD
RUN!!
FLEE FOR YOUR LIVES!
WE'VE BEEN DISCOVERED--!!

ARRRGHH!!

CRUSH ALL OPPOSITION! DESTROY ANY WHO DEFY YOU!
WE MUST WIN THE HAMMER--

--OR FACE THE ETERNAL WRATH OF LOKI!
MOVE, SALLA!
NO! I WON'T LEAVE YOU!
YES, YOU WILL! NOW!!

PUSHING THE YOUNG WOMAN TO SAFETY, DARGO TURNS TO FACE THE BRUTAL INVADERS...
WHO ARE THESE CREATURES? WHERE'D THEY COME FROM?!
THEY'RE SLAUGHTERING MY PEOPLE--AND WE DON'T HAVE A CHANCE!

CAN'T FIGHT THEM WITH MY BARE HANDS! I NEED A WEAPON!
INSTINCTIVELY, THE VALIANT TEENAGER REACHES OUT...

AND, NO SOONER DO HIS HANDS GRASP THE NEAREST OBJECT, THAN--
--THE ENTIRE AREA IS SUDDENLY BATHED IN A BURST OF LIGHT!

LIGHT AS BLINDING AS A FIERY BOLT OF LIGHTNING!

AND, SOME DISTANCE AWAY...
THE HAMMER--!!
WHAT IS IT, MASTER? WHAT'S WRONG?!
SOMEONE HAS UNLEASHED ITS POWER! SOMEONE--

"--WORTHY ENOUGH TO POSSESS IT!"
SOMETHING'S HAPPENING TO ME! I'M CHANGING... CHANGING!!

I CAN FEEL MY BODY BURSTING WITH POWER--POWER THAT'S ALMOST BEYOND HUMAN COMPREHENSION!

THE ANCIENT LEGENDS ARE TRUE! THEY MUST BE!!
I HAVE SOMEHOW BEEN TRANSFORMED INTO THE MIGHTIEST WARRIOR OF ALL TIME! THE LEGENDARY THUNDER GOD!
THIS REALLY IS HIS HAMMER, AND I--
I AM THOR!!

HIS BLOOD BOILING WITH EXCITMENT, THE YOUNG WARRIOR TURNS TO BATTLE...
WHIRLING HIS HAMMER FASTER AND FASTER... FASTER THAN EVEN THE MORTAL EYE CAN FOLLOW ...HE CREATES A RAGING TORNADO...

AND THEN...
NOW SHALL YOU FEEL THE ANGER OF THOR!!
W-WE'RE HELPLESS BEFORE SUCH UNRELENTING FURY!

NOTHING COULD RESIST IT! NOTHING!!
EEYYII!!!

DID YOU SCAN?
TOOK'EM ALL ON!
BLEW'EM AWAY!
WHO IS HE?
WHO CARES!

OUR PRAYERS HAVE BEEN ANSWERED! OUR GOD IS COME!
REJOICE! SALVATION IS AT HAND! MIGHTY THOR WILL SAVE US FROM THE OPPRESSION OF THE CORP!
I DON'T BELIEVE THIS! THESE STUPID SLACKERS ARE ACTUALLY WORSHIPING ME! ME!!

GET AWAY FROM ME, YOU FOOLS!
I'M NOT HERE TO FIGHT YOUR BATTLES FOR YOU!
I'M NOT A TOOL FOR YOU TO USE AGAINST THE CORPORATION!

HURLING HIS HAMMER UPWARD, THE MIGHTY THOR BURSTS OUT OF THE UNDERGROUND TEMPLE AMID A THUNDEROUS SHOWER OF CONCRETE DEBRIS...

AND, A FEW MINUTES LATER...
I NEED A PLACE TO THINK!
HAVE TO SORT THIS ALL OUT!

BUT AS SOON AS HE LANDS...
SOMETHING'S WRONG WITH THE HAMMER!
IT SEEMS TO BE PULLING AWAY FROM ME, TRYING TO FREE ITSELF FROM MY GRASP!
IT'S AS THOUGH IT REALIZES THAT I'M NOT ITS RIGHTFUL OWNER!

BUT, I KNOW HOW TO CONTROL IT!
ACCORDING TO ALL THE HISTORY BOOKS I'VE READ, ALL I HAVE TO DO IS TAP IT ONCE ON THE GROUND AND--
THW-OOM

WOW!

CONFUSED, SHAKEN BY THE EVENING'S STUNNING EVENTS, DARGO RETURNS TO HIS DORM-BLOCK TO THINK... TO PONDER... TO SEARCH HIS VERY SOUL FOR ANSWERS... AND, EARLY THE NEXT MORNING...
DID YOU HEAR?
HE'S RETURNED!
A GOD AMONG MEN!
I SAW HIM! TOUCHED HIS CAPE!

IT'S THE SIGN WE'VE BEEN WAITING FOR!
AT LAST! WE CAN BE FREE!
NOTHING--NOT EVEN THE VAST ARMIES OF THE CORPORATION--CAN WITHSTAND HIS POWER!
THE THUNDER GOD WILL PROTECT US!

OH, DARGO, THE REVOLUTION IS COME!
HAS IT? HOW CAN WE TRUST THIS THOR SLUG? HOW DO WE KNOW HE'S THE REAL THING?!

IT REALLY DOESN'T MATTER! HE'S ONLY A SYMBOL TO OUR PEOPLE!
A SYMBOL THAT COULD GET US ALL KILLED!
EVEN DEATH IS PREFERABLE TO SLAVERY!
IS IT?!

MEANWHILE AT CORP HEADQUARTERS...
PRODUCTION IS DOWN!
REVOLUTION IS IN THE AIR!

YOU WERE SUPPOSED TO SOLVE MY PROBLEMS... BUT THINGS HAVE GOTTEN WORSE!
CAN YOU EVEN IMAGINE HOW MUCH THIS REVOLT WILL COST ME IN LOST REVENUES?!
CALM YOURSELF, MR. CHAIRMAN.
EVERYTHING IS UNDER CONTROL.
IN THE EVENT A REVOLUTION DOES ERUPT, I ALREADY POSSESS THE NECESSARY RESOURCES TO CRUSH IT--TOTALLY AND WITHOUT MERCY--AT NO ADDITIONAL COST TO YOU.

YOU SLACKERS BELONG HOME IN BED!
WE'RE... SURROUNDED!!
CLEAR THE STREETS, OR PAY THE PENALTY!
DEATH TO THOSE WHO DEFY THE CORPORATION!
DEATH TO ALL REBELS!!

HOWLS OF PAIN AND DEATH SOON SEAR THE EVENING AIR, EACH NEW SCREAM STRIKING DARGO WITH THE FORCE OF A MORTAL BLOW...
WHY DIDN'T THEY LISTEN TO ME? WHY?
THE CORP RULES THIS LAND! IT OWNS US!

ONE MAN CAN'T CHANGE THAT! NOT EVEN ONE WITH THE POWER OF A GOD!
BUT, THERE ARE OTHER LANDS, OTHER CORPS...
WE CAN-- WE WILL-- BE FREE!

I MUST HAVE BEEN GIVEN THIS INCREDIBLE POWER FOR A REASON! A PURPOSE BEYOND MORTAL UNDERSTANDING!
I MUST USE IT! I MUST--

"--PROVE MYSELF WORTHY!!"
LOOK AT THEM FALL!
AGAINST OUR SUPERIOR FIREPOWER, AND THE BRUTAL SAVAGERY OF OUR NEW ALLIES, THESE POOR SLACKERS HAVEN'T GOT A--

--PRAYER!
CAA-THOOM!!

GET BACK, YOU MONSTROUS FIENDS! BACK, I SAY!
THIS IS NO UNARMED MAN OR HELPLESS WOMAN YOU NOW FACE!
IT IS ONE WHO WIELDS THE POWER OF THE THUNDER GOD HIMSELF!

NOTHING CAN WITHSTAND MY RIGHTEOUS FURY!
SEE HOW EASILY I PLUCK THIS CORP TRACKER FROM THE SKY!

NO LONGER WILL IT SERVE ITS EVIL MASTERS!

JUST AS YOU WILL NO LONGER THREATEN MY PEOPLE!
PWOOM!!

YOU ARE QUITE AN IMPRESSIVE LITTLE MAN ...FOR AN IMPOSTOR!
WHAT? WHO DARES--?!

BWAK!!
I AM TYRUS THE TERRIBLE--THE RIGHTFUL RULER OF ALL ROCK TROLLS!
I HAVE MET THE TRUE SON OF ODIN--THE REAL GOD OF THUNDER!
YOU ARE NOT HE!
YOU ARE ONLY A MORTAL MASQUERADING IN HIS GUISE.

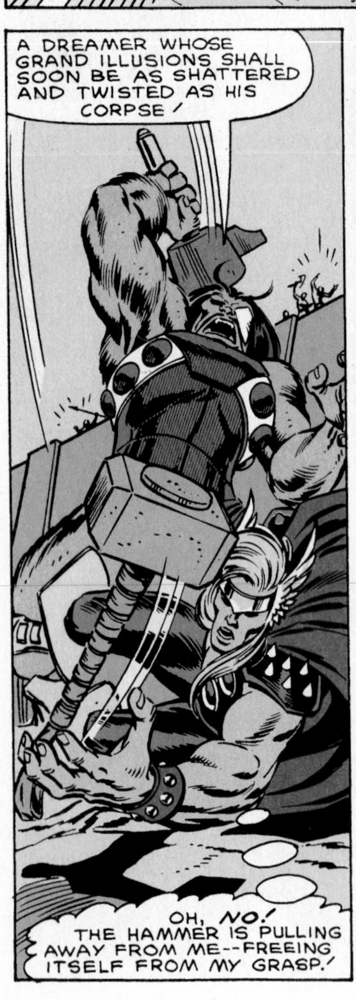

HE IS IN A PLACE WHERE NONE CAN REACH HIM!
AND, WITHOUT THE AID OF HIS MIGHTY URU HAMMER, HE CANNOT FREE HIMSELF!
THAT IS WHY CRAFTY LOKI AND I HAVE SO DESPERATELY SOUGHT THE HAMMER THROUGH THE CENTURIES!
TO PREVENT IT FROM EVER RETURNING TO HIM!

YOU'RE WASTING YOUR TIME, COWARD! RUNNING AWAY WON'T SAVE YOU FROM MY VENGEANCE!
YOUR MISERABLE LIFE IS ALREADY FORFEIT!
MORTALS MUST PAY THE ULTIMATE PRICE WHENEVER THEY HAVE THE AUDACITY TO INTERFERE IN AN AFFAIR OF GODS!
THE HAMMER--! IF ONLY I CAN REACH IT BEFORE HE RENEWS HIS ATTACK!

GOT IT! BUT, WILL IT OBEY ME--OR TRY TO ESCAPE AGAIN?

I'VE GOT A FLASH FOR YOU, TYRUS--GODS HAVE NO BUSINESS BUTTING INTO THE AFFAIRS OF MORTALS, EITHER!
BRAKA...

- -THWOOOM!!
YOU SHOULDN'T HAVE SIDED WITH THE CORP! SHOULDN'T HAVE ATTACKED MY PEOPLE!

YOU'RE GOING TO PAY FOR ALL THE MISERY YOU'VE CAUSED!
I SWEAR YOU'LL PAY!!
BRATTCHH!

DESPERATE, DRIVEN BY PAIN AND FURY, TYRUS SUDDENLY SPRINGS FORWARD...
I REFUSE TO ALLOW A MERE MORTAL TO DEFEAT ME!
THE DISGRACE WOULD BE TOO GREAT!

SO POWERFUL IS THE FORCE OF TYRUS'S ON-SLAUGHT THAT IT CAUSES THE VERY PAVEMENT TO COLLAPSE BENEATH THE TWO WARRIORS!
DOWN, DOWN, THEY PLUMMET--

MEANWHILE, AT CORP HEADQUARTERS...
DO YOU HAVE ANY IDEA OF WHAT'S HAPPENING OUT THERE?!
THOSE STUPID SLACKERS ARE SETTING FIRE TO MY FACTORIES-- DESTROYING BILLIONS OF DOLLARS WORTH OF EQUIPMENT!

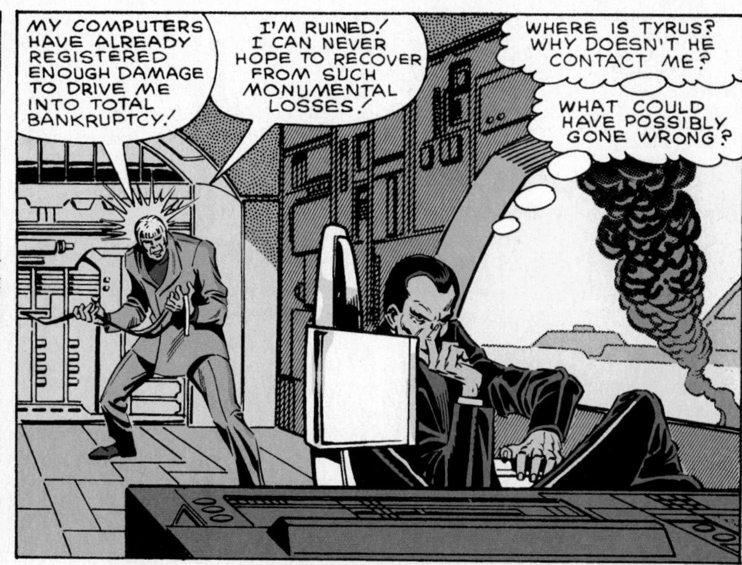
MY COMPUTERS HAVE ALREADY REGISTERED ENOUGH DAMAGE TO DRIVE ME INTO TOTAL BANKRUPTCY!
I'M RUINED! I CAN NEVER HOPE TO RECOVER FROM SUCH MONUMENTAL LOSSES!
WHERE IS TYRUS? WHY DOESN'T HE CONTACT ME?
WHAT COULD HAVE POSSIBLY GONE WRONG?

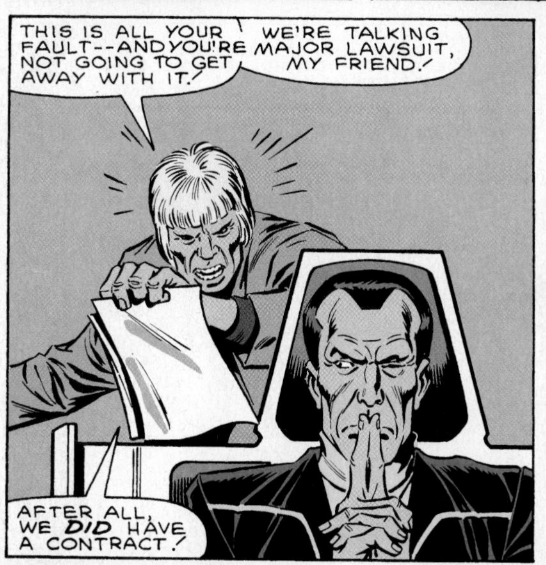
THIS IS ALL YOUR FAULT--AND YOU'RE NOT GOING TO GET AWAY WITH IT!
WE'RE TALKING MAJOR LAWSUIT, MY FRIEND!
AFTER ALL, WE DID HAVE A CONTRACT!

THAT CONTRACT IS NOW VOID, MORTAL--

--AS IS YOUR VERY LIFE!
KAR-
BAM!!

LOOK! SOME SLACKER HIT CORP CENTRAL!
THEY'LL BE COMPLETELY DISORGANIZED NOW!
WE DID IT! WE WON!!
WE CAN FLEE TO ANOTHER LAND BEFORE THEY CAN STOP US!
WE CAN FORM OUR OWN CORP!
BUT, WHO WILL LEAD US? WHO WILL TELL US WHAT TO DO?

I'VE BEATEN ALL THE TROLLS--AND DRIVEN AWAY ALL OF OUR ENEMIES!
WITH THIS HAMMER, I COULD SEIZE CONTROL! I COULD TRULY BE A GOD AMONG MEN!
NO! MORTAL MAN WAS NOT MEANT TO WIELD SUCH POWER! IT WOULDN'T BE GOOD FOR ME--OR MY PEOPLE!

THIS HAMMER BELONGS TO ANOTHER--ONE WHO DESPERATELY NEEDS IT--ACCORDING TO TYRUS!
I MUST RETURN IT! NOW! BEFORE I AM TEMPTED TO KEEP IT FOREVER!
WHIRLING THE HAMMER AT A SPEED WHICH DEFIES DESCRIPTION, THE YOUNG WARRIOR SHATTERS THE BARRIERS WHICH SEPARATE THE DIMENSIONAL PLANES--

--AND OPENS A MYSTIC GATEWAY INTO A DISTANT, MIND-STAGGERING REALM!
GO! RETURN TO YOUR TRUE MASTER!
SOMEHOW I SENSE THAT THIS PATHWAY WILL LEAD YOU TO HIM!

WILL IT EVER REACH THE REAL GOD OF THUNDER? WILL THE TRUE THOR BE ABLE TO SAVE HIMSELF NOW?
I'LL NEVER KNOW!
BUT, I CAN HOPE...AND PRAY!

ELSEWHERE, AT THAT VERY MOMENT...
NO!!

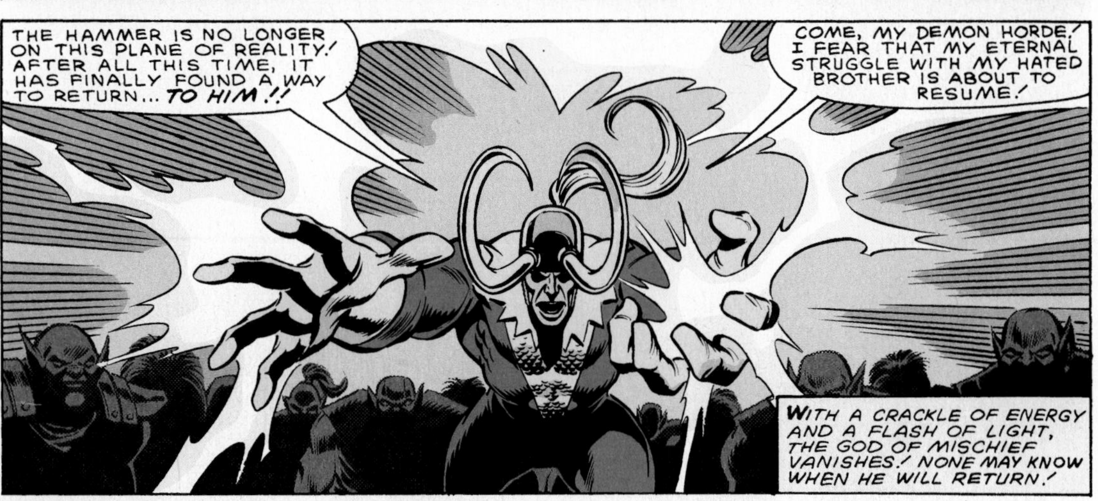
THE HAMMER IS NO LONGER ON THIS PLANE OF REALITY! AFTER ALL THIS TIME, IT HAS FINALLY FOUND A WAY TO RETURN... TO HIM!!
COME, MY DEMON HORDE! I FEAR THAT MY ETERNAL STRUGGLE WITH MY HATED BROTHER IS ABOUT TO RESUME!
WITH A CRACKLE OF ENERGY AND A FLASH OF LIGHT, THE GOD OF MISCHIEF VANISHES! NONE MAY KNOW WHEN HE WILL RETURN!

MEANWHILE...
SALLA! SALLA, I'VE FOUND YOU AT LAST!
YOU'RE ALL RIGHT. YOU'RE ALIVE!
DARGO--!

WE DID IT, DARGO! OUR PEOPLE ARE FREE AT LAST!
I TOLD YOU THAT ALL WE NEEDED WAS A LITTLE FAITH!
YOU WERE RIGHT, MY LOVE!

THE CORPORATION IS FINALLY DEAD--BUT, WHAT WILL RISE FROM ITS ASHES?
WHAT WILL BECOME OF OUR PEOPLE NOW?!
THAT IS FOR THE PEOPLE THEMSELVES TO DECIDE!

FREEDOM IS THE MOST PRECIOUS GIFT OF ALL--BUT IT MUST BE CONTINUALLY EARNED AND NURTURED--AS WELL AS CHERISHED--OR IT WILL DIE!
WE'VE BEEN GIVEN A NEW LEASE ON LIFE TODAY--A SECOND CHANCE! PERHAPS, WE CAN LEARN FROM OUR PAST MISTAKES!
PERHAPS, FINALLY, WE CAN PROVE OURSELVES WORTHY...
THE END

MARVEL COMICS
THE 1ST ISSUE OF A STUNNING NEW EPIC!
THE MIGHTY THOR
1991 MARVEL ENT. GROUP INC.
$1.00 US
$1.25 CAN
433
JUNE
02450
APPROVED BY THE COMICS CODE AUTHORITY
THERE'S A NEW THUNDER GOD IN TOWN!!

WHEN ARCHITECT **ERIC MASTERSON** STAMPS HIS WOODEN WALKING-STICK UPON THE GROUND, HE I
TRANSFORMED INTO THE NORSE GOD OF THUNDER. ARMED WITH HIS ENCHANTED HAMMER, HE IS AT ONC
MASTER OF THE STORM, LORD OF THE LIVING LIGHTNING, AND ONE OF THE STRONGEST WARRIORS
WHO EVER WALKED THE EARTH! STAN LEE PRESENTS . . .

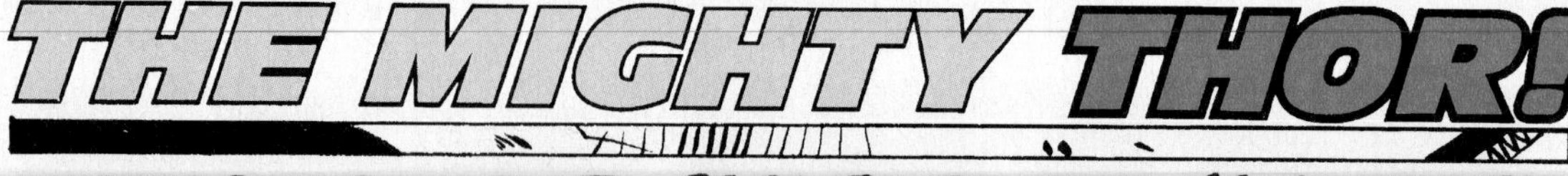

"WHOSOEVER HOLDS THIS HAMMER!"

LOKI, GOD OF EVIL, IS NO MORE!

HOWEVER, DEEP WITHIN THE SUBTERRANEAN CANALS WHICH SNAKE BENEATH THE ISLE OF MANHATTAN, PROWLS HIS MOST BRUTAL HENCHMAN... ULIK THE UNTAMED, MIGHTIEST OF ALL ROCK TROLLS!

BEGINNING A STARTLINGLY BOLD NEW DIRECTION!

THE *THUNDER GOD* MUST THINK ME DEFEATED! *HE IS WRONG!*

E'ER SINCE OUR LAST BATTLE*, I HAVE *HIDDEN* WITHIN THESE SEWERS! GATHERING MY *STRENGTH!* MARSHALING MY *POWER!*

* SEE THOR #431 FOR DETAILS -- MAC THE TROLL

RON FRENZ & TOM DEFALCO PLOT, PENCILS & WORDS — AL MILGROM FINISHED ART — CHRIS ELIOPOULOS LETTERER — MIKE ROCKWITZ COLORIST — RALPH MACCHIO EDITOR

AND NOW SHALL ULIK HAVE HIS REVENGE!
NEVER AGAIN WILL I BE HUMILIATED BY THE MIGHTY THOR!
MY BRAWN IS GREATER! MY RAGE IS BOUNDLESS!

THOUGH HE HAS APPARENTLY VANQUISHED THE CUNNING LOKI, I AM THE MIGHTIEST OF ALL WHO LIVE--
--AND THE SON OF ODIN WILL DIE!
I KNOW EXACTLY WHERE I MUST GO TO LURE HIM INTO BATTLE!

AND, AT THAT VERY MOMENT...
KRAKATOOM!
I STILL CAN'T QUITE ACCEPT THE FACT THAT THE ORIGINAL THOR IS REALLY... GONE!

THE GODS OF ASGARD BANISHED HIM FROM THIS PLANE OF REALITY SHORTLY AFTER HE DESTROYED LOKI!
AND THEN, FOR REASONS WHICH I MAY NEVER UNDERSTAND, THEY TRANSFERRED HIS POWER TO ME!
WHY ME?! I'M JUST NOT WORTHY OF THIS RESPONSIBILITY!
I DON'T KNOW WHERE THEY STASHED HIM, BUT I'M DETERMINED TO FIND THE TRUE THOR, AND RESTORE HIM!
MR. MASTERSON--?

YES, NURSE... WHAT IS IT?
YOU CAN VISIT MISS AUSTIN NOW!
SHE'S IN THE INTENSIVE CARE WARD, AND I'M AFRAID THAT SHE STILL HASN'T REGAINED CONSCIOUSNESS!

POOR SUSAN! LOKI REALLY DID A NUMBER ON HER!
THAT'S WHAT FINALLY DROVE THE THUNDER GOD OVER THE EDGE--
--AND CONVINCED HIM THAT MANKIND WOULD NEVER TRULY BE SAFE WHILE HIS BROTHER LIVED!

YOU CAN ONLY STAY A FEW MINUTES!
IT'S MY FAULT LOKI WENT AFTER SUSAN!
HE STRUCK AT HER BECAUSE OF MY LINK TO THE REAL THOR!

SHE LOOKS SO FRAGILE... SO HELPLESS!
SHE WAS ALWAYS THERE WHEN I NEEDED HER! SHE WAS SO GOOD AT HER JOB AS MY PERSONAL ASSISTANT THAT I GUESS I JUST STARTED TAKING HER FOR GRANTED!
I NEVER REALIZED HOW MUCH SHE MEANT TO ME BEFORE NOW!
HANG TOUGH, PRETTY LADY! I SWEAR THAT NO ONE ELSE WILL BE MADE TO SUFFER LIKE THIS AS LONG AS I POSSESS THE POWER OF THOR!

CONCLUDING HIS BEDSIDE VISIT, ERIC IS GREETED IN THE WAITING ROOM BY THE FAMILIAR FACE OF JERRY SAPRISTI...
HOW'S SHE DOING, ERIC?
PROBABLY A LOT BETTER THAN YOU! AT LEAST SHE'S GOT PEOPLE TO TAKE CARE OF HER!
AS WELL AS COULD BE EXPECTED!

WHAT DO YOU HAVE, BUDDY?
YOU RECENTLY LOST CUSTODY OF YOUR SON, YOUR ARCHITECT BUSINESS IS STARTING TO FAIL, AND NOW THIS!
ERIC, I DON'T KNOW IF YOU'VE EVER MET SUSAN'S ROOMMATE... LEENA MORAN!
SO THIS IS THE LEGENDARY ERIC MASTERSON!

I NOW UNDERSTAND WHY SUSAN WAS ALWAYS GUSHING ABOUT YOU!
YOU ARE QUITE THE CUTIE!
UH... THANKS!
YOU MAY SEE HER NOW, MISS MORAN!

ER... THAT LEENA IS QUITE A HANDFUL!
I'M SO BAD AT THIS! WISH I KNEW WHAT TO SAY!
THE GUY IS REALLY HURTING!

ER... YOU LOOK LIKE YOU COULD USE A SHAVE AND SOME FRESH CLOTHES!
YOU BEEN HOME SINCE THE ACCIDENT?
I'LL BE GOING SOON!
UH... GOOD IDEA...

KRAKABOOM!
LISTEN TO THAT THUNDER ROAR!
IT ALMOST SOUNDS LIKE A GROWL OF ANGER!
YES...
...AND IT'S GOING TO GET A LOT WORSE!

MEANWHILE, OUTSIDE...
THESE NEW INFRARED VISORS THAT RIGGER WHIPPED UP ARE INCREDIBLE, MAD DOG!
PERFECT FOR NIGHT VISION AND WEATHER LIKE THIS!
YEAH, YEAH... JUST WAKE ME UP IF YA SEE ANY CUTE NURSES!
GO EASY ON THE ENTHUSIASM, JOCK! YER EAGER BEAVER ROUTINE IS STARTING TA ANNOY ME, AND I'VE GOT A GUN!
TRAUMA CENTER
POLICE
I TAKE IT YOU AREN'T THRILLED WITH THIS PARTICULAR DUTY, SIR.
LET'S JUST SAY THAT I DIDN'T VOLUNTEER FOR CODE: BLUE TA PLAY NURSEMAID!
LIEUTENANT STONE THINKS THE AUSTIN GIRL MAY STILL BE IN DANGER... BUT WHO WOULD WANT TO HARM HER NOW... AND WHY?!
THE WOMAN IS NAUGHT BUT A PAWN! A PLAYTHING TO BE USED... AND QUICKLY DISCARDED!
MORTAL LIVES ARE TOO BRIEF, TOO FRAGILE TO HOLD ANY OTHER VALUE TO A ROCK TROLL!
OH, WOW! A FULL-FLEDGED CELEBRITY!
IF WE'RE REAL LUCKY HE'LL AUTOGRAPH OUR GUNS AT HIS ARRAIGNMENT!
NY PD CODE BLUE
JUMP, MAD DOG! JUMP! IT'S THAT ULIK CHARACTER-- THE ONE THAT INSPIRED STONE TO FORM CODE: BLUE!
BOAM!
BOAM!
LOOK SHARP, JOCK! WE CAN REALLY IMPRESS THE NURSES BY MAKING LIKE HEROES!

THAT SOUNDS LIKE GUNFIRE!
HOLY--! A MONSTER IS ATTACKING THE POLICE! SMASHING THROUGH THEM LIKE A BATTERING RAM!
ULIK... AND IT'S OBVIOUS WHY HE'S COME!

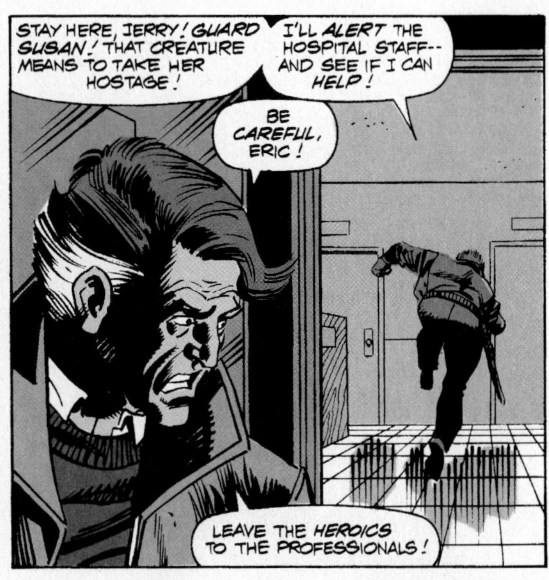
STAY HERE, JERRY! GUARD SUSAN! THAT CREATURE MEANS TO TAKE HER HOSTAGE!
I'LL ALERT THE HOSPITAL STAFF-- AND SEE IF I CAN HELP!
BE CAREFUL, ERIC!
LEAVE THE HEROICS TO THE PROFESSIONALS!

I REALLY WISH I COULD DO THAT, PAL--BUT I HAVE NO CHOICE!
LIKE IT OR NOT, I'VE BEEN GIVEN A DUTY... A RESPONSIBILITY THAT I CAN'T IGNORE!

O-BOY! THIS IS SO CRAZY! I... I ALMOST CAN'T BELIEVE THAT I'M ACTUALLY GOING THROUGH WITH IT!
NO SENSE PUTTING IT OFF ANY LONGER--!

I JUST HOPE THAT I DON'T MAKE A COMPLETE FOOL OF MYSELF--AND END UP CAUSING MORE HARM THAN GOOD!!

MEANWHILE...
YOU SURE THOSE GIZMOS PACK ENOUGH WALLOP, RIGGER?
THEY'LL DO THE JOB, FIREWORKS!
GET THEM INTO POSITION-- AND FORGET THE DEBATE! WE AIN'T GOT A WHOLE LOT OF OPTIONS HERE!
DO NOT FLATTER YOURSELF, MORTAL!
YOUR LIFE IS ALREADY FORFEIT!
POLICE

I HAVE ONLY BEEN TOYING WITH YOU! SAVORING THE INEVITABLE MOMENT OF YOUR DESTRUCTION! YOU--A MERE MORTAL--WHO DARES TO CHALLENGE A ROCK TROLL!

HE'S SO MUCH FASTER... STRONGER THAN I REMEMBER! GOT TO STOP HIM BEFORE ≷UGN≶

STONE IS DOWN!

KNOWING THE LIEUTENANT, HE'S JUST RESTING--PLANNING A NEW STRATEGY--AND I'D HATE TO BE IN OLD UGLY'S SHOES WHEN HE GETS UP!

IN THE MEANTIME, I'LL JUST PROVIDE A LITTLE DISTRACTION--!

≷UNNN≶

FOOL! YOU LEAP INTO THE JAWS OF DEATH!

NOT QUITE--UNLESS THAT'S A REFERENCE TO THE SEWER-LIKE AROMA OF YOUR BREATH!

MY MAMA INVESTED GOOD MONEY IN GYMNASTIC LESSONS--AND THEY PAID OFF!

THERE--! I EVEN MANAGED TO PLANT THE SECOND TRANSMITTER!

STOP PATTING YOURSELF ON THE BACK, JOCK--AND GET OUTTA THERE!

THE THIRD BABY IS FINALLY IN PLACE, RIGGER! GO! GO!

WHAT'S THE DRILL, RIGGER? WHAT EXACTLY IS THAT GIZMO SUPPOSED TO ACCOMPLISH?
IF IT WORKS, OUR UGLY FRIEND GETS ENCASED WITHIN AN ELECTRIFIED STASIS FIELD!
AND, IF IT DOESN'T--?!
A CERTAIN WELL-KNOWN CHAIN OF ELECTRICAL SUPPLIES OWES MY ESTATE A FULL REFUND... AND A SINCERE APOLOGY!
I'LL SAY ONE THING FOR YOU, LADY--YOU DON'T LACK CONFIDENCE!
POLICE
POLICE

BZZZZ - AKKKK!
YAHOO! RIGGER, MY GIRL, YA JUST EARNED YOURSELF A PATENTED SENSES-SWIRLING KISS!
FORGET IT, DOG! I'D RATHER COZY UP TO ULIK!

BUT THEN...
STAND BACK! STAND YOU, ER... YE... AWAY!
VERILY, SHALL THE GOD OF, UM, THUNDER CLOBBER YONDER VARLET!
"CLOBBER?!"
SAY WHAT--?
POLICE
THOR, NO--! STOP! YOU'LL OVERLOAD THE FIELD, AND--

KRAKA-CHOOM!
URGG

UNNN! MY FIRST APPEARANCE WAS LESS THAN SWEET!
WHAT WILL I DO FOR AN ENCORE-- TRIGGER AN EARTHQUAKE?!
THOR BLEW IT BIG TIME, LIEUTENANT!
THIS GADGET IS JUST A HUNK OF FUSED WIRES AND MELTED METAL NOW!
FORGET IT, RIGGER--AND HELP THE OTHERS WITH CROWD CONTROL!
I'VE GOT A HUNCH THE REAL TROUBLE IS JUST STARTING--!
AT LAST! I HAVE DRAWN YOU OUT OF HIDING, THUNDER GOD!
I AM DETERMINED TO CRUSH YOU--AND FINALLY PROVE THAT I AM TRULY THE STRONGEST OF ALL!

BUT WAIT! THERE IS SOMETHING... DIFFERENT... ABOUT YOU... AND IT IS FAR MORE THAN THAT SCRAGGLY FACIAL HAIR!
APPEARANCES CAN BE CHANGED... BUT NOT SCENTS!
YOUR'S HAS BEEN SUBTLY ALTERED!

THAT CAN ONLY MEAN THAT YOU ARE AN IMPOSTER! A DECEIVING FRAUD!
SO MUCH FOR MY CLEVER IMPERSON-ATION!
I HAVE A CLEAR SHOT AT HIS HEAD--BUT THE REAL THOR DOESN'T FIGHT LIKE THAT!

BUT THEN, EVEN AS ERIC HESITATES... THE MERCILESS ULIK STRIKES!
YOU SOUGHT TO PLAY ME FOR A FOOL--AND MUST NOW PAY FOR SUCH TREACHERY!
B-TOOK!

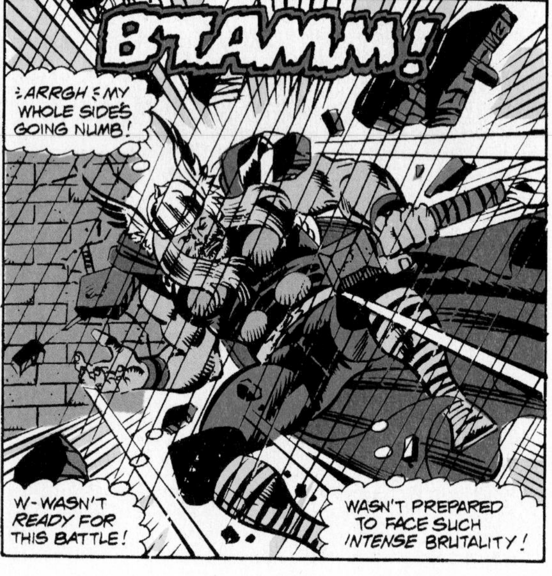
BTAMM!
ARRGH! MY WHOLE SIDE'S GOING NUMB!
W-WASN'T READY FOR THIS BATTLE!
WASN'T PREPARED TO FACE SUCH INTENSE BRUTALITY!

WHO ARE YOU? WHY DID YOU ATTEMPT THIS FUTILE MASQUERADE?!
WHERE IS THE REAL THOR?!
ANSWER ME! ANSWER ME, OR I SWEAR THAT I SHALL--

BAH! YOU ARE AS UNWORTHY OF WRATH.. AS YOU ARE OF MY STRENGTH!
TELL THE TRUE THUNDER GOD THAT ULIK STILL AWAITS HIM!

AND NOW--
--BEGONE!!
PA-WOK!

LIKE A HELPLESS, BROKEN RAG DOLL, THE BLOND ADVENTURER IS CONTEMPTUOUSLY HURLED INTO THE NEARBY HOSPITAL...
KA-PLASH!

AND THEN, WITH A CASUAL SWIPE OF HIS MASSIVE HAND, ULIK EFFORTLESSLY RIPS A PING HOLE IN THE PAVEMENT BENEATH HIS FEET--!
BAH! I HAVE WASTED TIME ENOUGH HERE!
LOOK OUT! HE'S TRYING TO ESCAPE!

EVEN AS THE CODE: BLUE TEAM SPRINGS FOWARD, THE PITILESS ROCK TROLL LEAPS TO THE SUBWAY PLATFORM BELOW--!
STAND ASIDE, YOU TREMBLING WEAKLINGS--
--OR SUFFER THE FATAL CONSEQUENCES!

BATTERED, BRUISED, AND THOROUGHLY DISENCHANTED WITH HIMSELF, ERIC MASTERSON SLOWLY STUMBLES TO HIS FEET...
I COULDN'T HAVE SCREWED UP WORSE IF I TRIED!
SHOULDN'T HAVE LET ULIK GET THE UPPER HAND ON ME!
I MAY HAVE THE REAL THOR'S STRENGTH--BUT I LACK HIS COMBAT EXPERIENCE--AND HIS CONFIDENCE!

APPEARANCES TO THE CONTRARY, I'M NO MUSCLE-BOUND SUPER JOCK! I'M ONLY AN ARCHITECT WHO HAS NO BUSINESS PLAYING HERO, AND--
BZZZT!
WHAT THE--?!

IT'S THOR'S AVENGERS I.D. CARD!
THE WAY MY LUCK'S BEEN GOING, THEY PROBABLY NEED HIM TO SAVE THE WORLD FROM IMMINENT DESTRUCTION!
CAPTAIN AMERICA CALLING THOR!
THIS IS AN A-1 PRIORITY! REPORT TO AVENGERS MANSION IMMEDIATELY!

CAN'T LET CAP SEE MY BEARD! HE'S BOUND TO REALIZE THAT I'M A FAKE--AND I'M NOT PREPARED TO ANSWER HIS QUESTIONS!
ER, THOR CAN'T COME TO THE PHONE NOW!
HE'S, UM, OUT TO LUNCH!

OUT TO LUNCH--?!

I...CAN'T BELIEVE I REALLY SAID THAT!
YEAH, I'M OUT TO LUNCH ALL RIGHT... IF I THINK I CAN SUBSTITUTE FOR THE REAL THUNDER GOD!
WAIT UP, THOR--!
WE HAVE TO TALK!
OH, NO!

CAN'T DEAL WITH STONE NOW! HE SAW THOR KNOCK OFF LOKI!
I'M SORRY, LIEUTENANT-- BUT I AM NEEDED ELSEWHERE!
THAT WASN'T A REQUEST, MISTER. WE HAVE A FEW UNRESOLVED MATTERS TO DISCUSS!
YEAH, WELL, WE'LL DISCUSS THEM ALL RIGHT--

--BUT, WE'LL DO IT LATER!
SOMETHING'S VERY WRONG HERE! THE BIG GUY JUST AIN'T TALKING OR ACTING LIKE HIMSELF!
AND, NOBODY CAN GROW A FULL BEARD IN A DAY!

THIS IS TURNING OUT TO BE A TOTAL FIASCO!
I COULD HAVE BEEN KILLED FIGHTING ULIK!
AT LEAST... I THINK I CAN DIE!
THERE'S SO MUCH I STILL HAVE TO LEARN ABOUT THOR'S POWERS AND--

WHOA! I...I'M FLYING!
I INTUITIVELY TOSSED THE HAMMER...BUT I... I DON'T KNOW HOW TO CONTROL IT!

YEOW!

THAT DOES IT! I'VE GOT TO GET A HANDLE ON THIS THUNDER GOD BIZ--AND FAST!
I WAS DOING JUST FINE ON PURE INSTINCT...UNTIL MY MIND GOT IN THE WAY!

THIS IS NO GAME! I CAN'T AFFORD ANYMORE MISTAKES!
I HAVE BEEN GIVEN INCREDIBLE POWER!
I MUST START TAKING IT SERIOUSLY-- AND TREATING IT RESPONSIBLY!
POWER WITHOUT RESPONSIBILITY... IS POWER WHICH IS DESTINED TO BE ABUSED!

AND SO, SOMETIME LATER...
HOME... AT LAST!
I...I'M FINALLY STARTING TO ENJOY FLYING... BUT THE LANDINGS STILL MAKE ME NERVOUS!

WHAT A MESS! ULIK DID A REAL JOB ON MY COSTUME!
I'D BETTER CHECK HIS PERSONAL BELONGINGS FOR A SPARE!

NO SUCH LUCK! HE ONLY PACKED HIS SUIT OF ARMOR!
THIS HELMET ISN'T BAD, BUT I CAN'T EVEN IMAGINE THE TYPE OF UNDERWEAR I'D NEED.

WHAT AM I WORRIED ABOUT? I'M AN ARTIST! A FEW QUICK SKETCHES CAN EASILY SOLVE THIS PROBLEM-- AND UPDATE THOR'S IMAGE IN THE PROCESS!

EVEN A THUNDER GOD CAN DO WITH AN OCCASIONAL NEW LOOK!
AFTER ALL, IT IS THE NINETIES!
BESIDES, IF I'M REALLY GOING TO BE THE NEW THOR--

KRAKABOOM!
--I'LL HAVE TO DO IT MY WAY!
UNABATED, THE THUNDERSTORM CONTINUES TO RAGE ALL THROUGH THAT NIGHT, AND INTO THE FOLLOWING DAY!

THEN, ON THE MORNING OF THE THIRD DAY, LOWER MANHATTAN'S PEERLESS MEAT PACKING PLANT IS SHAKEN BY A VIOLENT TEMPEST--
KRAKABOOM!

-- OF UNEXPECTED NATURE!
KRASH!
ULIK HUNGERS--!
RUN! I-IT'S SOME KIND OF MONSTER!
SOMEBODY OUGHTA CALL THE UNION-- AND FIND OUT HOW THIS IMPACTS OUR OVERTIME!

GO! GET OUT OF MY SIGHT!
I WISH TO DINE IN PEACE! MMMRRR!
YOU GOT IT, PAL! I DON'T WANNA SEE WHAT YOU HAVE FOR DESSERT!

BUT, EVEN BEFORE THE RAMPAGING ROCK TROLL CAN COMPLETE HIS FIRST COURSE...
ULIK HAS BEEN SPOTTED! ALERT CODE: BLUE!

QUICK TIME, PEOPLE! THIS IS OUR CHANCE TO NAIL THAT PERP!
YA
HOO!
POLICE
POLICE

AT THAT PRECISE MOMENT, ACROSS TOWN...
IS THE JARLSON ORDER READY?
SPOTLIGHT COSTUMES &
CUSTOM TAILORING
KENT

WHAT A HUNK!
...RISCICA REFUSED TO COMMENT ON ALLEGATIONS THAT HE KNOWINGLY FALSIFIED THE BUDGET!
I HAVE IT RIGHT HERE!
SALE
WE KNEW YOU WERE IN A RUSH--SO OUR CHIEF TAILOR WORKED THROUGH THE NIGHT!
I APPRECIATE THE SERVICE!

AND, IN LOCAL NEWS... A MEAT PACKING PLANT ON THE LOWER WESTSIDE WAS REPORTEDLY ATTACKED THIS MORNING BY A--
YOU SUPPLIED US WITH A VERY INTRIGUING DESIGN!
I'D, UM, LOVE TO SEE HOW IT LOOKS ON YOU!
MAYBE THAT CAN BE ARRANGED!

DO YOU HAVE A PLACE FOR ME TO CHANGE?
THE SPECIAL POLICE TASK FORCE KNOWN AS CODE: BLUE IS CURRENTLY ON THE SCENE!
NEWS BULLETIN
YES, THERE'S A ROOM IN THE BACK!

FEEL FREE TO CALL ME IF YOU NEED HELP SLIPPING INTO ANYTHING!
I'M SURE I'LL DO JUST FINE ON MY OWN!
WHEW! I COULD REALLY GET USED TO HAVING A PHYSIQUE LIKE THIS!
I JUST HOPE THIS NEW LOOK WORKS...

MESSING WITH AN ICON LIKE THOR'S COSTUME CAN BE REAL CHANCY!

YOU NEVER KNOW HOW ANYBODY'S GOING TO REACT!

BUT, SOMETIMES YOU'VE JUST GOT TO GO WITH YOUR GUT!

WHAT'S THE WORST THAT COULD HAPPEN?
THE GUYS IN CHARGE OF ASGARD COULD REALLY HATE IT... AND CANCEL MY RUN AS THE THUNDER GOD!

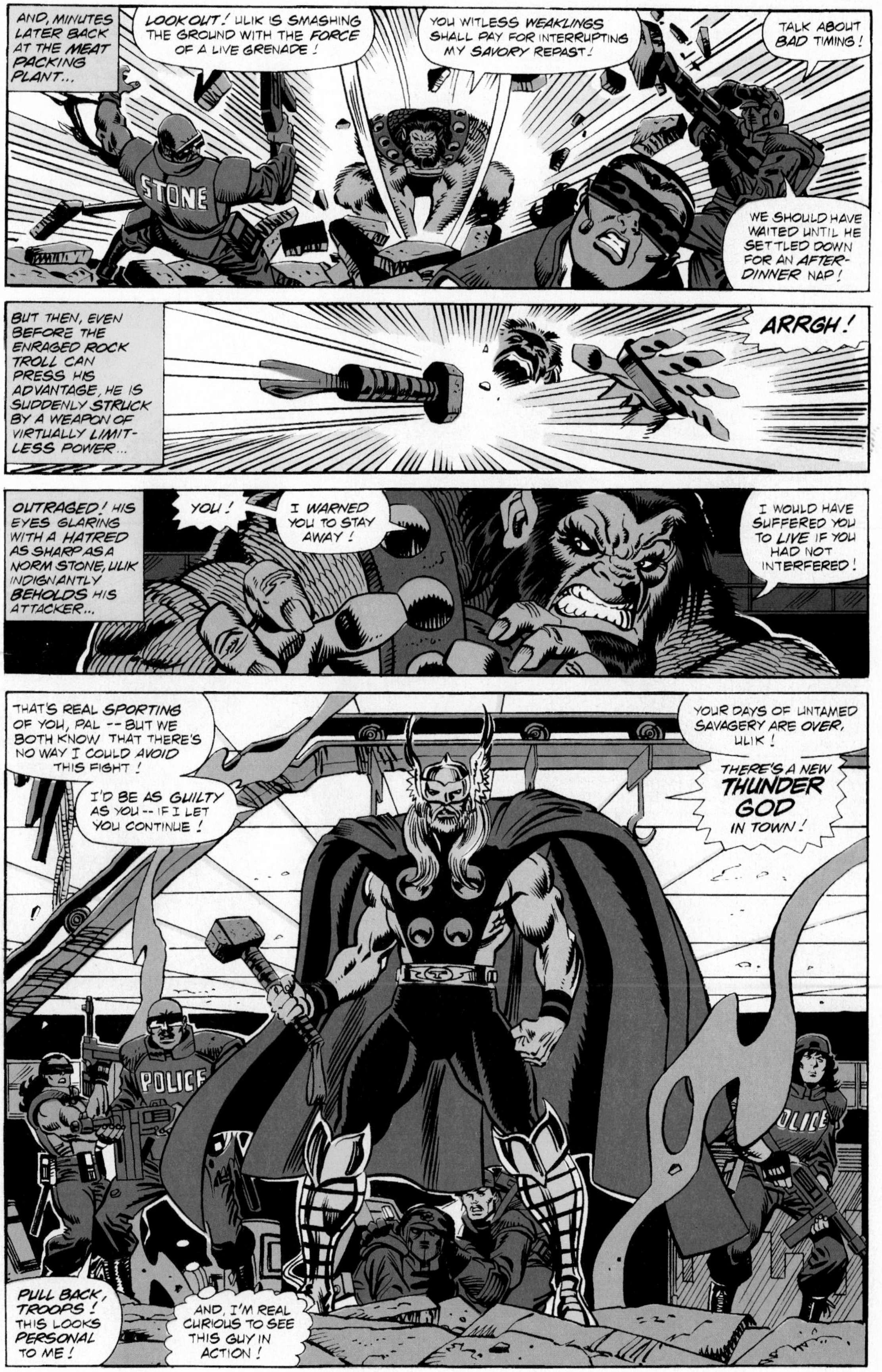

THAT'S REAL SPORTING OF YOU, PAL -- BUT WE BOTH KNOW THAT THERE'S NO WAY I COULD AVOID THIS FIGHT!

I'D BE AS GUILTY AS YOU -- IF I LET YOU CONTINUE!

YOUR DAYS OF UNTAMED SAVAGERY ARE OVER, ULIK!

THERE'S A NEW THUNDER GOD IN TOWN!

POLICE

POLICE

PULL BACK, TROOPS! THIS LOOKS PERSONAL TO ME!

AND, I'M REAL CURIOUS TO SEE THIS GUY IN ACTION!

YOUR MASQUERADE IS NAUGHT BUT A FOOLISH PRETENSE!
YOU ARE AN INSULT--AN ATROCITY--TO THE TRUE SON OF ODIN!
CRUSHING YOU WILL BE AKIN TO OVERPOWERING A HAPLESS FLEA!
TALK IS CHEAP, ULIK!
A MAN IS MEASURED BY THE QUALITY OF HIS DEEDS...NOT THE QUANTITY OF HIS WORDS!
ARE YOU GOING TO FIGHT--
--OR JUST KEEP TALKING ABOUT IT?!

YOUR ARROGANCE IS WITHOUT PEER! I WILL SUFFER IT NO MORE!
NOTHING CAN SAVE YOU NOW! YOU WILL PAY THE ULTIMATE PRICE! THE FINAL PRICE!
DEATH TO THE FALSE THUNDER GOD!

EVEN AS ULIK HURTLES HIMSELF FOWARD, HIS TARGET SUDDENLY SPRINGS ASIDE--DODGING HARM'S WAY!
NO! THE REAL GOD OF THUNDER WOULD HAVE FACED MY ONSLAUGHT! HE WOULD NEVER LEAP TO SAFETY!
THAT'S TRUE!
BUT, AS YOU'VE ALREADY POINTED OUT--

--I AIN'T HIM!
BA-KRASH!

YOU ARE A COWARD!
A DISGRACE TO THE GOD WHOSE HAMMER YOU WIELD!

A TRUE WARRIOR OF ASGARD FOLLOWS CERTAIN RULES OF COMBAT--AND HONOR!
HE DOES NOT RESORT TO UNMANLY TRICKS!
HE DOES NOT RUN AWAY!

SWOKK!
IS THIS THE POINT WHERE YOU START INSULTING MY MOTHER?!
DO YOURSELF A FAVOR, ULIK--AND SAVE THE PONTIFICATING FOR SOMEONE WHO CARES!

THIS IS NO GAME TO ME!
I HAVE ONLY TWO OPTIONS... VICTORY OR DEATH!
AND I'M DETERMINED TO WIN!

T-THAT AIN'T NO THOR I REMEMBER!
POLICE
NO... HE AIN'T!

I'M SICK OF CRETINS LIKE YOU WHO WANTONLY CAUSE DESTRUCTION, AND CARELESSLY THREATEN INNOCENT LIVES--
--AND THEN, HAVE THE COLOSSAL BRASS TO EXPECT MERCY AND FAIR PLAY FROM THE GOOD GUYS!
IT'S THE NINETIES, PAL!
THOSE DAYS ARE OVER!

ULIK THE UNTAMED EXPECTS NO MERCY-- AND GRANTS NONE!
I LIVE SOLELY FOR ONE PURPOSE-- ONE DESIRE-- TO DEMOLISH ALL MY FOES!
TO ANNIHILATE ALL THOSE WHO WOULD DEFY ME!
EVERYONE NEEDS A GOAL, BUDDY!
HOWEVER, YOURS IS TOTALLY WACK-O!
YOU'LL NEED A LOT MORE THAN A FEW TONS OF DETROIT'S FINEST AS LONG AS I POSSESS THE ENCHANTED HAMMER OF THOR!
THEN, YOU MUST POSSESS IT-- NO LONGER!!
THOKK!
THAT VEHICLE SERVED ME WELL! IT WAS NAUGHT BUT A DISTRACTION!
AT LAST, YOU STUPID SURROGATE! NOTHING STANDS BETWEEN US... SAVE DEATH!
BIG MISTAKE, ULIK!
BIG MISTAKE!

YOU KEEP CHARGING FORWARD -- LEAPING AT ME -- AND STICKING YOUR UGLY FACE OUT!
SO THIS IS ONLY NATURAL!
Y-YOUR CAPE--!

I CANNOT SEE!
I DO BELIEVE THAT YOU'RE FINALLY GETTING WITH THE PROGRAM!
OF COURSE, YOU'LL PROBABLY WHINE THAT THIS IS ONE OF THOSE UNMANLY STUNTS THAT WOULD BE BENEATH THE REAL THUNDER GOD!

THOK!
I DON'T CARE!

WUMP!
YOU HEAR ME?

BTAMM!
I DON'T CARE!

TRY TO STAY CONSCIOUS A LITTLE LONGER, ULIK!
THERE'S A NEW MESSAGE FOR THIS NEW DECADE, AND I'D REALLY HATE FOR YOU TO MISS IT!
PAY ATTENTION! I'M ONLY GOING TO SAY IT ONCE--!

BA-CHOOM!
THE GOOD GUYS CAN PLAY HARDBALL, TOO!

KRUMP!
I...I GUESS WE SHOULD MOP UP!
YEAH... RIGHT!

A GUY COULD REALLY GET USED TO POWER LIKE THIS!
TOO BAD IT DOESN'T BELONG TO ME!
YOU DID GREAT, THOR! I'LL JUST GO GET YOUR HAMMER AND -UFF- I... CAN'T EVEN BUDGE IT!
DON'T STRAIN YOURSELF, FRIEND!

IT TAKES A SPECIAL KIND OF STRENGTH TO LIFT THIS BABY!
A STRENGTH BORN OF FAR MORE THAN MERE MUSCLE!
A STRENGTH WHICH I HAVE FINALLY BEGUN TO EARN THE HARD WAY!
H-HE RAISED IT SO EASILY-- SO EFFORTLESSY!

YEAH, MAYBE I CAN DO THIS!
AT LEAST FOR THE DURATION...
WHOSOEVER HOLDS THIS HAMMER, IF HE BE WORTHY, SHALL POSSESS THE POWER OF THOR

AND SO, SHORTLY...
THOSE OMNIUM STEEL HANDCUFFS SHOULD HOLD ULIK!
THEY MAY NOT BE NECESSARY WITH THE FIGHT KNOCKED OUT OF HIM!
I CAN'T IMAGINE HOW IT WAS DONE, BUT IT'S REAL OBVIOUS THAT SOME SERIOUS CHANGES HAVE BEEN MADE!
YOU'RE A WHOLE NEW THOR-- AREN'T YOU ?!
IN SOME WAYS, WE ARE VERY DIFFERENT!
IN OTHERS, QUITE THE SAME!
STONE

I GO BACK WITH THE ORIGINAL! I CAN'T EXACTLY SAY WE WERE FRIENDS... BUT I'D STILL LIKE TO KNOW WHAT HAPPENED TO HIM!
SO WOULD I!
AND, I WILL FIND OUT!
I'D BE HONORED TO HELP!
POLICE

THANK YOU, LIEUTENANT! I APPRECIATE THE OFFER!
BUT NOW, THERE'S SOMETHING ELSE I MUST DO--!
TAP! TAP!
THE RAIN--! IT'S STOPPING! IT EASED UP THE MOMENT YOU TAPPED YOUR HAMMER!
THE HEAVENS HAVE MOURNED LONG ENOUGH!

CHECK OUT THAT RAINBOW!
I'VE GOT A HUNCH IT'S GOING TO BE A GLORIOUS DAY IN THE NEIGHBORHOOD!
WELCOME ABOARD, MISTER!
IT'S A PLEASURE TO BE HERE, LIEUTENANT!
IF EVERYONE IS DONE PATTING THEMSELVES ON THE BACK, LET'S BREAK FOR LUNCH!
FIGHTING ROCK TROLLS IS HUNGRY WORK!
SO SAY WE ALL!

NEXT ISSUE:

ERIC MASTERSON BEGINS A QUEST IN SEARCH OF THE *ORIGINAL THOR!* A QUEST WHICH LEADS TO THE GATES OF *ASGARD* AND A BATTLE ROYAL WITH THE *WARRIORS THREE* AND THE STUNNING *LADY SIF!*

DON'T MISS...

"IF HE BE WORTHY--!"

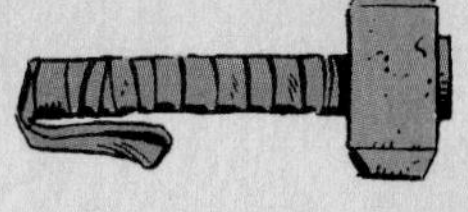

Thor Annual #17 pinup by Dan Panosian & Scott Marshall.

THE MIGHTY THOR HAS A BONE TO PICK WITH JUST ABOUT EVERYBODY IN THE COSMOS. THE SILVER SURFER AND WARLOCK WANT TO STOP HIS MADNESS BEFORE IT GETS OUT OF HAND.
STARTING IN THOR #468 AND CONTINUING THROUGHOUT SILVER SURFER, WARLOCK CHRONICLES AND WARLOCK AND THE INFINITY WATCH. FOLLOW THOR'S GALAXY SPANNING TOUR OF DESTRUCTION.
WITNESS
BLOOD AND THUNDER
Mike DeCarlo '93

Thor Corps #1 pinup by Mike DeCarlo, promoting the "Blood and Thunder" Thor crossover.

DC Comics, Inc.
BOOK: THOR ISSUE/MONTH: #384 15

INSTRUCTIONS FOR TWO-PAGE SPREAD: BUTT PAPER AT EDGES, TAPE ON BACK. DO NOT OVERLAP AT CENTER: EACH HALF SHOULD MEASURE 10⅝" wide, FULL SPREAD = 21¼" wide.

11

Thor #384, page 11 art by Ron Frenz & Brett Breeding

Courtesy of HeritageAuctions.com

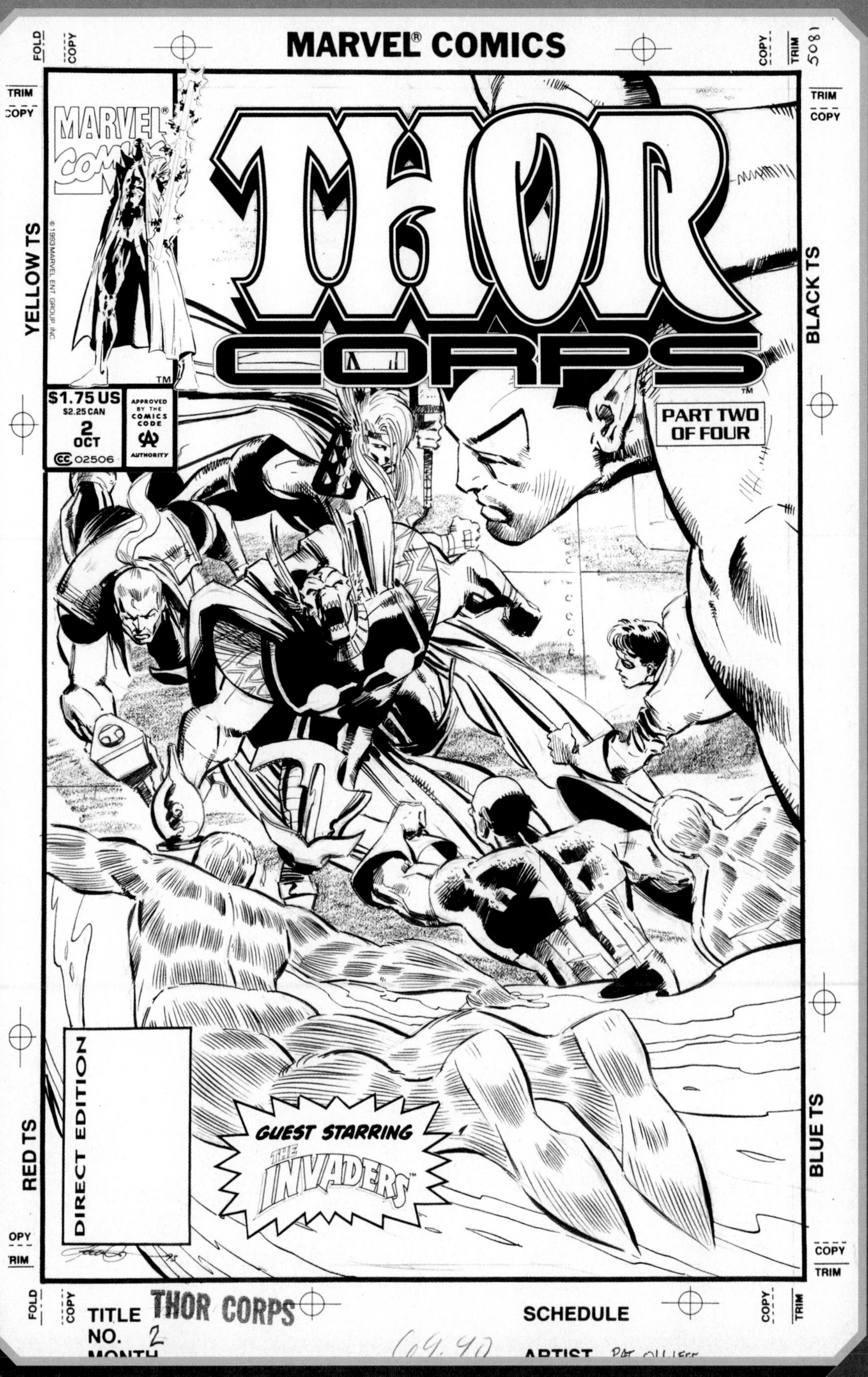

Thor Corps #2 cover art by Patrick Olliffe

Courtesy of HeritageAuctions.com

Thor Corps #4 cover painting by Lou Harrison